THE MULTIFAMILY MILLIONAIRE
VOLUME II

The
MULTIFAMILY
MILLIONAIRE

Create Generational Wealth

by Investing in

Large Multifamily Real Estate

Volume II

BRIAN MURRAY AND
BRANDON TURNER

BiggerPockets®
PUBLISHING
Denver, Colorado

Praise for
Brandon Turner's Books

How to Invest in Real Estate:
Winner of Indie Press Awards 2019
First and Second Place CIPA EVVY Awards 2019

"An insider's perspective, full of encouragement and resources for new-comers. ... Interested readers will find the book substantially useful as a starting point."

—*Kirkus* Review on *How to Invest in Real Estate*

"I only wish this book had been written in 2005 when I was starting my real estate investing journey!"

—Ken Corsini of HGTV's *Flip or Flop Atlanta*
on *How to Invest in Real Estate*

"There are very few books that provide a detailed, step-by-step frame-work for accomplishing real estate success. Brandon Turner's *[Rental Property Investing]* does that and does it in a way that puts financial freedom through real estate within reach of anyone who wants it."

—J Scott, Author of *The Book on Flipping Houses*

"I wish I had *[Managing Rental Properties]* before I made all of my expen-sive property management mistakes! Brandon and Heather Turner have covered the biggest challenges for landlords and solved each one with step-by-step systems."

—Chad Carson, Author of *Retire Early with Real Estate*

Praise for Brian Murray's Crushing It in Apartments and Commercial Real Estate

---

**Gold Award Winner,
Nonfiction Book Awards**

**Gold Award Winner,
2018 Robert Bruss Real Estate Book Awards**

"A strong choice in a crowded category."

—*Publishers Weekly*

"Newbies and professionals alike will benefit from this volume, which is chockfull of insight and solid investing advice."

—BlueInkReview.com

"The mistakes he names can be learned from, and his transparency makes his stories of success both exciting and inspiring."

—*Foreword* Clarion Review

The Multifamily Millionaire, Volume II: Create Generational Wealth by Investing in Large Multifamily Real Estate
Brian Murray and Brandon Turner

Published by BiggerPockets Publishing LLC, Denver, Colorado
Copyright © 2021 by Brian Murray and Brandon Turner
All rights reserved.

Publisher's Cataloging-in-Publication Data

Names: Turner, Brandon, author. | Murray, Brian Harold, 1968-, author.
Title: The multifamily millionaire , volume II : create generational wealth by investing in large multifamily real estate/ by Brandon Turner and Brian Murray.
Description: Includes bibliographical references. | Denver, CO: BiggerPockets Publishing, 2021.
Identifiers: LCCN: 2020945827 | ISBN 9781947200401 (Hardcover) | 9781947200425 (pbk.) | 9781947200418 (ebook)
Subjects: LCSH Residential real estate--Purchasing. | Real estate investment. | Apartment houses. | House buying. | BISAC BUSINESS & ECONOMICS / Real Estate / General | BUSINESS & ECONOMICS / Real Estate / Buying & Selling Homes | BUSINESS & ECONOMICS / Investments & Securities / Real Estate
Classification: LCC HD1382.5 .T87 v.2 2021 | DDC 332.63/24--dc23

Printed on recycled paper in the United States of America
10 9 8 7 6 5 4 3 2 1

Dedication

The Multifamily Millionaire, Volume II,
is dedicated

by Brian to Alexa, Jackie, Ryan, and Kyle,

and by Brandon to Rosie and Wilder.

Our children are our "why."

TABLE OF CONTENTS

PREFACE

Whatever you are thinking, think bigger.

—TONY HSIEH

I (Brian Murray here—and throughout this book anytime you see "I," it's me talking!) was one of thirty multifamily investors from around the country who had convened in Las Vegas, lured by a shared interest in learning from one another and raising our game. The first morning, we sat around a conference room listening attentively as each person took a turn going to the front of the room to present. One by one, the investors introduced themselves, discussed what they were working on, what they were struggling with, and how they could help others.

Everybody's presentation was unique, and they were uniformly impressive. Even though many of the attendees had been investing for only a few years, they were acquiring apartment communities with hundreds of units—and some had accumulated multifamily portfolios that numbered in the thousands. It was humbling. And it was a wake-up call.

I walked into the event thinking I had done pretty well for myself, and by most standards, that was true. Without raising any outside capital, I had amassed a respectable portfolio of properties, including more than 500 multifamily units. However, many of the folks in attendance had portfolios that dwarfed mine.

Perhaps even more impressive were their eye-popping goals—this was a group of people who were thinking BIG. They were amazing and inspiring. I was surrounded by fellow real estate entrepreneurs who had found solutions to many of the constraints that were limiting my own growth. I was fascinated by the things I learned and the people I met that day, and I knew it was time to level up.

This type of gathering is called a mastermind, a concept introduced by the author Napoleon Hill in 1925 and later expounded on in his renowned book *Think and Grow Rich*. The idea is to convene a group of peers to share advice, learn from one another, help one another, and grow.

Attending a mastermind might sound cool, but to be completely frank, attending this event was outside my comfort zone. I almost didn't go, and I certainly didn't know what to expect—but thank God I decided to attend. The two days I spent surrounded by other investors at this mastermind led to rapid, dramatic changes in my real estate investing— changes that would significantly affect me, my family, and my future.

How could that one event have so much impact? For one, it drastically changed my perspective. It challenged some of my long-standing beliefs and self-imposed limitations. It made me recognize that while I'd been successful up to that point, I'd reached a plateau in my investing. When it was my turn to present to the group, the other investors at the event offered their objective feedback. They complimented me on what I had accomplished on my own, but they also put a spotlight on my untapped growth potential—and I realized it was time to chart a new course.

Within the next six months, I had started a real estate meetup and joined two additional masterminds. I met many more people operating at a high level who shared my passion for entrepreneurship, real estate, and giving back. These people would make valuable introductions, teach me important lessons, and become my close friends. I would partner with them, sell properties to them, and invest in their deals.

The following years brought sweeping changes to my investing. I committed to raising my game to a whole new level. I set goals that were beyond anything I'd previously contemplated or believed possible.

I did a self-assessment and realized that I couldn't reach those goals on my own—and that I didn't want to. My experience up to that point had proven that going it alone can be lonely and limiting. I opened myself up to partnerships, and I went even further outside my comfort zone by entering new geographic markets and delegating far more responsibility for my existing portfolio. I embraced change. And I grew.

All of this was exciting and motivating. Sure, it was stressful at times, and of course it was hard work, but it was also fun and transformational. My portfolio has grown exponentially since I first sat at that mastermind table and opened my eyes to a whole new realm of possibilities.

What about you? Do you want to scale up in multifamily real estate investing? If so, Brandon and I are here to help make that a reality—because if we can do it, so can you. If you're determined to 10x or 100x your portfolio or buy your first hundred-plus-unit apartment complex, we want to share everything possible to improve your chances of success.

The first volume of *The Multifamily Millionaire* is a comprehensive resource for investing in small to medium multifamily properties. It provides a solid foundation for real estate investors who are either just getting started or in the process of growing their portfolio, and we believe the strategies in Volume I can be instrumental in achieving the dream of financial independence through real estate. If you haven't read Volume I, we highly encourage you to do so.

We wrote Volume II for the investor who wants to really go BIG in multifamily. It assumes a baseline of knowledge that you can get from Volume I or through firsthand experience investing in small to medium properties. We'll delve into strategies that can help you get to the next level and lay out a game plan designed to guide you every step of the way.

While more advanced, these strategies are not necessarily new, groundbreaking, or all-encompassing. That said, we believe that Volumes I and II of *The Multifamily Millionaire* cover more ground than any resource previously available. Still, there's no limit to how much you can learn about multifamily real estate—every single chapter could be expanded into a book of its own.

Experienced investors might be familiar with some of the methods we'll cover. However, based on countless conversations with investors of all levels, we've learned that strategies that seem obvious to some can be new to others, and we don't want to make any assumptions. We've encountered experienced investors who have never come across ideas that many others would consider standard practice, and we've spoken with newbies whose fresh perspectives have enabled them to identify approaches that are truly innovative. This book is intentionally inclusive, because we recognize that investors will benefit from the information we share to differing degrees depending on their level of experience.

Even so, it's unlikely that even the most experienced investors will have implemented all the strategies contained in this book. Hopefully, you will walk away with at least one new way to raise your game. And if you pick up and implement even one idea from Volume II, we're confident you'll realize a pretty great return on your investment in this book!

Finally, we would be remiss not to acknowledge that investing in large multifamily properties is not for the faint of heart. These investments can sometimes be complicated. The amount of risk involved is proportionate to the size of the deal. And there are no shortcuts—taking things to the next level requires commitment, drive, and hard work. People don't achieve extraordinary things without taking risks, making sacrifices, and encountering setbacks and failures along the way. But those who succeed hustle and persevere regardless—and that's how they win.

If none of that scares you, then something is wrong, because it should. However, if your excitement, determination, and work ethic are strong enough to overcome your fears, you might be ready for this new challenge. It is our sincere hope that you find tremendous value in this book and achieve great success in your investing. We don't want you to do what we've done. We want you to do more.

Now get out there, roll up your sleeves, and crush it!

INTRODUCTION

*If people aren't calling you crazy, you aren't
thinking big enough.*

—RICHARD BRANSON

"I just don't want to see you ruin your life," the broker said in a patronizing tone that made me want to reach across the table and strangle him. "You seem like a nice guy," he continued, "but it's pretty obvious you haven't done this before. Some very experienced investors have looked at this property and passed on it. You just don't know what you're getting yourself into."

Maybe he had a point. After all, he was the big-shot broker from out of town in a fancy suit who had been doing this for decades. And he was right—I (this is Brian Murray, by the way, and it usually will be my stories throughout the book unless stated otherwise) didn't have a lot of experience, and the property I had under contract was in distress. I certainly didn't fit the profile of a typical buyer. In fact, a small investor acquiring a property of this size was far enough outside the norm that some might consider it reckless and inappropriate.

Still, the way he said it really irked me—and that infuriating smile of his, I decided, was just a little too big. He may have been well intentioned, but he struck me as a bit too smug and condescending. I imagined if he had a puppy at home, he'd speak to it the same way he was speaking to me. In fact, I half expected him to reach over and pat me on the head... maybe offer me a treat. As if on cue, his voice interrupted my thoughts. "Would you like another donut?" he asked, still beaming.

In hindsight, I realize my negative reaction probably had less to do with his demeanor and more to do with my own insecurities and the hard truth of his words. Despite any displays of outward calm, under the surface I was waging an internal war—fighting to suppress a cacophony of doubts and fears. I was trying to buy my largest property to date, and a lot of naysayers were making me second-guess myself.

Fortunately, while the broker's words played on my anxieties, they didn't deter me. I moved forward with the deal and eventually managed to turn that property around, creating massive value as occupancy improved, income climbed, and expenses came down. Even so, the broker was at least partially right, because when you take on a challenging project, it's never really as easy as just "turning the property around"—which almost makes it sound like flipping a switch.

Although most aspects of multifamily investing aren't complex, it takes a lot of work and can be a bumpy road, to say the least. You can expect lots of trial and error, and plenty of setbacks along the way. I did make a lot of mistakes, just as people thought I would—not only on my first multifamily but on all the others that followed. Some mistakes were small, some were big, and while some may have been unavoidable, others were downright embarrassing. All in all, I've gotten a real education.

The lessons I learned as I grew my portfolio would prove valuable over the long run, but they didn't pay the bills. Still, if I messed up so many times, how did I manage to pull it off? How did I avoid bankruptcy and not ruin my life, as some people had predicted?

While many factors contributed to my positive outcome, the most important is this: *Multifamily investments are forgiving by their very nature* and offer a number of benefits that are unique within the investment world.

The Benefits of Large Multifamily

Large multifamily investments share the same advantages as most rental real estate, including wealth creation through cash flow, appreciation (forced and passive), tax savings, and amortization, which result in the accumulation of equity as you pay down your debt. Brandon calls these the four wealth generators of real estate—and for good reason. Given enough time, these four glorious generators can be further magnified through leverage and compounding to create abundant wealth.

In addition, multifamily assets can serve as an effective hedge against inflation, provide diversification to your investment portfolio, and offer a degree of recession resistance not found in other asset classes, which we will explore in more depth in a later chapter.

These are all advantageous, but let's not overlook the obvious. The benefits you can realize by owning investment real estate are directly proportional to the size of your holdings. All things being equal, owning a multifamily property that is ten times as large will generate ten times the cash flow, ten times the tax benefits, and so on. What *won't* increase by a factor of ten? The work that goes into it.

That's not to say that investing in large multifamily properties isn't a lot of work, but efficiencies of scale do come into play. For example, the work that goes into the underwriting, due diligence, and closing of a 150-unit apartment complex is not ten times as much as for a 15-unit complex. It might be closer to 50 percent more work, if that.

Other benefits of investing in larger multifamily properties include:
- Better lending terms than you can get for smaller multifamily properties
- Diversification of income across more tenants
- Efficiencies of scale in operations
- More opportunity to force appreciation through value-add
- More leverage and negotiating power with vendors
- More well-qualified buyers when it's time to sell
- Greater interest from people who would like to invest in your projects

The income diversification aspect of large multifamily properties is particularly important. Let's say you own a hundred-unit apartment building and you make a mistake that causes you to lose a tenant—or three. Most likely the resulting 1 to 3 percent drop in income is something you can learn from without missing a beat.

Most new property owners have at least a 25 percent cushion built into their cash flow, which, if necessary, can help them muddle through some pretty big gaffes, surprises, or dismal circumstances. On top of that, if you have an amortizing mortgage, you're paying down your debt every month, which is building equity, in effect creating a reserve that could be cashed in someday in a time of need.

Finally, large multifamily properties offer the advantage of allowing owners to force appreciation on an even larger scale by taking steps to boost income or reduce expenses. A change that might yield modest results in a smaller property, such as the installation of low-flow plumbing fixtures or a modest increase in rents, can create surprising amounts of equity in a large multifamily.

As already stated, multifamily properties tend to be forgiving by nature. They operate with momentum and once they're headed in the right direction, they can power through most setbacks without significant consequences. If you make as many mistakes as I have, it's reassuring to know that it's going to take a lot to derail the train.

Even though we took somewhat different paths, Brandon and I shared a penchant for finding ways to make improvements that paid some pretty big dividends right from the start. We both overcompensated for our blunders by constantly identifying problems and coming up with solutions; unlocking value by fixing things, improving things, making things more efficient. It might be something as simple as installing higher-efficiency lightbulbs. Or it might involve mustering up the fortitude to deal with unsavory situations. We have both tackled problems that would make most people's skin crawl—all along, showing lots of love and attentiveness where before there was neglect.

This value-add approach turned out to be one of the keys to surviving and then thriving for both of us, especially early in our investing careers. By incessantly seeking out and implementing strategies to boost income and cut expenses, we were able to generate the cash we needed not only to overcome our mistakes and setbacks but also to purchase additional properties and grow our portfolios. After we added enough value to a property, we would refinance it and pull cash out to do more deals, which in turn continued to fuel our growth.

That said, while focusing on value-add real estate investments can be lucrative and allow you to grow without raising outside capital, it isn't easy and it's not for everyone. Over the years, as Brandon and I have grown our respective portfolios and expanded geographically, we've both learned how to invest more passively by relying on the knowledge and experience of partners and third-party associates to get things done. Our earlier hands-on experience has proven invaluable as we underwrite deals and oversee property managers. We've also realized the benefits of raising capital to fund our acquisitions, which has accelerated our ability to buy large multifamily properties while providing the satisfaction of creating wealth for others who invest in our deals.

The Downsides of Large Multifamily

After hearing all the benefits of investing in large multifamily real estate, perhaps you're motivated to dive in. If so, we wouldn't blame you. It's a decision we've both made—but if large multifamily properties are so wonderful, why doesn't everyone invest in them? There are many reasons, but let's review the most common and legitimate ones.

First and foremost, while investing in large multifamily properties can be lucrative, it's no walk in the park. This type of investing requires a lot of hard work and sacrifice. We've had the pleasure of meeting dozens of investors who have grown portfolios of 1,000-plus units. The one thing they all have in common? A strong work ethic.

This should not be surprising, as hard work is a powerful force that can lead to positive results in any field of endeavor. In an interview with *60 Minutes*, the actor Will Smith said, "I've never really viewed myself as particularly talented. I've viewed myself as slightly above average in talent. Where I excel is ridiculous, sickening, work ethic." Among the highest achievers in real estate, you'll often find this same level of determination, sometimes bordering on obsession.

Even when the work is divided among a team of partners, there is always more to be done. That said, you have a choice about how far and how fast you grow a business. You don't need to have 500 units in the first year or 2,000 in the second—and you certainly wouldn't be expected to do everything yourself, nor should you. There are plenty of excellent property management firms and other vendors out there who can make your life easier.

Investors who are in it for the long haul need to have balance in their lives. Just know going in that if you want to excel in the multifamily world, you can't offload everything. That may be disheartening for people who were under the illusion that real estate investing is an entirely passive activity. However, real estate is a business like any other and it doesn't magically run itself, especially in growth mode.

Are there passive paths to wealth in multifamily investing? Absolutely. If you want to invest on a large scale but don't want to put in the work, you can invest in other people's deals. There are lots of syndicators out there looking for limited partners who are willing to invest in their multifamily projects. These investments come with no responsibilities or authority—you just have to write a check.

The downside of this passive approach? You won't have any control over the outcome, and there is generally less upside. That said, these limitations can be a fair tradeoff for people whose commitments or priorities won't allow for active involvement.

The Myths of Large Multifamily

In an ideal world, decisions regarding whether to invest in multifamily would be driven by an objective evaluation of the pros and cons, in conjunction with one's own personal goals and circumstances. Unfortunately, decisions about large properties are often made for the wrong reasons. There are many convincing myths out there. Let's take a look at four of the most pervasive.

Myth No. 1: Large Multifamily Is Too Complex

While there are more moving parts to large properties and analyzing them is more involved, in most cases they really aren't that much more complex than small ones. Most aspiring investors have heard this at one point or another, but few actually believe it.

When a new investor first enters a large apartment complex with an eye toward owning and operating it, they are likely to feel overwhelmed. The sheer vastness of the asset and fear of the unknown create anxiety, which can drive people to discard the idea.

When that same investor considers a single-family home, a condo, or a duplex, they probably feel a greater sense of familiarity and comfort. They have probably lived in a similar property, and it seems more manageable. Most new investors feel they can handle a small condo. How complicated could it be?

What is a 150-unit apartment complex? It's 150 single apartments. It's seventy-five duplexes or fifty triplexes. At a high level, the issues you deal with are the same. If you can manage a single condo unit, you can manage a large apartment complex—especially since you're most likely going to have a third-party management company to handle day-to-day operations. You can hire people to help with anything else you don't have the time for, don't have the knowledge or skills for, or just don't want to do yourself. You can also partner. When you invest in a large multifamily deal, there's a lot more potential profit to split with other people.

Myth No. 2: Most Investors Can't Afford to Buy a Large Property

This is a particularly powerful and prevalent myth, primarily because it is rooted in a grain of truth. Most people *don't* have enough money to buy a large apartment building. In fact, even investors who have already accumulated a respectable portfolio of smaller multifamily assets may not be able to make the leap on their own.

But here is the *real* truth: The vast majority of people buying these large assets are not using their own money. They raise money from others and keep some of the equity for their trouble. In fact, in the world of large multifamily, the rarity is the investor who has enough cash to *not* need other people's money.

There are many ways to structure the acquisition of large assets, and we'll review those in more detail later. Just know that cash is not a prerequisite for making a large multifamily acquisition.

Myth No. 3: There Are No Good Deals

The market moves in cycles, and valuations can be high or low relative to other periods in time. However, at every stage in the cycle, there's a seemingly incessant chorus of people predicting a pending decline or complaining that things are overpriced. The truth is that there are *always* good deals, regardless of where we may be in the market cycle.

Of course, we should clarify what a "good deal" actually is, since that can clearly be subjective. We would define a good deal as one that cash flows at a high enough level to generate returns satisfactory to the investor, with enough of a cushion built in to weather any storms you're likely to encounter along the way. If you have a long-term horizon and can lock in debt at an interest rate that will achieve these results, your downside is limited. A good deal should also have a potential upside that will allow you to force appreciation and increase the value of your investment.

Are there deals out there that can achieve these kinds of returns? While it can seem impossible at times, the answer to this question is *always* yes. The question is, how difficult are they to find, and how hard are you willing to search to find them? If you're relying entirely on public sources like the internet and broker listings, finding strong deals can be challenging and you're likely to get discouraged. But there are many other ways to find deals, which we'll delve into later on.

Myth No. 4: You Need a Ton of Experience

This myth is also rooted in a grain of truth. Real estate investment experience is undoubtedly a valuable asset for diving into the world of large multifamily, but lack of it is not a deal breaker.

We've observed that prominent investors can travel a wide array of paths to achieve their goals. Some start with smaller properties and work their way up, using "The Stack" method, which we outlined in Volume I. These investors begin with a small property and exponentially grow their portfolio by making increasingly larger acquisitions, gaining knowledge, experience, and capital along the way. Other investors team up with partners who have the experience they lack. Still others leverage valuable skills they acquired through an education or career that, on the surface, may seem entirely unrelated to real estate.

Is experience valuable? Undoubtedly. Does a lack of experience preclude you from buying a large multifamily property? Absolutely not.

Large Multifamily Is Within Your Reach

One of the greatest takeaways from all my experience with larger properties is a conviction that investing in large multifamily deals is within the reach of most real estate investors. There are ways to overcome any limitations you may face as well as the mistakes you'll undoubtedly make.

If you currently own rental real estate or have owned rentals in the past, you've almost certainly laid a solid foundation for moving up to larger multifamily properties. Everything you've learned and experienced will improve your chances of success.

What if you haven't owned rental real estate and are just getting started? You'll need to dig in and really educate yourself—a process that, by the way, should never stop. If you haven't already done so, read Volume I of *The Multifamily Millionaire*, then read this book, then go back and read them both again.

You'll also need to network and build relationships, because going it alone as a newbie is a recipe for disaster. You'll need to do a ton of work and take on the things that others aren't willing to. However, if you're determined enough, patient enough, and prepared to do whatever work is necessary, becoming a large multifamily investor and creating generational wealth is almost certainly within your reach.

In the first volume of *The Multifamily Millionaire*, we discussed a common problem: Many real estate investors stay within their comfort zone for far too long. They get comfortable with their small portfolio—or with no portfolio—and although their heart and soul yearn for growth and expansion, they stay small because their fear speaks louder than their ambition. This book is designed to be an antidote to fear. We want to arm you with the detailed, tried, tested, and true knowledge you need to rise to your full potential.

A decade ago, I didn't listen to Mr. Condescending Smile. Instead, I stepped outside my comfort zone and discovered an incredible life on the other side. May this book be your guide as you take your business to the next level—toward becoming a multifamily millionaire and creating generational wealth.

KEY TAKEAWAYS

- Before deciding whether to invest in large multifamily properties, you'll need to weigh a number of advantages and disadvantages.
- Common myths about large multifamily real estate are that it's too complicated, the properties are not affordable, there are no good deals, and you need a lot of experience. All of these may have a grain of truth but are simply challenges that can be overcome.
- Despite what many people may say or believe, investing in large multifamily deals is within the reach of most small real estate investors.

Note from the authors: Throughout this book, we wanted to not only "tell" you about the path to large multifamily success—we wanted to share actual examples from our experience. The following is the first in a series of end-of-chapter anecdotes that chronicle real-life examples of large multifamily projects. We hope these ongoing stories leave you inspired, educated, and entertained.

River Apartments: Part I

I still remember the phone call. The CEO of a real estate investment firm was going to be in town soon and wanted to meet me. His company owned River Apartments, a 115-unit multifamily project in the area, and they'd decided it was time to sell—hopefully to me.

The call was not entirely unexpected. The multifamily property in question had caught my attention several years earlier, so I had reached out to see if they might be willing to sell. When they said no, I continued to reach out every six months or so. The message was the same every time I checked in: "No, and if we change our mind, we'll let you know." Well, true to his word, the CEO was now letting me know.

It can be difficult to find good multifamily deals, so I make it a point to plant seeds like this all the time. When the owner of a property I'm interested in eventually decides to sell, I'll be the first one they call, and I can reap what I sowed. It's worked for me before, and it worked again this time.

During my meeting with the CEO, I discovered that the property was an affordable housing project that was currently operating under a contract with the U.S. Department of Housing and Urban Development (HUD). This meant that the government was subsidizing the rent to help the residents afford their housing, and in exchange the property owner was subject to a wide range of operating restrictions, inspections, and reporting requirements. However, the CEO explained that the contract was about to expire. Knowing the local rental market, I thought that converting the apartments from HUD to market-rate housing could be a great opportunity to unlock some value.

Soon after our meeting, I entered into negotiations and started doing some preliminary underwriting. What I found wasn't pretty on the surface. Staffing was literally double what it should have been for a project of this size, and maintenance costs were exorbitant beyond reason.

The CEO acknowledged that there were plenty of opportunities to cut costs and used this angle to try to persuade me that there was upside potential—something I was already sold on. He explained that his company was ready to pull up stakes in the area and wanted to make a deal soon so they could redeploy the proceeds to another project they had lined up. He encouraged me to look beyond the numbers, which were ugly.

As it turned out, the seller didn't know the half of it—things were worse than either of us could have imagined. Since the property was local, I asked around. Eventually, I tracked down some of the contractors who were routinely doing work there, one of which I had an excellent relationship with. It was a painting contractor who gave me the first clue as to what was really going on at River Apartments, and it was shocking.

What a mess this project was. Why did I like this property again? It was about to become a lot harder to remember.

To be continued...

Chapter One

DEFINING YOUR INVESTMENT CRITERIA

The successful warrior is the average man, with laser-like focus.

—BRUCE LEE

One of the wonderful things about real estate investing is that there are so many different types of properties and ways to create wealth by investing in them. Even within the world of large multifamily investing you have a wide range of property types, classes, sizes, values, and markets. While it's great to have so many choices available, the breadth of possibilities can also be overwhelming.

One of the keys to improving your chances of success in multifamily investing is to narrow your focus by defining your investment criteria. In Volume I we talked about the importance of establishing crystal-clear criteria—CCC. This means thinking through all the possible investment strategies as well as the type, location, condition, and price of the property you're seeking and your target returns, so that you can narrow your search down to a manageable level. Defining the specific strategy and characteristics of the property you're seeking is not only advantageous but also necessary from a practical standpoint.

At any given moment, there are more multifamily properties for sale than you could ever hope to evaluate. LoopNet.com claims to have more than 500,000 multifamily properties listed for sale, but that's just the tip of the iceberg. There are far more properties listed on other sites, not to mention the millions of off-market properties that are potential candidates for acquisition.

For example, the commercial real estate data tracking company Reonomy has more than 4 million multifamily properties in their database. If you were to spend just ten minutes evaluating each property in their database for twelve hours a day, seven days a week, it would take more than 150 years to go through them all. That doesn't leave much time for anything else, so narrowing down what you're looking for is probably a better approach.

Clarity and specificity will also allow you to better develop knowledge and expertise. The more focused your investment criteria, the easier it is for you to educate yourself about asset type, geographic area, prices, rents, trends, and so on. If your focus is too broad, your knowledge will tend to be shallower and harder to maintain. Focus allows you to go deep, which is how you gain expertise.

In his best-selling book *Awaken the Giant Within*, Tony Robbins attributes his ability to make quantum leaps forward to controlled focus, which he says is "like a laser beam that can cut through anything that seems to be stopping you." Robbins calls this principle "concentration of power" and offers this observation: "One reason so few of us achieve what we truly want is that we never direct our focus; we never concentrate our power. Most people dabble their way through life, never deciding to master anything in particular." There is truth here, and you would be well served to consider concentrating your power in your real estate investing. Defining your investment criteria is the first step.

Having deep knowledge about a specific property type and geographic area also puts you in a better position to readily recognize and execute on opportunities. You'll get to know what market rents are, what is typically included in those rents, what the supply and demand is for different unit types, what amenities are popular, how properties are being valued, what areas are growing or declining, and more.

This means that when a deal comes to market, you'll be able to quickly and accurately determine what it's worth. You're more likely to avoid making mistakes and be able to take full advantage of opportunities that may be overlooked by others—plus you'll have the network in place to execute on them. Having deep knowledge of a specific property type and market can also help you build credibility.

One of the challenges you'll face each time you raise your game in the multifamily world is gaining the respect of people in a position to help you realize your goals. Among those important people are brokers, lenders, and investors, and you'll want to establish relationships with them.

All these people will expect you to clearly and concisely communicate your investment criteria. Nobody is going to be inspired by someone who seems adrift and unclear about what direction they're headed. Brokers will assume you're wasting their time. Lenders will assume you have no idea what you're doing. Investors will run for the hills. But if you can speak with authority on your investment, you can make a positive first impression and lay the foundation for a mutually beneficial relationship.

What to Consider Before Selecting Investment Criteria

Understanding and appreciating why it may be necessary to define your investment criteria doesn't make it any easier to choose what to focus on, but there are some steps you can take to narrow things down.

Self-Evaluation

The first step in defining your investment criteria is to do a self-evaluation. The goal of this exercise is to determine what type of property is best suited to your strengths, weaknesses, and personal goals. Some of the things you'll want to consider include your skill set, your access to capital, where you live, your knowledge and experience, your risk tolerance, and your personal preferences. If you're working with partners, you'll evaluate the strengths and weaknesses of the team as a whole.

For example, you'll want to consider your team's access to capital. If you know that you can raise $1 million in capital, you're likely looking at a purchase price of $3 million to $4 million, depending on the scope of planned capital expenditures and the terms of the debt you can secure. If you're interested in a particular class of property and geographic area, you'll know how much investors are typically paying per unit and can estimate how many units you are looking for.

There are no hard-and-fast rules for performing your self-evaluation. Ideally, it is an exercise in objective judgment—the same type of judgment you'll apply when ultimately selecting your investment criteria.

Competitive Advantages

The multifamily world is very competitive, and the bigger you go, the stronger the competition, driven by more savvy competitors and fewer available properties. Based on your self-assessment, challenge yourself to identify potential competitive advantages. What can you do better than other investors? What are you willing to do that other investors are not? Think about both your current strengths and those that you're willing to develop. Is there a specific approach to investing you could leverage that will create an advantage over the competition?

When Brandon and I reflect back on when we first started out as investors, our biggest weaknesses were similar—we both had limited knowledge and experience, and we both lacked capital. However, we were also both willing to educate ourselves, work much harder than most people, and consistently motivate ourselves to take on challenging and stressful projects.

These strengths were best leveraged by investing in our local markets, where we could be more hands-on: Brandon on the Olympic Peninsula in western Washington, and me in upstate New York. On opposite ends of the country, we took on distressed properties that we could turn around, mostly by necessity. Distressed properties were priced lower, so they were more within reach financially, especially since the sellers of such assets tended to be more open to creative financing deals.

Contrast our situation with that of an investor who has a significant amount of capital to deploy and too many obligations to put a lot of time into their multifamily properties. This investor's circumstances would better align with a turnkey investment strategy that prioritizes the acquisition of newer, stabilized properties that will be managed by a third party. The returns on such a property will be lower but more stable. They can create value through rent growth over time while equity grows through principal paydown. With limited hands-on involvement, there is no need for projects to be local, so this investor might look across the country and choose a specific market or two they find most appealing.

Somewhere in between the distressed-property turnaround and the turnkey asset is a more middle-of-the-road strategy called value-add. Value-add is the bread and butter of many large multifamily investors. The idea is to force appreciation by making improvements to the property that will boost income and reduce expenses. Investors will typically upgrade units and add amenities to command higher rents.

The value-add approach is popular because it avoids the high risk associated with distressed assets but still offers the opportunity for attractive returns. Due to this approach's prevalence and potential, we have included an abundance of value-add resources, which we'll share later in this book.

Vision and Goals

Brandon had just left a real estate conference where he was surrounded by investors doing big deals—much bigger than he was doing. Just as happened to me at my first mastermind, he was made acutely aware of how much higher his potential was by surrounding himself with those at a higher level, and he made a commitment to get outside his comfort zone, to graduate to larger deals.

Knowing he needed to lead with a strong vision, he picked up the book *Vivid Vision* by Cameron Herold and read it cover to cover on a flight from Denver to Salt Lake City, and on the following seven-hour flight to his home in Maui he carefully crafted a three-year vision for himself and his team using Herold's methodology. When he touched down at his final destination, he had specifically laid out where he was headed. This was the beginning of Open Door Capital, which soon led to our partnership and, several years later, the very book you're reading right now.

When you're ready to take your multifamily investing to the next level, having a clearly defined vision and specific goals is extremely important. Therefore, if you haven't already done so, take the time and effort to establish your vision and goals.

If you've already defined your vision and goals, consider whether they need to be updated. Taking things to the next level often requires a shift in mindset and a clearly defined path. If you don't know what your target is, it's very difficult to take aim.

To achieve your goals in multifamily real estate investing, you'll need to purchase properties, and which properties you acquire will be one of the most important determinants of whether you meet your goals and fulfill your vision. Your investment criteria must align with your vision and goals.

Now that you have completed your self-evaluation, identified your competitive advantages, and created a vision and goals, you're ready to define your investment criteria. Your investment criteria will consist of a list of attributes associated with the location you choose to target and the property itself.

Location

The first parameter you should consider when defining your multifamily investment criteria is the geographic market. Your target location can be broad or narrow. Some multifamily investors pick a specific region of the country, while others choose states, counties, or cities, or even particular neighborhoods in or around those cities.

In industry jargon, the major markets are called primary markets, the smaller surrounding cities and towns are called secondary markets, and more rural areas are called tertiary markets. All else being equal, multifamily properties in primary markets tend to be valued more highly than those in secondary and tertiary markets. Does this mean you should target primary markets? Not necessarily. Higher valuations are usually associated with lower returns. Investors are sometimes willing to trade the benefits of an urban location for stronger cash flows.

When establishing your buying criteria, it is advantageous to narrow your target market as much as possible while still providing adequate investment opportunities. Having access to more deals is one reason some investors focus on markets in or near large metropolitan areas. Striking the right balance between staying focused and getting enough deal flow isn't easy and may take some trial and error, especially when there are so many considerations that may affect your decision. Additional factors that investors tend to consider when selecting a market include:

- **Proximity to Home:** While you can invest anywhere, there are many advantages to living close to your projects (or having a partner reside there). Investing locally makes it easier to keep a close eye on things and stay aware of activities and developments that might influence investment decisions. If you're considering investing outside your immediate area, reasonable access by car or direct flight should weigh in a market's favor. Visiting a project monthly or quarterly can help improve the likelihood of meeting your objectives.

- **Familiarity:** If you don't live nearby, the next best thing is for you or a partner to have some close familiarity with a market. This could be a place where one of you used to live or attend school or currently have friends and family.
- **Population:** As already touched on, there are pros and cons to investing in urban versus rural areas. You may find that more rural areas have less competition and lower prices, but in general, metropolitan areas with higher populations have more jobs and a renter base that tends to be viewed more favorably by both investors and lenders. As a result, many investors set minimum populations as part of their investment criteria, with common thresholds being metropolitan statistical areas (MSAs) of 100,000 or 200,000 people. Perhaps even more important than population size is population *trends*, which can drive the demand for housing.
- **Job Growth:** Low unemployment and high job creation represent opportunity. Jobs attract residents and spur economic growth, creating a strong foundation for multifamily investments to perform well. Job growth increases demand for apartments and can trigger increases in market rental rates.
- **Employment Base:** It's a good idea to analyze the source of jobs in the area. Ideally, the employment base will be diversified and not too dependent on any one employer. Large employers that are less cyclical and more recession-resistant—such as government, health care, and education—are also desirable.
- **Crime:** While every city has crime, some have higher crime rates than others. Even within a particular city, crime rates fluctuate from neighborhood to neighborhood. You're better off investing in one of the safer neighborhoods. High crime doesn't have to be a deal-breaker, but it can hamper the growth and prosperity that will elevate a property over time.
- **Demographics:** Ideally the demographics of an area will align well with the type and class of property you want to invest in. Pay particular attention to household income levels, which can help determine whether there is the capacity for most residents to pay rent.
- **Housing Market:** Multifamily properties tend to perform better in communities where there is a strong housing market. To an extent,

rentals are competing with homeownership. High housing prices often indicate that a place is considered desirable to live in and can support higher rents.

- **Supply:** You won't be investing in a vacuum. There will be competition. The strongest markets will attract developers, and new construction can increase supply. If a large number of units are under construction, the result can be a housing surplus, and this oversupply can lead to lower occupancy and rent suppression.

- **Landlord-Tenant Laws:** Tenant-protection laws, including rent control, in some states and cities have made it progressively more difficult for landlords to prosper. As legal burdens increase, the implications are significant. How landlord-friendly a market is will become an increasingly important factor influencing investment decisions.

- **Valuation Levels:** The ideal target market is one that isn't at the top of every investor's list. If a market is already hot, you may find excessive competition and property valuations that are too rich to achieve decent returns. If you can identify a market that is in the beginning stages of an upward swing, you'll be able to get in early, acquire properties at reasonable prices, and benefit from the rent growth and price appreciation that will closely follow the job growth and economic development.

- **Micro Considerations:** When drilling down to location on a micro level, some factors to consider include proximity to major employers, the quality of the school district, access to major highways, nearby retail and restaurants, local crime levels, and the overall desirability of a specific neighborhood. Neighborhoods are sometimes ranked with a letter classification to reflect their desirability. Class A neighborhoods are the nicest, most prosperous areas, while Class B neighborhoods tend to be more middle class. Class C neighborhoods are generally more blue-collar, low-to-moderate-income areas, while Class D are not always ideal investing areas.

- **Proximity to Retailers:** You can sometimes draw conclusions about an area by looking at which retailers and restaurants are located nearby. Some investors will require their assets to be within a certain distance of a specific store or restaurant chain, such as Walmart or Starbucks. The idea is to leverage the research done by a corporation's site selectors, who have already determined that such locations are viable for investment from the standpoint of the local population, demographics, and growth trends. In addition, the opportunity to live in close proximity to certain retail or restaurant locations may also be appealing to renters.

As you can see, there are many factors worth considering when trying to choose a target market location—but don't get overwhelmed. Most multifamily investors will pick just a few criteria that are most important to them and apply those. No market is perfect. Your best bet is to prioritize the characteristics of a market that are most important to you and try to find an area that offers the best compromise. You can always make changes later.

Property

Once you've decided on a geographic market to target, you'll have to decide on what kind of multifamily property you'd like to invest in. Among the factors to consider are type, class, age, price, size, occupancy, and target returns.

Type

Large multifamily properties come in many forms. While there are no industry-wide standard definitions, Freddie Mac breaks down multifamily types as follows:

- **High-Rise:** A building with nine or more floors and at least one elevator
- **Mid-Rise:** A multistory building with an elevator, typically in an urban area
- **Garden-Style:** A one-, two-, or three-story apartment development built in a garden-like setting in a suburban, rural, or urban location; buildings may or may not have elevators
- **Walk-Up:** A four- to six-story building without (as the name implies) an elevator
- **Manufactured Housing Community** (mobile home park): A community in which the operator leases ground sites to owners of manufactured homes
- **Special-Purpose Housing:** A multifamily property of any style that targets a particular population segment

- **Student Housing:** A multifamily property of any style in which at least half the units are intended for students attending a nearby learning institution
- **Senior Housing:** A multifamily property of any style that is dedicated to housing senior citizens
- **Subsidized Housing:** A multifamily property of any style that caters to renters with low incomes or special needs and is made affordable by rent and income restriction

Another category of multifamily housing not included on this list but frequently referred to in the industry is "workforce housing," which is unsubsidized housing that is affordable to most low- and middle-income households. Workforce housing and subsidized housing are both popular choices for investors seeking properties that are recession-resistant.

Class

Just as neighborhoods are classified, large multifamily properties of all types are further categorized as Class A, Class B, Class C, and Class D depending on their age, overall condition, and attributes. These letter grades are used to help industry professionals estimate the quality of a property. Unfortunately, the classifications are somewhat ambiguous. What constitutes a particular class is relative, so it can vary significantly depending on what market you're in. That said, we can outline some general guidelines.

Class A multifamily properties are those considered to be of the highest quality in terms of construction, materials, and amenities relative to other properties in the same market. They tend to be newer properties, typically constructed within the past ten years, or sometimes older buildings that have been extensively renovated. Class A properties are also usually situated in the most attractive locations. They present well and command the highest rents.

Class B multifamily properties are a step down from Class A in terms of age and amenities. They are likely to have been constructed within the last twenty years and have good-quality construction with little deferred maintenance.

Class C multifamily properties are older properties with more limited or dated amenities. They will show some age and deferred maintenance. Finishes, fixtures, and appliances are often dated.

Class D multifamily properties are older, dilapidated properties that tend to be in less desirable locations. They are distressed due to some combination of low occupancy, disrepair, crime, and overall bad management.

Class A and Class B assets located in major markets are the most attractive investments for large institutional buyers and lenders. They are usually stabilized properties with limited opportunity to add value, though B properties can sometimes command higher rents if they are upgraded. As a result of the superior quality of these properties, investors can secure better financing terms with the properties commanding premium prices.

Class C and D assets are priced lower and can sometimes be more challenging to finance, but they also tend to offer the most opportunity to add value through improvements. Depending on the state of the property, the successful execution of value-add projects can be costly, disruptive, and labor-intensive. However, the returns can be attractive, making these properties enticing for highly motivated investors seeking to create equity.

Age

Although basic age assumptions are built into each asset class, some investors prefer to be even more specific and insist on a range of years in which a property was built. Your investment strategy will determine the ideal property age for you.

For example, if you're looking for a fully stabilized property with low maintenance, you'll want something constructed within the past ten years. If you're seeking to add value, you'll want something older. Properties with dated finishes and features can sometimes present a great opportunity to renovate and increase rents. However, beware that properties that are too old or neglected may require you to replace major systems, which can be a substantial undertaking.

Price

When defining your buying criteria, you'll want to set a price range, which is generally limited by how much cash you have access to. If you're going to purchase a Class A or Class B property, you can usually finance as much as 75 to 80 percent of the purchase price. You'll also need to budget for closing costs and any improvements you might have planned.

For example, let's say you have access to $2.3 million and you estimate $30,000 in closing costs plus an additional $270,000 for post-closing cash needs. Subtracting the $300,000 from $2.3 million leaves $2 million for a down payment. Assuming a lender will finance 80 percent of the acquisition, the $2 million would cover 20 percent of the purchase price, meaning the purchase price would be $10 million. Since there are many variables here, you might want to set a target price range that is a little broader, say $6 million to $12 million.

For Class C and Class D properties, the same amount of cash is likely going to translate to a lower purchase price. That's because your lending terms will probably be less favorable and you'll need a higher renovation budget. In this case, the target price range might be $5 million to $10 million.

Sometimes creative financing options can reduce the amount of cash required for closing. For example, a seller may extend a loan for a higher percentage of the purchase price than you can get from a bank, or they may extend a loan that supplements bank financing. These types of arrangements have the potential to raise the target purchase price.

Size

Target size is defined by the number of units. How many units you can acquire will be driven in large part by the target price range and average price per unit for your target asset class in your chosen market. For example, if you are looking for Class C properties with apartments priced at $8 million in a market where the average price per unit for Class C apartments is $80,000, you'll be looking for properties with about a hundred units. Since the price per unit can vary according to the specific location, features, and floor plans, you'll have to work within a range.

Occupancy

Some investors are more willing than others to take on a property with low occupancy levels. The primary concerns associated with low occupancy are limited cash flow and lending restrictions. Most lenders like to see a minimum occupancy rate of 85 percent. Once you drop below that, your borrowing options become more limited *and* you're taking on additional risk.

Target Returns

Large multifamily investors usually have specific target returns in mind in order to feel comfortable with a property acquisition. These metrics vary widely and will be covered later in the book, but they primarily come into play when you're doing your underwriting. The returns you're seeking will determine how much you can pay for a given property.

Note that the criteria you or your team establish are internal metrics. You would not typically share these financial targets with a broker or anyone else helping you find a deal. However, if raising capital, you would communicate these metrics to your investors.

Other Property Attributes

This chapter covers only the most common investment criteria—the list is not intended to be comprehensive. Each investor will have their own opinions and priorities and will set their criteria accordingly. For example, some investors will not consider properties that are located in a flood zone. Others rule out certain physical or mechanical features; for instance, many investors will avoid properties with flat or mansard-style roofs due to poor drainage, higher maintenance costs, and shorter life spans.

Sample Investment Criteria

To give you a general idea, below is an example of an actual large multi-family investor's buying criteria. What you elect to target and the criteria you choose to apply may be similar or entirely different.

- **Location:** Primary and secondary cities throughout the Southeast with population trending upward
- **Type and Class:** Class C garden-style or walk-up workforce housing with reposition opportunities
- **Age:** 1980s construction and newer, but will consider others on a case-by-case basis
- **Price:** $5 million to $12 million, with $1.5 million to $3 million in funds provided
- **Size:** One hundred units or larger
- **CAP Rates:** Market rates
- **Roof:** Pitched roof construction preferred
- **Value-Add:** Looking to acquire assets with opportunities to add value through physical improvements or better property management

This set of investment criteria is pretty typical and would be effective.

The "value-add" potential of a property may require a bit more digging and could be assessed afterward, but everything else is straightforward enough that the requirements can be readily applied to a high volume of deals.

Now that you're armed with everything you need to know to set your investment criteria, it's time to take a look at how to structure a large multifamily deal. Deciding how to structure a deal is something you need to prioritize and do early on. In fact, even though the options available to you are sometimes specific to a particular deal, there is little sense finalizing your investment criteria if you haven't considered how you plan to pay for your investment. Only when you've determined your sources of capital can you set a target price range and associated property size.

KEY TAKEAWAYS

- It is practical, advantageous, and necessary to have crystal-clear investment criteria when getting started in large multifamily investing.
- When defining your investment criteria, you should consider what type of property will best leverage your (and your partners') strengths, weaknesses, and personal goals. The investment criteria should also align with your vision and goals.
- The criteria most commonly defined include a property's location, type, class, age, price, size, occupancy, and target returns, but there is no industry-wide standard. Every investor's priorities are different, and you can set your investment criteria accordingly.

River Apartments: Part II

I was pretty excited about River Apartments because the property met all our investment criteria. First, it was a Class C multifamily with more than a hundred units, which is exactly what we wanted. It was also in a good location in our target market. Finally, I was cautiously optimistic that we could acquire the property at a price that would allow us to hit our target returns. The only thing I still wasn't sure of was whether the property offered the kind of value-add potential we were looking for. Now I was busy investigating opportunities to boost income or cut expenses.

As I started digging into the operations at River Apartments, I decided to track down local contractors who had done work there to find out what they knew about the property. A painting contractor confided that the property's maintenance staff would purchase large quantities of paint directly, but then ask him to include his own paint supplies in his quotes and invoices.

According to the contractor, the property management staff would then take home the paint they purchased and use it or sell it. This was shocking on multiple levels. Not only was there outright theft, but considering how many maintenance personnel were on the payroll, the painting should never have been outsourced to begin with. The contractor shared his suspicions that this might be the tip of an iceberg, and my research supported this assertion.

While I didn't have hard proof of crimes being committed, my research indicated that theft was rampant. For example, according to the expense history, most of the appliances should have been replaced over recent years, but when I did unit walk-throughs, I observed them to be old. Equipment had been purchased but wasn't on-site. When I visited their office, staff members sat around doing nothing. Others were clocked in but couldn't be located.

The seller shared the dreadful financial statements for the prior two years, which served as the basis for a valuation. They wanted to wash their hands of the entire mess, and I couldn't blame them. You might be thinking that I should have run screaming from this deal and never looked back. However, I'm a value-add investor, so I absolutely love buying properties that are a mess. Overstaffing? Great. Bad management? Love it. Rampant theft? Even better. Eliminating such things are surefire ways to quickly boost value in a property turnaround.

In general, the worse the management of a property is, the more I like it. If I can bring in better management and see that a property is operated to its full potential, I can almost assuredly boost income and reduce expenses. In this case, the final box of our investment criteria list was definitely checked in a big way.

Would my strategies for turning properties around work at River Apartments? Or was I the one about to get robbed? There was only one way to find out.

To be continued...

Chapter Two

STRUCTURING MULTIFAMILY DEALS

Empty pockets never held anyone back. Only empty heads and empty hearts can do that.

—NORMAN VINCENT PEALE

The first time I heard somebody use the term "capital stack," all I could think of was a big pile of cash. I was pretty sure "first position" had something to do with dance—and when I heard someone reference "mezzanine debt," I thought it was somehow related to stadium seating options. Maybe "mezzanine debt" was a season-ticket financing plan? Eventually I educated myself on such things, but I probably should have made the effort to know the lingo a little sooner.

As you start to do bigger multifamily deals, it's helpful to understand how larger investors look at projects and get a better grasp of the terminology, some of which isn't widely used for smaller properties. An important part of that perspective is understanding deal structure, which is often no more complicated than for a duplex, but on occasion, it can get much more so.

At a high level, there are two types of capital that are used to fund a deal: debt and equity. The capital can come from different sources, and the sources are layered on top of one another to cover the cost of the project. Combined, these layers make up what is referred to as the capital stack (not to be confused with the real estate strategy known as The Stack, which we outlined in Volume I).

The capital stack reflects not only the sources but where each source falls relative to the others in terms of first rights of repayment should the property not perform. Capital stacks are often depicted graphically in the shape of a pyramid. At the bottom are the people or entities who would get paid first if everything falls apart, which means this is the place on the pyramid where capital is the least at risk. In most deals, the lenders are at the bottom of the capital stack.

The equity you contribute out of pocket is almost always going to be at the top of the pyramid. You are not going to get paid until the debt obligations are fulfilled, so your funds are at the greatest risk, but you also have the greatest exposure to the upside. In general, the risk declines as you go lower in the capital stack, but so do the returns.

Debt

Debt is the cornerstone of most deals. In most large multifamily transactions, debt covers anywhere from 65 to 80 percent of the purchase price. That said, Brandon and I have both done all-cash deals for which we didn't borrow any funds as well as deals for which we've financed 100 percent of the purchase price.

Many investors with limited cash resources dream of purchasing a multifamily property with all debt and no equity. While buying a multifamily property with no cash out of pocket is possible, finding these opportunities is exceptionally challenging. Over the past decade I have been involved in hundreds of deals, but I've funded only two properties with 100 percent debt, and both were facilitated through strong lender relationships.

The reality is that you'll need at least some cash to close most deals, although it doesn't necessarily have to be your own cash. While closing without much cash or even walking out of closing with a check in your pocket might seem exciting, you should be cautious about structuring deals this way. Just because you come across a situation that allows you to put in less cash doesn't mean it's the right thing to do. Taking on debt involves risk, so you must be careful not to overextend yourself.

Both Brandon and I have employed creative financing techniques when we knew properties would generate more than enough cash flow to safely cover our debt service. On other occasions we have each walked away from opportunities to use high leverage because we weren't able to identify enough opportunities to add value or didn't want to take on the higher risk associated with the debt.

How much debt you can secure typically depends on the specifics of the property and the deal you negotiate. We'll cover debt and the entire lending process in detail in upcoming chapters, but the amount of debt most lenders are willing to extend is in large part dependent on how much cash a property is generating and its ability to cover the mortgage payments.

In terms of the capital stack, the largest debt is most commonly found at the bottom of the stack in the first position, which is secured by the property. The debt in first position is also called the senior debt. What is the significance of being in the first position? Basically, if you were to default on this loan, this note holder can foreclose and would be paid before anyone else in the capital stack.

Sometimes there will be a lender in a second position that extends mezzanine debt, which is subordinate to the senior debt. This second position in the capital stack fills the gap between senior debt and equity. For River Apartments, the mezzanine debt was extended by the seller. Another example of mezzanine debt is when developers get landowners to partner with them or finance the land portion of the deal through construction.

If there is ever a foreclosure sale, the lender in the second position would get paid only if there are proceeds left over after the first lender is made whole. Banks are not generally comfortable with the risk of being in the second position, so this debt is more likely to be secured from the seller or a private lender. There are some lenders out there, usually debt funds, who do only mezzanine debt and charge a higher interest rate to offset the higher risk.

Below is an example of a potential capital stack:

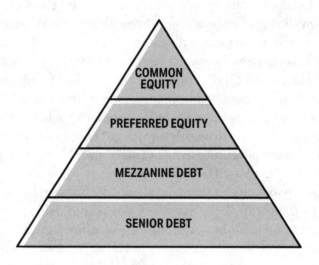

Equity

Equity is the cash portion that sits at the top of the capital stack. In most situations, you will either put this cash in yourself or secure it from partners or investors. For development projects and major restorations, however, equity will often come from a variety of creative sources such as federal and state historic preservation tax credit programs, low-income housing tax credits, state and local development grants, and in some limited cases even the EB-5 Immigrant Investor Program.[1]

A savvy entrepreneur with expertise in these programs can sometimes put a development deal together with very little of their own cash, though the devil is in the details. Most of these types of programs can get complicated and will involve long and arduous slogs through bureaucracy, politics, and paperwork. In many cases, you may find yourself looking at multiple years of development efforts before a project will actually cash flow, and most grant programs require you to front the cash and apply for reimbursement after the work is complete.

For more traditional multifamily acquisitions, the three most common ways to cover the equity portion of a deal are to contribute all the cash yourself, do a joint venture with other investors, or syndicate the deal. Each of these options comes with its own advantages and disadvantages.

---

1 https://www.uscis.gov/working-in-the-united-states/permanent-workers/eb-5-immigrant-investor-program

Going Solo

The first option is to cover all the cash requirements of a deal by using your own capital. The legal entity of choice for going solo on a multifamily deal is the single-member limited liability company (SMLLC). (We cover other options in Chapter Twenty.) The biggest advantage to funding a deal yourself is that you can have 100 percent ownership and control of the property. The downside is that you have to come up with the funds. They might come from your personal savings, the sale of other investments, a line of credit, or anywhere else you can drum up some cash.

For my first deal, I drained my retirement account, which I don't recommend. After that, I tried to avoid using my meager personal savings. For most of my deals I was able to secure the necessary cash from adding value to properties in my portfolio and doing cash-out refinances. Using this approach, I was able to accumulate a portfolio of more than 500 units, plus a handful of office and retail properties. I did a couple of joint ventures along the way, pooling my resources with partners. Later, after more than a decade of going it alone, growing organically, and being perpetually cash poor from reinvesting all my profits into more deals, I decided to partner and start syndicating. This allowed me to take my portfolio to the next level, accumulating units in the thousands.

Joint Venture

A joint venture basically entails teaming up with other active investors to do a deal together. The most common way to structure a real estate joint venture is by forming a multi-member LLC, but there are many other potential legal entities you could use. (Again, see Chapter Twenty for more on this topic.) The advantages of a joint venture include the ability to leverage the skill sets and connections of multiple people, as well as the ability to share the workload. Perhaps more importantly, you can pool resources and acquire properties that are larger than you could manage by yourself.

The downside of joint ventures is that you're taking on all the potential perils and pitfalls of investing with partners. You won't be able to keep all the equity either, and depending on how the operating agreement is written, you may not have full control. That said, you are getting a smaller ownership stake in what is likely to be a much larger deal, so you could consider it a wash from an equity standpoint.

A joint venture requires a lot of up-front communication to make sure everyone is on the same page. Responsibilities and ownership should be defined in the operating agreement and can be divided in any way that is agreeable to the parties involved.

How much each partner contributes toward the cash required for closing is also flexible. Cash contributions can be split equally among the partners, or they can be divided to reflect the relative amount of responsibility each partner assumes for, say, the acquisition or day-to-day operations. It's not uncommon, especially in smaller multifamily properties, for one party to put in all the cash and one to put in most of the work, or "sweat equity."

That said, all partners in a joint venture must have some active role in the investment, even if it's minor. If any of the owners are 100 percent passive, then the investment could technically be considered a security and subject to securities law. If you want to accept money from 100 percent passive investors, the deal should be structured as a syndication.

Syndication

A syndication is a limited partnership that involves the pooling of money from passive investors to fund a deal. In return for contributing cash, these passive investors, who are limited partners, get part ownership and a preferred share in the profits. By preferred, we mean that the people who invest in your syndication would be the first ones to receive a defined portion of the returns after debt obligations are met. This means you will have two types of equity—common and preferred.

As shown in the earlier illustration of a sample capital stack, preferred equity sits above debt but below common equity. As the one who pulls the deal together, you would be a general partner and hold common equity (sometimes called sponsor equity), which sits at the top of the capital stack and is subordinate to all other debt and equity holders. As a general partner and common equity holder, you are paid last.

On the downside, syndications are significantly more complicated than joint ventures from a legal standpoint, and they usually involve giving up a lot of equity. Depending on how much of the capital you are raising from the limited partners, your ownership stake can end up being severely diluted compared to going solo.

That said, giving up a hefty chunk of equity to passive investors can be fulfilling because it provides you with the opportunity to create wealth for others. However, the real beauty of syndicating a deal is that it allows you to buy properties far larger than you would otherwise be able to afford.

Some syndicators contribute cash of their own alongside the passive investors, but many syndicators raise all the necessary capital from others. That's the big attraction of syndication for a number of investors: *You can buy large multifamily properties with no cash!*

Syndication has become popular because it enables investors to successfully scale to large levels relatively quickly. We've met syndicators who have amassed thousands of units in just a few short years by raising capital to fund their deals. In fact, the fund we own grew from zero to more than 1,000 units in eighteen months thanks to syndication. It's a great strategy but also a complex one, so in the next two chapters we're going to dig deeper into syndication and raising private capital.

KEY TAKEAWAYS

- The two types of capital used to fund a deal are debt and equity, both of which can come from different sources. They are layered on top of one another to make up the capital stack. Where each source falls relative to the others in the capital stack reflects the order of repayment if the project fails.
- Debt is the cornerstone of most deals and is usually in the first position at the bottom of the capital stack. Equity/cash is at the top and is last in line for repayment.
- The most common ways to come up with equity are to contribute the cash yourself, form a joint venture, or do a syndication. Each option has its own advantages and disadvantages.

River Apartments: Part III

While some investors may have been deterred by all the theft going on at River Apartments, I was pretty excited about it. Firing the thieves and replacing them with competent, law-abiding people seemed like a surefire way to reduce expenses. However, even though my heart was warmed by the glowing potential for value-add, I still had to get the property at a fair price and figure out how to structure the deal in a way that would work well for me. I knew this could pose a challenge because I didn't have a lot of equity to invest.

Fortunately, the seller was highly motivated, and the sorry state of affairs at River Apartments gave me some pretty good leverage. After some back-and -forth, we agreed on a purchase price. During negotiations, I also got the seller to agree that they would extend owner financing in the amount of $500,000. This mezzanine debt would be subordinate to the first mortgage and security interest lien held by the bank and was extended at favorable terms. The historical cash flows were sufficient to service the combined bank and seller debt, which gave me a high level of confidence in light of my plans to dramatically improve the property's financials right out of the gate.

The $500,000 in owner financing was extremely helpful to me as the buyer while still being palatable to the seller. The seller's debt was fairly low, and since I would be using bank financing to cover 75 percent of the purchase price, the seller would still receive enough proceeds at closing to pay off their debt and pull out a significant amount of cash.

This is an approach I have used for numerous commercial transactions and continue to use today. During negotiations, I will often wait until later in the process to introduce owner financing in exchange for offering a higher price. I will also negotiate other credits that will allow me to reduce the amount of cash I need to close. Sellers will sometimes agree to these kinds of concessions if doing so will allow them to secure a better price.

For this particular deal, the primary concession I sought (in addition to owner financing) was a closing credit for the massive amount of deferred maintenance at River Apartments. In exchange for accepting the property "as is," I received a deferred-maintenance credit from the seller at closing.

While a deferred-maintenance credit can be for any amount, I decided not to define a specific dollar amount so it wouldn't affect my bank financing. Instead, I included a clause in the purchase agreement for a credit equal to the balance of the seller's reserve escrow accounts on the day we closed.

In cases where a seller has owned a property for a long period of time, as this one had, their reserve account balances tend to grow rather large. Accordingly, I included the following clause in the purchase agreement, even though I had no idea what the existing reserve balance might be:

> Buyer accepts Property "as-is" and Seller agrees to provide Buyer with a credit at closing for deferred maintenance in an amount equal to the balance of the Seller's reserve for replacements account that was established in accordance with the terms of the Seller's mortgage. Seller shall continue to make required reserve deposits and shall not withdraw funds from the reserve for replacements account prior to closing without approval of the Buyer.

I figured I had nothing to lose. There were surely at least some funds in there, and since the seller's mortgage was taken out a long time ago, I surmised it could pay sizable dividends. The seller didn't object to the clause, and I hoped for the best.

I felt good about the terms of the deal I had negotiated, and the seller was happy to have found a buyer who was willing to ignore the hideous financials—but a signed contract is just the beginning. I felt as if the safety bar had dropped down and locked me in place at the beginning of a scary roller-coaster ride. Turns out that was an accurate premonition—it was going to be quite a thriller.

To be continued...

Chapter Three
SYNDICATION

*It is one thing to fill your own pockets. But I've got
to tell you, when you also make money for other
people, the joy is huge.*

—GLENN GONZALES

The best thing about participating in a meetup or mastermind is the opportunity to meet other investors. At one of the first events I attended, I found myself in conversation with an investor who was doing syndications. "It's really amazing how you've grown your portfolio," she said. "I can't believe you haven't raised any capital yet. You really funded everything yourself? How did you do that?"

"Yeah, it's true," I responded. "I've focused mostly on value-add projects, and once I add value, I do cash-out refinances and use the proceeds to buy more properties. I've been pretty religiously reinvesting everything back into my portfolio."

"Wow, that's impressive. You've obviously done a lot of hard work. If you reinvest everything and keep buying more properties, how do you pay yourself?" she asked.

"Well, I kept my day job for the first seven years I was investing, plus my wife works. And now I get some book royalties, so that helps pay the bills," I explained with mixed emotions.

I was proud of the portfolio I'd grown, but after more than a decade of sacrifice, I was getting tired of always being cash poor. I had accumulated a $50 million portfolio but felt like I was perpetually scraping every last dollar together for the next deal. "I've recently started to take more owner distributions," I added before realizing that probably made me sound only slightly less pathetic. Some mastermind members had exotic sports cars in the parking lot. I wondered what they would think if they knew I was still driving a pickup with well over 100,000 miles on it. Another investor had recently labeled me the King of Delayed Gratification. This wasn't entirely true, because I found gratification in my work and other areas of my life. But it *was* true with regard to money, and I would have liked to enjoy more of the fruits of my labor.

"Why haven't you done any syndications?" she asked. "You can raise the capital and do bigger deals without having to keep depleting your personal savings. Syndicating is a lot of extra work, but maybe you could start to keep some of that cash your portfolio generates." I started to explain all the reasons I don't syndicate but quickly stopped. I was hearing myself from her perspective and realized that none of my reasons were very good. They sounded a lot more like excuses, and I don't like to make excuses.

The hard truth was that I learned about syndication late in my investment career, and when I finally did, it seemed way too complex and beyond my comfort zone. I'd rationalized my decision to avoid it in a number of ways, and what I was doing seemed to be working fine. I hadn't revisited that decision, but now, surrounded by syndicators, it was becoming obvious to me that syndication *was* a viable option and worth considering. Not only that, syndication would be consistent with my desire to help others achieve wealth through real estate. It was clearly time to take a fresh look at things.

"You know," I said. "I think that's something I'm going to be taking a closer look at."

What Is Multifamily Syndication?

If you want to go big in multifamily but don't have the capital to make your dream a reality, syndication may be the answer. Basically, syndication allows you to raise capital by selling equity or issuing debt in a deal to passive investors. These investors contribute cash, entrusting you with their money in exchange for the opportunity to share in the profits and the tax benefits of depreciation as limited partners.

Meanwhile, as the syndicator you retain a portion of the equity and profits to compensate you for pulling the whole thing together and overseeing the project. Your ownership stake will be diluted, but you can retain control and avoid a large cash outlay.

Taking on limited partners is a great responsibility. By committing money to your project, these investors are placing their trust in your ability to manage the project and deliver the projected returns. The added pressure associated with this arrangement can sometimes deter multifamily investors from syndicating deals. In response to this concern, syndication attorney Mauricio Rauld once noted that "if you are worried about the prospects of losing investors' money, then you are exactly the kind of person we need in this industry. It's those who don't care about their investors' money and don't treat it with respect that are the ones who shouldn't be doing it."

How comfortable you are with syndication is a matter of how you choose to view it. Remember that what you're really doing is providing *opportunity*—a chance for people to invest in real estate projects that would otherwise be out of reach. As a syndicator, you're committed to doing a lot of hard work and allowing people to join you for the ride. If you successfully execute on your plans, you're in a position to create wealth for a lot of people, not just yourself. This goal can be motivational, and bringing it to fruition can be fulfilling.

In terms of practicalities, there are many different ways to structure the partnership and compensation, and syndicators can get creative as long as they comply with federal and state regulations. Bear in mind that the limited partners who are putting in the cash do not have an active role in the project; instead, they are expecting you to generate the return for them. As such, they are passive investors, and the sale of equity or debt through a syndication is considered a securities transaction (similar to a stock offering). Therefore, it falls under the purview of the U.S. Securities and Exchange Commission (SEC) and the state securities regulators.

We will review the types of syndications available to you, the associated restrictions, and how to comply with them later. They may seem complicated, but in practice they are manageable for most investors willing to put in the necessary time and effort.

Dispelling the Myths

Among the challenges for people interested in learning more about syndicating real estate deals is the limited amount of information available. In addition, on the surface, syndication can seem complicated and out of reach. There's lots of jargon and acronyms along with plenty of references to federal law that will be unfamiliar and, understandably, intimidating.

As a result, many investors are quick to reject syndication as a viable option. Brandon and I used to count ourselves among them. But once we had each done a number of syndications, we both realized that our earlier concerns were misplaced. Are there cumbersome legal and regulatory requirements? Yes. Is there complicated documentation? Absolutely. Then why were we wrong to rule out syndications due to their complexity? Because we failed to consider all the resources available to us—the companies and attorneys out there who will gladly take care of the difficult parts.

After all, it's not your job to understand every statute and regulation. That's what those companies and attorneys are for. Your job is to put all the pieces of the syndication puzzle together. All you need is enough of a general understanding so you can have an intelligent discussion with your expert support team. It's really the legal requirements that are challenging, and a good, experienced securities attorney can take care of everything that needs to be done and guide you through all the compliance.

Syndication Structure

Syndications are typically structured as limited liability companies or limited partnerships, which have two types of partners: general partners (GPs) and limited partners (LPs).[2] The GPs are considered the sponsors of the syndication and are the ones who pull the deal together and oversee

---

2 LLCs have members (as opposed to LPs) and managers (as opposed to GPs), but for the purposes of this chapter we will use the more typical GP and LP.

all aspects of the project. GPs are also liable for the project's financial obligations, including debts and any potential litigation. The LPs are passive investors who contribute most or all of the cash necessary to close and execute on the project plan. In exchange, LPs earn a share of the profits and the tax benefits associated with depreciation of the investment property. LPs are not involved in management, and they have no responsibility for debts or exposure to liability beyond their initial investment.

General Partners

The GPs find the deal and underwrite it, negotiate a price and get the asset under contract, conduct due diligence, secure financing and sign the loan documents, and manage the asset for the life of the project. GPs in real estate syndications are also referred to as sponsors, syndicates, or syndicators. Some real estate investors do syndications as the sole GP, but they're more commonly done in teams in order to divide and conquer. Having multiple GPs is an opportunity to leverage different skills and resources, which is helpful given the breadth of what's involved.

When partnering, consider the GPs' roles and responsibilities, which include the following:

- **Pre-Close Work:** This includes sourcing the deal, underwriting, due diligence, and transaction management.
- **Pre-Close Money:** This includes the fronting of all at-risk capital spent prior to closing, including deposits, the cost of due diligence, travel, and so on. This capital is considered at risk because it could be lost if the project doesn't close.
- **Key Principal:** Lenders will require that one of the GPs have relevant experience, sufficient net worth, and enough liquidity to satisfy their guidelines; that person will be designated as the key principal (KP). Requirements vary, but you should expect a net worth requirement equal to the size of the loan, and liquidity (cash assets or equivalent) equal to 10 percent of the loan amount post-close.
- **Asset Management:** The asset manager is responsible for oversight of property management, or "managing the manager," and addressing operational issues that arise over the life of the project. This role involves a longer-term, ongoing commitment compared to pre-close responsibilities.
- **Investor Management:** Investor relations start during the equity raise but continue throughout the project. Investors will expect

updates and answers to their questions. LP distributions will also need to be managed throughout the life of the project.

- **Raising Capital:** Building relationships and raising money from LPs is one of the most valued and important roles of any GP.

In exchange for all these demands, the GPs keep a percentage of ownership in the project. The amount of equity retained by GPs can vary widely, depending on such things as investor expectations, project returns, the level of risk involved, and what the rest of the compensation structure looks like. I have seen GPs get anywhere from 10 to 90 percent ownership, but in the majority of syndications, GPs retain between 20 and 35 percent, with 30 percent being most common.

If you have only one GP, they get the whole 30 percent. In that case, you can either do all the work yourself, hire people to do some of it, or outsource some of it to third parties, depending on your preferences and the resources at your disposal. If there is more than one GP, you will need to divide the equity among the team.

Every partnership must decide how to allocate equity fairly in consideration of the value associated with the tasks and the risk involved. The exception to this is raising capital, which has come under SEC scrutiny due to the transactional nature of awarding equity in direct exchange for raising money. In the past it was common for syndicators to award a percentage allocation of the total GP equity (or the portion of equity that goes to the GP) based on the amount of capital each partner brought in.

This practice began to result in GPs that had numerous "capital raisers" who had no other role in the project. The capital raisers looked and smelled like they were operating as unlicensed brokers. Most syndicators that are legitimate cosponsors rely on what is called the issuer exemption under Rule 3a4-1 of the Securities Exchange Act of 1934 to avoid being considered a broker.[3] In order to fall within this exemption, each syndicator must generally (a) not be compensated with "transaction-based compensation," (b) have substantial duties in the deal, (c) primarily work on those substantial duties (as opposed to primarily working on the capital raise), and (d) not be in the business of raising capital.

To stay compliant with SEC rules, it is therefore advisable to not think of these GPs as capital raisers but rather as integral members of the

---

[3] https://www.sec.gov/rules/final/1985/34-22172.pdf

sponsor team who are providing valuable contributions to the deal and only incidentally raising capital as just one of their many functions. At a minimum, you should avoid linking their equity directly to the amount of capital raised (since transaction-based compensation is the hallmark of broker activity) and make sure they have other roles and responsibilities that justify their percentage of ownership.

Limited Partners

The LPs are passive investors in the deal. The liability exposure of LPs (as opposed to that of GPs) is limited to the amount of their initial investment, so their personal assets are protected. LPs cannot be sued and are not on the loan, even though they are entitled to a share of the profits.

The share of profits and depreciation awarded to LPs varies widely, but it is common for LPs to get priority treatment through a "preferred return" that pays them a percentage on their investment before anything gets split with the GPs. This structure effectively awards the LPs a higher share of the profits than would be expected based on their percentage of ownership.

It's worth noting that preferred returns are not guaranteed. Offering preferred returns simply means that all the cash flow available for distribution will first go to the LPs until their preferred return is reached. If there is less to distribute, they will get less. Some preferred returns are cumulative, meaning that if returns fall short in a given year, they carry forward and build up until they are paid. Cumulative returns may or may not be compounding, which means that the shortfalls that get carried forward will earn interest at the preferred rate until they are paid.

Preferred returns can be any amount, though 5 to 10 percent is usual, with the most common being 7 percent. Higher preferred returns tend to be associated with higher-risk projects or occur in structures that have more limited upside. For example, an LP might get a 10 or 12 percent preferred return but no share of profits beyond that level, which essentially makes these LP investments look more like a debt instrument.

More commonly, profit splits will change as different return thresholds are reached. For example, let's say there is a project with a 7 percent preferred return and a 70/30 LP/GP split. For this project, the LPs would get profit distributions awarding them a 7 percent return on their investment, and only profits above that level would be subject to the 70/30 split. Having multiple levels like this where the compensation structure changes is called a waterfall.

Another syndicator might elect to structure their offering with an 80/20 split across the board, meaning that profits are split 80 percent to the LPs and 20 percent to the GPs at all levels without any waterfall. This is a more straightforward approach, but whether it's better is debatable. Removing the waterfall rewards the GPs with distributions even when returns are low while reducing the GPs' participation in the upside. From an LP standpoint, the straight split eats into their profits when returns are modest but allows them to more fully participate in the upside if things go better than expected. There are pros and cons to every structure, so consider all your options carefully.

Types of Syndications and Investors

At a high level, there are several types of syndications to choose from, and these are driven by regulatory requirements. When you syndicate, you're actually selling a security and subject to the same regulations that govern the sale of private stocks. Both the SEC and the states have extensive and complicated regulations governing the offering and sale of any type of securities to the general investing public. The purpose of these regulations is to protect the interests of the everyday investor.

Generally, when you are selling a security, you must either (a) register your security with the SEC or (b) find an exemption to registration. Fortunately for real estate investors, there are a variety of exemptions that can be claimed in order to avoid the need to register your offering and secure approval from the SEC. Each exemption has specific rules and restrictions, and it is incumbent on syndicators to keep records detailing how they complied with the rules of the specific exemption they plan to claim.

On a fundamental level, the exemptions are based on the premise that offerings will be restricted to sophisticated or high net worth individuals, who are knowledgeable enough to look out for their own interests. These individuals are therefore deemed capable of making their own decisions and better weathering any adverse consequences.

There are three specific exemptions from registration that are most appropriate for multifamily investors that will be covered in this chapter: Regulation D, Rule 506(b); Regulation D, Rule 506(c); and Regulation A.

Of these, the most widely used exemption is Rule 506(b). This exemption is particularly appealing to real estate investors because it offers an attractive combination of limited complexity and flexibility regarding who can invest. It also "preempts" state regulations, so you don't have to worry about complying with state securities laws other than the anti-fraud provisions and filing some notice paperwork (known as Form D or "blue sky" filings).

Syndicating Under Rule 506(b)

If you do a syndication under Rule 506(b), you can raise an unlimited amount of money and can offer your syndication to accredited investors and up to thirty-five sophisticated nonaccredited investors. However, there are some restrictions and limitations to be aware of.

Perhaps the most notable restriction for syndications under Rule 506(b) is that you cannot publicly advertise or generally solicit your offering. The most common way of proving that you did not advertise or generally solicit your offering is to have a pre-existing, substantive relationship with your prospective investors. This substantive relationship should be documented, since it will be your burden to prove the substantive nature of the relationship. Still, as long as you can demonstrate that you had a substantive relationship prior to the commencement of your investment offering, you should be able to satisfy the no-advertising requirement.

As briefly mentioned above, while you can have an unlimited number of accredited investors, you will be limited to only thirty-five sophisticated nonaccredited investors, as defined in Rule 501 of Regulation D of the Securities Act. The SEC considers all investors either accredited or nonaccredited depending on whether they meet this definition. An accredited investor is allowed to participate in investments such as syndications regardless of what exemption you choose to rely on. The idea is that these investors (by virtue of their wealth) have the sophistication and wherewithal to invest in potentially risky investments and withstand any potential losses.

So what exactly is necessary for an investor to be considered accredited by the SEC? It's pretty straightforward in most cases. The individual must meet one of the following two criteria:

- Income of more than $200,000 (or $300,000 together with a spouse) in each of the last two years, with a reasonable expectation of income above these thresholds in the current year, or

- Net worth over $1 million, either individually or together with a spouse (excluding the value of their primary residence).

For a 506(b), the syndicator need only have a reasonable belief that the investor is accredited. Therefore, passive investors often self-verify whether they meet these criteria.

The most unique aspect of Rule 506(b) is that you can accept investments from up to thirty-five sophisticated nonaccredited investors. This makes a 506(b) syndication particularly attractive for real estate investors who have friends and family who would like to invest but don't meet the SEC's definition of accredited investors.

What does the SEC mean when they say an investor must be "sophisticated"? This does not mean that they have to be cultured and fashionable, or that your crude, beer-swilling uncle can't invest in your project. Instead, the SEC expects you to ensure that any nonaccredited investors have enough financial savvy to know what they're doing, and that the investment is suitable for them.

Just to be on the safe side, it's a good idea to have a series of conversations to assess each LP's financial situation, goals, and previous investing experience to make sure they are suitable. It's also advisable to keep records documenting such conversations.

The downside of accepting cash from nonaccredited investors is that it increases the scope of disclosures that you need to prepare, which is significant. This is one reason why some syndicators prefer to limit their offerings to accredited investors only. Nonaccredited investors are also likely to make smaller investments, and those investments can sometimes represent a significant percentage of their net worth. This can lead to high levels of concern from the nonaccredited investor(s), particularly when a project has an unanticipated setback or isn't going well. Concern can sometimes manifest itself in unpleasant ways, such as incessant questions and demands. If anxiety escalates to panic, things can get dramatic, which could be uncomfortable, especially when it comes to people you have long-established relationships with.

Syndicating Under Rule 506(c)

If you would like to advertise your deal to the public and can forgo raising money from nonaccredited investors, you should consider syndicating under Rule 506(c). These syndications are restricted to accredited investors, but they have a huge advantage over 506(b) offerings, which is that under 506(c) you are allowed to advertise or generally solicit your offering publicly, which can help you reach new investors and raise more capital. This makes a 506(c) particularly appealing to syndicators who have achieved some level of professional notoriety, have large social media followings, or developed other platforms with significant reach.

With a 506(c) offering, GPs are expected to take "reasonable steps to verify" that each of the LPs meets the criteria for accredited investors. Passive investors cannot self-verify, as they can for a 506(b) deal. The verification process typically involves third parties and may entail the review of bank statements, tax returns, or other documentation demonstrating an LP's income and net worth. Another common option is to have each of the LPs secure written confirmation of accredited investor status from a licensed attorney, securities broker, or CPA.

Overall, 506(c) offerings are considered more appealing than 506(b)s. The average investment per LP is higher, you don't have to be concerned about publicly promoting your offering, and the disclosure requirements are less onerous than those provided to nonaccredited investors.

Many syndicators feel compelled to start off with 506(b) offerings because their network of potential investors is probably full of people that aren't accredited. Over time, it's common for these syndicators to expand their investor network with the goal of migrating to 506(c) offerings. For a more limited number of syndicators, it may also make sense to consider a Regulation A exemption.

Regulation A

The Regulation A (Reg A) exemption from SEC registration requirements is a little more complicated and less widely used than 506(b) and 506(c), and probably not appropriate for most investors. Originally passed in 1936, Reg A was significantly overhauled in 2015 as a result of the JOBS Act of 2012. The updated Reg A (commonly known as Reg A+), was split into two tiers, with Tier 1 (similar to the original Reg A) allowing offerings of up to $20 million and Tier 2 covering offerings of up to $50 million. Few syndicators took advantage of Tier 1 due to its limitations, but the Tier 2 exemption has been gaining in popularity.

The appeal of Reg A+ is due to the freedom to market the offering broadly, the eligibility of nonaccredited investors, and not having to worry about registration in every single state where you have investors (as is the case with Tier 1 and the old Reg A rule). This combination of benefits overcomes the major limitations of the other two options: 506(b) allows for up to thirty-five nonaccredited investors but prohibits marketing, while 506(c) allows marketing but does not allow nonaccredited investors. However, Reg A+ also comes with its share of downsides.

One of the challenges of claiming a Reg A+ exemption is that before proceeding with an offering, you must file a statement on Form 1-A with the SEC for review and qualification. Often referred to as a mini IPO, the submission must include copies of the proposed disclosure documents that will be provided to investors. Only after the SEC reviews and approves your offering can you proceed with accepting LP investments.

This process can take upwards of six months, so you would have to initiate it well in advance of raising equity, which is challenging from a timing standpoint. Due to this requirement, it is difficult to conduct a Reg A+ offering for project-specific syndications since you typically don't have time to wait for the SEC to approve your deal. Reg A+ is more often used by syndicators putting together a fund that has no closing deadlines.

The need for SEC approval requires a lot more involvement from your securities attorney as the attorney must negotiate with the SEC attorneys until the offering is approved. This makes the compliance cost of Reg A+ offerings substantially more expensive. In addition, the syndicator must provide the SEC several ongoing reports, including annual reports, quarterly reports, exit reports, and audited financials, adding more to the compliance costs.

In terms of raising capital, under Tier 1, you can raise up to $20 million in any twelve-month period. In addition to requiring SEC qualification, Tier 1 offerings must be qualified by state securities regulators, although there are no ongoing reporting requirements. State qualification is the primary reason most syndicators forgo Tier 1, as they would need to follow the securities laws of every state where they offer their syndication. Under Tier 2, you can raise up to $50 million in any twelve-month period. Tier 2 offerings, however, do not need to be qualified at the state level, since they are "preempted" by the federal rule.

Finally, Tier 2 comes with significant investment limitations. While you are able to market the offering and accept investments from non-accredited investors, their investments are capped at 10 percent of the greater of their (and their spouse's) annual income or net worth (excluding the value of their primary residence). The implications of this are significant. In addition to all the extra verifications, disclosures, and reporting requirements, you will likely get more but smaller investments, and end up with a much larger pool of LPs to manage.

Fees

In addition to sharing in the profits, the GPs in a syndication are usually compensated through a variety of fee structures. The fees are tied to events or activities that can be very time-consuming. If not for fees, it would be hard for GPs to rationalize or sustain the amount of work that goes into all aspects of a syndication. The following are the most common fees:

- **Acquisition Fee:** Collected at the time of closing, the acquisition fee is usually based on a percentage of the purchase price and allocated proportionally to each GP's equity share. This fee is typically between 1 and 4 percent, with most falling around 2 to 2.5 percent.
- **Finance/Refinance Fee or Loan Guarantee Fee:** Some syndicators will charge a finance fee for securing debt on the project, which is usually based on a percentage of the mortgage amount. This fee is more commonly assessed on a refinance than on an initial mortgage. It is typically between 1 and 3 percent of the new loan, with most falling around 2 to 2.5 percent. A loan guarantee fee is sometimes incorporated when the GPs must personally guarantee the mortgage, and this is usually about 1 percent of the loan amount.
- **Asset Management Fee:** Most syndications assess a monthly asset management fee, which is based on a percentage of the project's gross income. This fee is typically between 1 and 3 percent, with most falling around 2 to 2.5 percent.
- **Disposition Fee:** This is typically between 1 and 4 percent, with most falling around 2 to 2.5 percent.

While these are the most common fees found in syndications, there are no real standards, and some syndicators can get pretty creative with what they charge. In the end, it's important to strike a balance and ensure that the GPs' interests are aligned with those of the LPs. The more fees you charge, the more challenging it is to deliver attractive returns.

Excessive fees will also make it much more difficult to find deals that work and to make competitive purchase offers.

Funds

As a syndicator, you have the option of raising money for individual projects or multiple projects. When you do multiple projects, the syndication is called a fund. The exemptions, guidelines, and restrictions associated with a fund are basically the same as for individual projects, but funds do offer a unique advantage for the LPs: Pooling multiple projects into one offering mitigates single-asset risk by providing diversification. Some projects might do exceptionally well, while others may fall short. The more you can combine under a single fund, the more likely they will balance out and allow you to achieve your target returns.

You can raise money in a fund for specific, pre-identified assets or in a "blind pool," meaning that investors entrust you to deploy their cash in opportunities as they arise, which allows you to act quickly and be opportunistic.

Key Documentation

Once you've figured out what type of syndication you're going to offer and how you're going to structure the distributions, you'll need to assemble some important documents in cooperation with your securities attorney. To do this properly, it's important to use an SEC attorney who specializes in syndications.

The Investment Summary

The first document you'll prepare is an investment summary, which is a high-level document that will serve as your primary marketing tool with investors. The investment summary is often structured in the form of a presentation and typically includes the following:

- An overview of the property and the market, highlighting the advantages
- A summary of financial information that may include metrics, such as projected cash-on-cash returns, equity multiples, average annual return, and internal rate of return
- Your plans for the property after closing and your exit strategy

- The team you have in place, their qualifications, and their track record
- Any restrictions or requirements for LPs, such as whether they need to be accredited and what the minimum investment is

It's worth investing a significant amount of effort into creating the most visually appealing and professional investment summary you can. While the biggest single factor influencing an LP's decision to invest is their relationship with the GPs, the investment summary probably comes in second. An ill-prepared investment summary will definitely not instill confidence and can give prospective investors second thoughts.

Private Placement Memorandum

Another critical document is the private placement memorandum (PPM), which is an expansive document designed to disclose all the risks involved in your deal, as well as provide a broad range of information and disclosures to prospective investors. The PPM should be drawn up by an experienced securities attorney to ensure compliance and protect you from liability.

The goal of the PPM is to provide every piece of material information an investor might require in order to make an informed decision. This includes details of the project, use of proceeds, projections, risks, disclaimers, entity and distribution structures, company and management information, insurance, tax considerations, and so on. The PPM includes exhibits such as the operating agreements, the subscription agreement, and an investor questionnaire.

A PPM contains a ton of information. Although it may have boilerplate provisions, each PPM should be specifically tailored to your unique deal. Yes, there is work involved in determining what needs to be included in a PPM, but not so much that it should deter you from considering syndication as a viable option for funding your deals. Again, let the experts, like your attorneys, focus on that, just as your CPA focuses on the taxes and your mortgage broker focuses on the financing.

KEY TAKEAWAYS

- Syndication involves raising capital by selling equity or debt in a deal to passive investors who become LPs and share in the profits and depreciation. Meanwhile, the GPs retain part of the equity and profits in exchange for overseeing all aspects of the project. Syndications offer a wide variety of possibilities for fee and profit-sharing structures.
- Syndications are subject to securities laws, and the three most common exemptions syndicators rely on are based on Rule 506(b), Rule 506(c), and Regulation A+. Each type of syndication has pros and cons based on the associated restrictions.
- The various requirements, language, and documentation associated with syndications can be complicated, but you can easily navigate them with the help of an experienced securities attorney.

River Apartments: Part IV

Going into negotiations, I really wasn't sure how I would pay for River Apartments, but I trusted that if I got a good enough deal, I'd find a way to make it work. At this point in my investing career, I hadn't done (or even considered) syndications, so that option was off the table.

In the end, I was able to work out a creative financing solution. Pending a satisfactory appraisal, I'd be able to borrow about 95 percent of the purchase price, so I would have to come up with only enough cash to cover the other 5 percent plus closing costs. I knew borrowing this much was risky, but the cash flow was more than enough to cover the debt payments, and I was increasingly confident that I could find ways to add value after closing. Once the property was under contract, I focused on further identifying these value-add opportunities and making sure I knew exactly what I was getting into.

Due diligence proved inordinately exciting as I continued to uncover prodigious amounts of malfeasance, but the real surprise didn't come until we were almost to closing. My entire plan to convert the project to market-rate housing was predicated on the pending expiration of the HUD contract, which seemed straightforward...until I got a call from my attorney. Closing was just around the corner, but he had some shocking news. "I just got off the phone with the seller's attorney," he said. "Apparently there was some kind of mix-up. HUD sent them a twenty-year contract extension—and one of their executives signed it and sent it back in."

"*What?*" I exclaimed. "Are you sure? That can't be right." I was absolutely stunned. I was so close to pulling this off. Everything was lined up and ready to go, but if this was true, it was bad. Really bad. Deal-killer bad.

As the news sunk in, I felt a pit in my stomach, and I was frustrated. At no time during my conversations with the seller had they indicated that the HUD contract would be extended, and they knew I planned to convert the project to market-rate housing.

So I picked up the phone and called the CEO, whom I had originally negotiated the deal with, to see what had happened. Surely there must be some kind of misunderstanding. "Yeah, it's true," he said. "When the contract came in, it just went through our normal processing. It never occurred to the people involved that anyone wouldn't want to sign it. You have to understand, in the affordable housing world, this kind of contract is like gold," he said. "You're set for twenty years. But I hear what you're saying," he added. "If you need to terminate the purchase agreement, I understand."

Not wanting to make any rash decisions, I told him I'd have to think about it and would get back to him. I've learned from experience that it's better not to make impulsive decisions when emotions are high or things seem to be at their worst. In the words of Colin Powell, "It ain't as bad as you think. It will look better in the morning." Besides, I didn't have a full understanding of HUD housing or what it entailed.

My gut still told me I had negotiated a great deal, so I clung to the hope that I could somehow salvage things. There was definitely an opportunity to add a lot of value, whether the project remained affordable housing or not. Or maybe I was just rationalizing because I didn't want to let go. I was an optimist and still clinging to hope. After all, what did I know about HUD projects and contracts? The answer soon became pretty clear—absolutely nothing.

To be continued...

Chapter Four
RAISING PRIVATE CAPITAL

YOU have the potential to greatly influence many people's lives in a positive way. And if you don't realize that potential, then you're being a little selfish because you're not giving to others and helping them reach their financial goals. Which, by the way, will help you reach yours too (and then some).

—JOE FAIRLESS

In an ideal world, everyone who wanted to invest in real estate would have access to all the capital they needed to purchase whatever properties they wanted to. Unfortunately, this is not the case for the vast majority of us. That includes both Brandon and me, since we both started with limited resources and were having enough trouble just paying the bills.

The cold, hard truth is that getting a loan can be a challenge. I tried for more than four years before I got my first commercial mortgage, while Brandon had to live in his first multifamily in order to qualify for an FHA loan. As hard as it is to get a commercial mortgage, it can be even harder to accumulate enough cash for the down payment and closing costs, which can be upwards of 20 to 30 percent of the purchase price. For most people, accumulating that much capital represents years of deep sacrifice.

How can you move forward and overcome these constraints? For some, the answer is simple—they can't. However, those not so easily deterred will look for other solutions. When you can't get a loan through traditional channels or come up with the cash to move forward, you're forced to be creative, both with deal structures and sources of capital. This is where private capital—meaning funds you secure from private individuals or firms that are seeking to put their money to work—comes into play.

In the last chapter, we covered syndication, which is one of the primary structures you can use to fund a deal. You can also secure private capital in the form of debt, from individuals or firms. Of course, none of this really matters if you can't actually get anyone to invest their cash. Establishing the connections and trust necessary to get people to lend you money or invest in your multifamily projects takes a lot of work. In this chapter we're going to focus on some of the keys to successfully raising private capital, whether through a syndication, a loan, or some other structure.

Mindset

If you're going to be raising capital, the first step is to embrace the right mindset. This means you will have to overcome any fears you might have. If you have an aversion to approaching people for money, take solace in the fact that you're not alone. Being uncomfortable with raising capital is completely natural, especially if you're a major introvert like me. However, there are ways to overcome those anxieties, starting with acknowledging your discomfort and educating yourself on what raising capital actually entails.

Let's get right to the heart of the matter: Asking other people for money can feel really awkward. For some, it can trigger a misplaced emotional response rooted in pride—and I do mean misplaced, because raising private capital is not about other people helping *you*. It's about you helping *them*. At a bare minimum, it's a mutually beneficial arrangement.

The best way to ensure the proper mindset is to follow the advice of the legendary author, salesman, and motivational speaker Zig Ziglar, who said, "Stop selling. Start helping." Another quote from Mr. Ziglar is equally applicable: "You can get everything you want in life if you will just help other people get what they want." Not only are these axioms true, but they are particularly relevant when it comes to raising capital.

Many people have an aversion to sales, and that can include both sellers and customers. Why? There are lots of reasons, and it doesn't help that we are constantly inundated with advertising and people trying to take our money. How do you get people to pay attention? *Stop selling. Start helping.*

The key to successfully raising capital is to focus on why people are motivated to invest or lend their money. You need to understand what they're seeking and *how you can help them*. People don't usually lend or invest just to be nice or because they pity you. It's a business transaction that fulfills a need. Investors are seeking a return on their capital, either in the form of interest or a share of the profits.

In fact, both of us are members of a small mastermind of wealthy individuals who gather semi-annually (and chat daily in a private Facebook group). The No. 1 topic of conversations with these folks is, *Where can I get a good return on my money*? In other words, the biggest problem for many wealthy individuals is the lack of opportunity, which you, the real estate investor, could help them solve!

When raising private capital, it's important to understand as much as possible about what the investor is hoping to accomplish. What level of risk are they comfortable with? Are they more interested in preservation of capital or a return on their capital? Are they looking to defer taxable gains? Trying to diversify their investment portfolio? Seeking something more stable than the stock market—maybe an investment secured by real property? Explore how your offering can be a solution to their needs.

Brandon and I have extensive experience on both sides of private capital. We have raised millions of dollars and invested millions of dollars passively in other people's deals. We have borrowed millions in private capital and lent millions to other people. Based on all this experience, what is our advice for mindset? Here is our unemotional, objective view of what it means to raise private capital: You are offering people opportunities to preserve and generate wealth through real estate. Period. You're not trying to force anyone. You're not begging, and you're not selling. You're *helping* people.

Some prospective investors who hear about your opportunity will be interested. Others won't be. Some will be excited and grateful. You won't know who's who until you start talking about real estate and letting people know about the opportunities that exist thanks to your industriousness and determination.

How to Get Started

We have established that people have needs, but why should anyone choose you? Because in addition to seeking financial benefits, investors want to have a sense of comfort with the person or team they are handing their money to. Trust is a powerful motivator.

Therefore, it makes sense to start with people you have a pre-existing relationship with—people who know you and are likely to have confidence in you. Maybe it's a neighbor or a drinking buddy. Maybe you've worked with them or gone to school with them, or you're in a club together. It doesn't really matter how you got to know them. The point is people feel more comfortable lending or investing money with someone they trust.

How do you expand beyond this inner circle and engender trust from people who don't know you? There are a wide range of strategies you could employ. Here are some of the most effective:

- **Referrals:** Referrals leverage the trust and legitimacy you've established with people who know you. If someone in your existing network recommends you or refers you to someone else, there is a foundation of trust by extension. How do you get referrals? Perhaps the best way is by performing exceptionally well and doing exactly what you say you're going to do. It's great if that track record is with real estate deals, but it could also be through any other type of professional work or investment.
- **Social Media:** Social media allows you to share information about yourself and your life that helps others feel as if they know you, even if you've never met in person. Post consistently and try to add as much value as possible to folks while occasionally mixing in personal posts to help you become relatable and familiar. Getting to

know someone virtually can translate to a level of trust and make people want to be involved in your deals.

- **Meetups, Seminars, and Industry Events:** Real estate meetups and other industry gatherings are magnets for people interested in putting their money to work in real estate. Even better, people are there to network and share common interests, which makes it easier for you to approach them and strike up conversations. It would be hard to find a better environment for expanding your network of prospective lenders and investors.
- **Reputation:** Over time you can build a personal brand and reputation that will help you overcome any reservations people might have. This will happen naturally as you interact with others and grow your portfolio, but you can also accelerate the process. In addition to using social media, you can build credibility and brand recognition by appearing on news programs and podcasts, winning awards, authoring articles or books, and making speaking appearances.

How and When to Approach People

Even before you have a deal lined up, it's a good idea to start planting seeds among the many people you interact with as you go about your daily life. The best way to communicate is to be genuine and let your excitement for real estate shine through. Talk about your plans and share your enthusiasm, because it's contagious. When people express interest, ask them whether they'd like to have you walk them through a sample deal to show them what it's going to look like. Then, when you get a deal lined up, the idea won't come out of the blue. It will feel somewhat familiar, and that familiarity breeds comfort and confidence.

Whenever someone wants to learn more, tell them about the project and offer to share a copy of the investment summary. But remember: Don't sell. Be completely honest about the full range of possible outcomes, the potential risks and rewards. Allow them to make their own decision about whether the project is right for them.

In our experience, people appreciate honesty and transparency. These qualities will lay the foundation for a healthy, longer-term business relationship. Even if they decide a particular opportunity is not right for them at that moment, if you make a positive impression, they may come back to you later.

If you want to advertise or reach out to people you don't have a pre-existing relationship with, remember that legal restrictions apply when raising money from passive investors. Therefore, if you're syndicating, you'll need to structure your deal in a way that best aligns with your planned approach in order to remain in compliance with securities laws.

Skin in the Game

When raising capital, perhaps the most common question you can expect from prospective investors is whether you (and any partners) are investing your own capital and, if so, how much. In fact, nearly *all* prospective investors have this question—they just might not ask it out loud.

If you're going to raise private capital, you must be prepared to answer this question or, even better, volunteer the answer proactively. Fair or not, the perception among investors is that there is no better way to ensure your interests are aligned with theirs than to have capital at risk under the same terms they do.

As a result, both Brandon and I have committed to investing alongside LPs in all our deals. We do this as a matter of principle and to satisfy investors. However, the truth is that investing our own capital doesn't make us any more motivated than we already are. Being entrusted with other people's money is a stronger motivator, and we have far more at stake in the form of our reputations and the time we put into our projects than with our capital.

If you don't have a lot of capital, how can you be expected to put skin in the game? In the case of a syndication, you could take a portion of your fees and invest that capital back into the deal on the LP side. You could also help investors understand and appreciate the non-monetary investments you're making. Let them know how seriously you take the syndication and how much is at stake for you personally.

When you're entrusted with other people's money, failure is not an option. *The No. 1 rule as a syndicator is to not lose people's money.* Return *of* capital is far more important for most investors than return *on* capital. Once you see things through that lens, it will—and should—color every decision you make.

Investor Management

As you approach investors and open up lines of communication, keeping a record of those contacts is essential. There are many platforms out there to help with this, such as CRM (customer relationship management) solutions. If you are syndicating, good record keeping can help ensure that you are compliant with any requirements for pre-existing relationships. It's also valuable from the standpoint of organization and efficiency.

Accurate record keeping becomes even more important once investors are making commitments and you have to ensure that proper documentation is in place. As involved and intense as the time period leading up to closing can be, it's really only the beginning. Keeping investors informed as a project goes through its entire life cycle is imperative.

Many investors will track everything in a spreadsheet, though this can be unwieldy. Fortunately, there are a variety of helpful online portals and software platforms available, such as AppFolio, InvestNext, Investor Deal Room, Investor Management Services, and SyndicationPro. These types of tools can make communication and documentation tracking much more efficient for both you and your investors.

Institutional Equity

If you have large cash demands or want to fill the equity needs of a multifamily project in one fell swoop, you can consider some of the larger private equity sources out there. Options include family offices, private equity firms, and institutional investors, such as pension funds, insurance companies, and hedge funds. These are the titans of the real estate private equity world, frequently doing deals in the hundreds of millions or even billions of dollars.

While these large players are operating at the highest levels, they can sometimes be a source of equity for large multifamily deals. The bigger players will typically have minimum deal sizes, and sometimes they are quite large.

Try to seek out equity sources that are appropriate to the size of your deals. For example, your $5 million multifamily project won't be of interest to Blackstone Group, one of the largest investment firms in the world, but you might generate some interest from a local family office. Family offices manage the wealth and investments for ultra high net worth families and individuals, generally with at least $100 million in assets, and can be a great source of equity for the right opportunities.

While securing equity from any of these cash-rich sources may sound appealing, there are good reasons why many large multifamily investors steer clear of them. Going into business with one of these firms isn't all fun and games.

Unfortunately, the downsides can be monumental. First, when someone brings a huge pile of cash to the table, they're in a position of strength when it comes to negotiating the terms of the arrangement. They're going to expect preferential treatment. Be prepared to give up more ownership, more control, and more of the project returns. They will name their price and you can expect it to be steep.

On the upside, you can potentially get all the equity you need to fund even the largest of deals—and all from one source. This basically bypasses the entire process of courting and managing individual investors, which can be both stressful and time-consuming. With such a large partner on board, you'll probably also be able to secure better debt terms. In addition, these firms can bring value through their experience, expertise, connections, and even leads on future opportunities. It could be the beginning of a long and fruitful relationship.

However, you'll need to ensure that your interests are aligned. Each firm has its own needs and seeks specific types of projects, deal structures, returns, and level of involvement. For example, some firms are content with a passive role, while others want to be more actively involved and provide operational support. If you're prepared to partner with a private equity firm, make sure that everyone's expectations are clearly communicated and mutually agreeable. If they're not, things are unlikely to go well.

Finally, you're taking on considerable additional risk when going with one large investor. What happens when your sole source of equity backs out at the last minute or demands that you change the terms of your arrangement with them? If you've raised money from individuals and the person who makes this demand is one of thirty, you can tell them to go pound sand. But if you're put in this situation by your sole investor, you'll find yourself between a rock and a hard place. Your deal is unlikely to be particularly meaningful to them, so you don't have much leverage to do anything other than agree.

Every firm conducts business differently, but their primary responsibility is not to you—it's to the people who have entrusted them with their money. They'll do what they need to do, even if it's not in your best interest. You have to respect that, which can be tough when you're getting squeezed. It's never easy to dance with a gorilla, so buyer beware.

Accessing Private Capital Without Raising Private Capital

Now that you have a better understanding of what it takes to raise private capital, what if it's not something you want to do? Maybe you're not a people person at all, and the process would cause you too much stress. Perhaps you have too many other responsibilities. Does that mean you need to rule out private capital entirely? Not necessarily. If you can't or won't raise capital yourself and don't have the resources to close deals on the scale you envision, you have four options:

1. Start smaller or wait until you can accumulate enough savings to do a large deal on your own.
2. Look for other creative ways to finance a deal without private capital.
3. Partner with somebody who will raise the capital—somebody who is more suited to this role or, even better, already has the experience and relationships to be effective. Remember, though, this person must have some other role(s) besides raising capital.
4. Hire or contract with somebody to raise capital on your behalf.

Legal Considerations

One of the most critical components of raising private capital is to get sound legal advice, both before you get started and throughout the process. You're wading into territory that can fall under a broad range of state and federal regulations, so you'll need the services of an experienced professional. Raising private capital is not an aspect of real estate you should tackle all on your own, unless you happen to be an attorney yourself or have extensive experience, and even then, it would be wise to consult with an expert.

If you're borrowing private money, you'll want to have an attorney draft the appropriate documentation and, when necessary, record the transactions. When you're planning to raise private equity, you'll want to engage the services of an experienced securities attorney. This is not a do-it-yourself situation and you should not trust templates you find online. You can research and develop familiarity with the process, but recognize that laws are constantly changing and can vary by state. Even most real estate attorneys will not have the experience or expertise to handle this on your behalf, so always use a securities attorney.

KEY TAKEAWAYS

- When raising private capital from individuals or firms to fund your project, it's important to embrace the proper mindset. You are helping people meet their needs by offering a way for them to invest in real estate. You are not imposing on them, and you are not selling them anything. You are sharing an incredible investment opportunity that you would like them to be a part of.
- To find private investors or lenders, start with people you know and then expand your network through referrals, social media, industry events, and taking steps to build your reputation. Share your excitement, talk about your deals, follow up with people who express interest, and keep records. It's all in the follow-up!
- There are larger sources of private equity available, such as family offices and institutional investors. However, before pursuing these options, be sure to carefully consider their advantages and disadvantages. Do plenty of due diligence and tread cautiously.
- Getting sound legal advice is essential, both before you get started raising private capital and throughout the process.

River Apartments: Part V

Up to this point, everything had gone better than I could have hoped for with River Apartments. I negotiated a great price on an off-market deal, and on top of that I had identified a ton of ways to add value. Even better, the use of creative financing would let me retain full ownership and should allow me to avoid the need to raise private capital. I say should because the bank financing was contingent on the appraisal, which I was anxiously awaiting the results of. If it came in too low, I'd have a gap to fill.

But right now, I had a larger and more immediate problem. The seller's CEO had just confirmed that they had inadvertently signed a renewal contract with HUD, which effectively dealt a death blow to my plans for turning the property into market-rate housing.

After my conversation with the CEO, I immediately began to do a ton of research and speak to as many people as I could to educate myself. Each time I spoke with somebody new, I asked who to call when they have HUD questions. Then I'd call that person.

Over the next couple of days, I got a crash course on HUD's Section 8 program and the significance of a Housing Assistance Payments (HAP) contract, such as the one the seller had extended. Here are a few key things I learned:

- I'd have more luck trying to stop the earth from rotating than I would trying to get HUD to overturn a fully executed HAP contract—and it would cost me a lot less in legal bills.
- There was an entire affordable housing industry out there that I had little familiarity with up to this point, and the market for properties under HAP contracts was healthy.
- Now that the HAP contract had been extended, acquiring the property would require a lengthy and cumbersome HUD approval. I gleaned from my discussions that this was no small task for the uninitiated.
- Properly managing a HUD property takes specialized knowledge and experience, which my team and I didn't have. I perused HUD's imposing *Housing Manager's Procedures Manual* and noted that it was an impressive 247 pages long.

Throughout the time I was conducting research, the CEO's casual remark kept repeating in my head: "In the affordable housing world, this kind of contract is like gold." Maybe he was still trying to sell me, but that seemed unlikely. Was it possible that the contract renewal was actually a good thing? I began to realize that my frustration was in large part due to the unexpected change, combined with my unfamiliarity with affordable housing. As I spoke to more and more people in the affordable housing world, I realized the CEO was right—the twenty-year HAP contract renewal would have real value to the right owner.

I called the CEO back. "I'd like to move forward with our deal. I'm sending over an extension so we can get the necessary HUD approvals in place." I hung up, then stared at my phone, wondering if I had just made a huge mistake. I despised bureaucracy and my experiences working with the government had been riddled with frustration. I looked forward to dealing with HUD about as much as I'd look forward to sticking a fork in my eye.

To be continued...

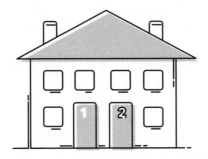

Chapter Five
MULTIFAMILY DEBT

The problem with leverage is that you need to pay it back. The biggest measure of success or failure is how entrepreneurs address and deal with leverage. If you are in the real estate business without leverage, that's like being a boxer in the ring without a glove.

—SAM ZELL

Debt is a powerful tool—far more powerful than most investors realize or appreciate until they've been in the business for a while. Debt can be used in traditional or creative ways to boost cash flows or dramatically leverage your purchasing ability. Harnessed properly, it can help you create a lot of wealth. But debt comes with risk, and the more you borrow, the more exposed you are.

The allure of leverage is a siren song to an investor hungry for more and bigger deals—and large-scale investors are not usually wired for moderation. However, too much of a good thing can lead to one's demise. And that's what makes debt so dangerous.

The creative use of debt was instrumental in growing both of our investment portfolios. It helped us retain more ownership than if we had raised capital, but a highly leveraged deal could have also been our undoing. Fortunately, we've always had a healthy dose of respect for and fear of debt. Neither of us wanted to lose everything we had worked so hard to build. Whenever the occasion arose to do a deal with little cash, we both made sure we had not only a very clear path to meet our debt obligations but also a healthy cushion to rely on in case of setbacks, which every investor will inevitably experience.

Given how important debt is, every aspiring large multifamily investor should understand how to make use of it. Doing so can dramatically improve your likelihood of success. You should also prioritize fostering relationships with experts who are in a position to help you navigate the world of debt to craft solutions that are most appropriate for your projects.

Mortgage Brokers and Mortgage Bankers

The larger the deal you do, the more you have at stake and the more significant debt becomes. Even small changes in terms can make a meaningful difference. Getting the right debt in place is even more critical when you're raising capital from investors who are trusting you to provide the optimal balance of risk and reward. As such, it makes a lot of sense to leverage the experience and connections of someone who specializes in debt. In the world of multifamily, one such person is a commercial mortgage broker.

A mortgage broker will help craft lending solutions and steer you toward options that will work well for your project and priorities. They will know which deals are the best fit for which prospective lenders, and shop your project around to secure the most competitive terms.

Once you choose a lender, a mortgage broker will also help assemble all the documentation necessary to ensure the application process goes as smoothly as possible. That may not sound like much, but getting assistance from someone with more experience than you is extremely valuable. There are any number of ways things can go awry, and dealing with lenders can be frustrating. For some people, going through the lending process can be about as much fun as rolling around naked in a field of cacti.

Another option is to work with a mortgage banker. Although some mortgage bankers have underwriting authority for smaller loans, in most cases, they still have to present the loan to a credit committee. In the end, there is little difference between a mortgage broker and a mortgage banker—working with either is fine.

Mortgage brokers and mortgage bankers come in all shapes and sizes, and you'll want to vet them carefully. Unfortunately, there are plenty of people out there who are quick to promise big things and fail to deliver. They'll convince you to work with them by tempting you with great lending terms, only to have them evaporate once you've invested a ton of time and effort in the approval process. In the end, you're left with few options because you've got a lot of sunk costs and a deal that needs to get closed.

The best way to find a good mortgage broker or mortgage banker is to speak with other multifamily investors about their experiences and ask who they'd recommend. It's a great topic to discuss with other investors at a meetup or on BiggerPockets.com. Fellow investors are likely to give you the unvarnished truth about their experiences, which is worth far more than any sales pitch from someone who's trying to get your business.

Mortgage brokers and mortgage bankers are incentivized to win your business because the support they provide doesn't come free. They will typically charge between .5 and 2 percent of the loan amount at closing. (You should avoid engaging a mortgage broker who wants an up-front payment.)

If you find a good mortgage broker, however, the fee will be money well spent. When a broker works with multiple lenders to get quotes, those lenders know they will have to be aggressive to win the business. While mortgage broker fees can add up, especially on large deals, the savings you'll realize over the long term as a result of better lending terms are likely to far outweigh the cost. You may end up with more proceeds, better rates, more years of interest only, and other terms that increase your project's returns.

Most mortgage brokers and mortgage bankers will have a broad range of lending options, and some will even have potential equity sources. The larger the firm or the stronger their expertise in a particular asset class, the more national and local relationships they are likely to have.

Traditional Lenders

There are numerous lending options for large multifamily properties, but investors are most likely to secure debt from portfolio lenders (such as banks), agency lenders (Fannie Mae, Freddie Mac, HUD), commercial mortgage-backed securities lenders (CMBS), and insurance companies. Each one these comes with its own advantages and disadvantages.

Portfolio Lenders

Also known as balance sheet lenders, portfolio lenders are the lifeblood for many investors, particularly those who are just getting started out or have deals that might fall outside the bounds of what larger lending institutions are comfortable with. Portfolio lenders are commercial banks, savings banks, community banks, or credit unions that originate mortgages and hold them in a portfolio instead of selling them to other institutions in the secondary market, as other types of lenders will do. In other words, they lend their own money and keep the debt in-house. That means these lenders can make decisions based on their own criteria instead of having to follow the strict underwriting standards that any agencies or investors purchasing their debt would demand.

Pros
- They are more flexible with regard to nontraditional properties and deal structures. For example, a portfolio lender is more likely to be comfortable with a major turnaround project or the use of subordinate debt. Also, they will sometimes make exceptions to their underwriting criteria.
- The lending process is frequently less rigorous than with national lenders or agency debt. There may be less paperwork and fewer third-party reports required. This can allow you to close faster and reduce closing costs.
- Reserve and escrow requirements are usually modest or even nonexistent.
- The loans are typically serviced in-house, and responsiveness is usually very good if any issues arise post-closing.

Cons

- Some portfolio lenders may not have a lot of experience with large multifamily deals.
- Terms are not generally very favorable, though this varies widely. Amortization periods and terms tend to be shorter, with higher rates.
- Most portfolio lenders will require the debt to be full recourse, which means you are personally liable for repayment. When nonrecourse is available, it will usually be at a higher interest rate.
- Smaller local banks and credit unions have related-party lending limits that can be reached pretty quickly if you're doing large deals. As a result, they may have to syndicate a deal (work with other lenders), which can complicate and delay the loan application process.

Agency Lenders

When multifamily investors refer to "agency lenders" or "agency debt," they mean loans that are backed by a government agency. Also known as government-sponsored enterprises (GSEs), the two principal agency lenders are the Federal National Mortgage Association (Fannie Mae) and the Federal Home Loan Mortgage Corporation (Freddie Mac). In addition to Fannie Mae and Freddie Mac, Federal Housing Administration (FHA) loan programs are available through the U.S. Department of Housing and Urban Development (HUD). Agency lenders do not lend directly to investors. The companies that source and underwrite loans for the agencies are called DUS (Delegated Underwriting and Servicing) lenders or seller servicers.

Pros

- Lower rates, interest-only periods, and longer amortization periods reduce your mortgage payment and improve cash-on-cash returns.
- Agency debt is nonrecourse, so there is no personal liability, subject to "bad boy" carve-outs (see Chapter Seven).
- You can lock in a fixed rate for a longer term, such as ten to twelve years or more.
- The loan process and documents are standardized and repeatable, which is especially important for repeat borrowers.
- Loans have a higher certainty of execution.

- There are a wide range of agency loan programs and terms available depending on your specific needs. One example is "green financing" programs, which reimburse energy-audit costs and provide preferential terms in exchange for improvements that will achieve specific conservation targets.
- Many agency lenders have a bridge to agency program for transitional properties, streamlining the refinance of value-add deals once a property is stabilized.
- Agency loans may be assigned to a purchaser once a property is sold.
- Many agency loan programs allow supplemental loans for the original borrower as well as subsequent borrowers (at the time of loan assignment or later).

Cons

- The loans typically come with significant reserve and CapEx requirements.
- The lending process usually proceeds at a slower rate than with local banks.
- Some agency lenders will originate and service loans in-house, while others will outsource the loan servicing. Dealing with a single entity is preferable when possible. Unfortunately, it can be hard to determine at the time of the loan application whether the agency lender will service that loan long-term. Also, if a deal is entering a distressed situation, a special servicer will be assigned.
- Subordinate debt is not allowed.

CMBS Lenders

The banks known as CMBS lenders or conduit lenders generally offer more competitive rates than portfolio lenders. CMBS are loans that are pooled together and converted into securities, which means they are sold on the secondary market. While CMBS lenders' rates may not be as competitive as those for agency debt, there is more flexibility with regard to projects and lending guidelines.

Pros

- Lending criteria are more flexible. CMBS lenders will accept deals that do not fit into agency programs.

- The loans are typically assumable. (Mortgage assumptions will be covered later in this chapter.)
- Loans are nonrecourse, so there is no personal liability, subject to "bad boy" carve-outs.
- Many CMBS lenders have a bridge to CMBS program for transitional properties, streamlining the refinancing on value-add deals.
- Some loans may allow mezzanine debt.

Cons
- There are usually pretty stiff prepayment penalties. The lock-out period is typically one to three years, followed by defeasance requirements designed to reimburse the lenders for the loss of interest resulting from prepayment of the loan.
- The loans are generally not serviced in-house. Loan servicing is outsourced, and customer service is notoriously subpar.
- Property tax, insurance, and replacement reserves are usually required.
- The certainty of execution is lower. Investors purchasing these securities can influence whether a deal is accepted as proposed.
- They do not offer supplemental loans.

Life Insurance Companies

Insurance companies generally lend money at competitive rates, but they take a conservative approach. They tend to be particular about who they lend to, the property type, and the location, preferring solid borrowers who are purchasing stabilized, Class A assets in top-tier metropolitan areas. Insurance companies count on collecting interest for an extended period of time. They structure their loans accordingly and are usually a good option only if you plan to hold a property for a long time.

Pros
- Interest rates are great, especially for lower-leverage loans.
- The loan process is relatively easy, with fewer forms and documentation requirements.
- You can lock in rates for long terms, sometimes fully amortizing.
- Some loans offer the ability to lock rates immediately.
- Lenders may be open to creative loan structures.

Cons

- Stringent lending standards rule out a significant portion of multifamily properties and borrowers.
- Lockout periods are long and defeasance requirements are expensive if you pay off the loan early.
- Leverage is low, often capped at 65 percent loan to value (LTV).

Creative Financing

You might consider looking beyond traditional lending options if any of the following apply to you:

- Aspects of your deal preclude the use of traditional debt.
- The terms you're able to secure through traditional channels are problematic.
- You're seeking to reduce the amount of cash required below levels available through traditional financing.
- You're able to secure superior returns or loan terms through a nontraditional approach.
- You need to close more quickly than is possible through traditional means.
- You need to accommodate a unique seller requirement.
- You have an aversion to traditional lenders.

Investors who like to use creative financing employ a handful of strategies. Among the most common are mortgage assumptions and seller financing.

Mortgage Assumptions

One of the most important things you can do in the early stages of a negotiation is to gain insight into the seller's financing and motivations. If there is debt in place, try to find out whether that debt is assumable and, if so, what the terms are. The easiest way to determine this is to ask for a copy of the note. Once you determine whether an assumption is allowable and would be of interest, you can incorporate the debt assumption into your underwriting and purchase offer. The most common reasons why a buyer might wish to assume debt include:

- The terms of the in-place debt are better than other options available to the buyer.

- The leverage available through the assumption of in-place debt is higher than what is possible through other options.
- The assumption process can sometimes be smoother, less costly, and faster than putting new debt in place. That said, the reverse can also be true. The favorability of the assumption process depends on the lender and their specific requirements.
- Lower purchase prices are sometimes possible in cases where the seller would be subject to a significant prepayment penalty.

Most sellers are comfortable with a mortgage assumption, as long as the buyer assumes responsibility for the costs associated with the assumption. As the buyer, you'll want to identify what the costs and cash requirements will be. Most mortgages that allow assumptions will have some sort of assumption fee, which you can expect to be about 1 percent of the outstanding principal balance. You'll likely also be responsible for all legal fees and the cost of any third-party reports, such as updated environmental reports, a new property condition assessment (PCA), or an updated appraisal.

If you are assuming a loan that has escrow and reserve accounts, you will also be expected to replace all the funds that have accumulated in these accounts. Depending on how long the seller has held the debt and how large the balances have grown, this can require a significant amount of extra cash at closing. For this reason, I have sometimes included a clause in my offers that requires the full balance in all the escrow and reserve accounts be transferred to the buyer at closing.

If you're assuming the debt on a distressed property, the purchase price may be lower than the seller originally paid or the value at which they may have refinanced when the debt was placed. The result can be a higher amount of leverage than the lender is comfortable with. In these circumstances, the lender is likely to impose conditions on their approval of the mortgage assumption, such as requiring an equity infusion to reduce the ratio of debt to the purchase price.

I have assumed many mortgages over the years and have been surprised at the degree to which negotiations come into play with the lender. Particularly in distress situations, lenders look at a mortgage assumption as an opportunity to improve their position in a property. As such, they are likely to ask for any variety of concessions to help mitigate their risk.

On multiple occasions I have been asked to establish a new "debt service escrow" that the lender would hold and draw from if I were to miss any mortgage payments. Typically, such an escrow would be released when some type of criterion is met related to the property's financial performance. Other times, lenders have asked for increases in the monthly reserve contributions or commitments to making specific capital improvements.

Any requirements a lender lays out are typically negotiable. Don't be afraid to push back and make your case. Usually a lender will listen to reason and accommodate some of your requests, but each situation is unique. Some agency and CMBS lenders are less flexible. I have also been in situations where the lender has stated their requirements to approve an assumption and refused to compromise at all. Your mortgage broker can be an excellent resource for guidance as to where you might find more flexibility and where you'd be banging your head against a wall.

Seller Financing

Most real estate investors assume that seller financing is an option only when a seller has no debt, but this is not the case. Yes, it's true that if a seller has no debt, they are in an ideal position to extend seller financing. I have encountered sellers in this position who have been willing to lend as much as 95 percent of the purchase price, but that is rare.

Sellers can lend any amount toward the purchase price, but the more debt you seek, the harder it will be to find an agreeable seller. If you're looking for a seller to lend a modest amount of the purchase price—say, 5, 10, or 15 percent—you're more likely to find takers, particularly if you're able to meet their price.

Beware, however, that a seller might perceive a buyer's request for financing as indicative of their inability to borrow through traditional channels due to a lack of qualifications. That's why presentation and communication are particularly important. Strategies that can help you deliver a seller financing offer from a position of perceived strength include the following:

- Don't include seller financing in your first offer. Instead, introduce it in a subsequent counteroffer. The lack of seller financing in the original offer will make a more positive first impression and create more confidence in the seller that you are a qualified buyer. The original offer establishes that you are not seeking seller financing due to a cash shortfall.

- Provide a compelling rationale for including seller financing in your offer. Seller financing will usually allow you to achieve higher leverage, which in turn reduces the cash you need to close. The lower cash invested then boosts your cash-on-cash return. You can explain to a seller (or to the broker who will deliver the offer) that seller financing is included as a component of your offer because it improves cash-on-cash return, which in turn will enable you to pay a higher price.
- Include multiple options with your offer, including one with traditional financing and one (or more) with seller financing. The seller will then clearly see that they can get a higher price for the property with the seller financing options. You can also include a table that shows the monthly payments and total amount you will pay over the term of the seller financing note, including final payoff. This will allow the seller to see the interest they will earn over the lifetime of the note.

Another argument in your favor, depending on what the seller plans to do with the proceeds from the sale, is that providing financing can offer significant tax benefits for the seller. The payments you make to the seller on their note will effectively spread their gain out over a longer time period and can be treated as an "installment sale," which sometimes results in a significantly lower tax rate.

If a seller is planning to do a 1031 exchange (see Chapter Twenty), the tax benefits of owner financing are more limited, though you can still secure a note from a seller who was entering into a 1031 exchange. In this situation the seller would be able to defer the bulk of the gain on the sale by exchanging into a replacement property. The portion of the proceeds they lend would then be subject to a capital gains tax, but those taxes would be paid slowly over many years as they received loan payments. Note that in this situation the seller has to pay taxes only on the capital gains associated with the principal portion of the monthly seller-finance payments. The interest is not considered part of their gain.

Subordinated Debt
When you secure seller financing for a very low portion of the purchase price, it is usually with the intention of stacking that debt on top of bank financing. As you recall from Chapter Two, this seller financing

is subordinated debt, which is in second position to the bank financing. The investment property is still collateral, but in the case of default, the debt obligation to the lender in the senior position would be satisfied first.

If you are planning to structure a deal using subordinate debt, you will most likely need to have a portfolio lender in the first position. Agency debt precludes the use of subordinate debt for the acquisition or at any point afterward. The portfolio lender will also want to see that your property is capable of meeting their lending criteria for both positions combined.

The other way to close the cash gap with a second loan is to secure debt that is not collateralized by the property. The debt could instead be secured by one or more other assets, or with a personal guarantee. The less collateralized the note is, however, the higher the perceived risk will be, so you'll receive less favorable terms.

Private Debt

As discussed in earlier in this chapter, you can also raise debt from private individuals or firms, though this can be challenging for larger deals. Your deal will have to be able to support debt terms strong enough to be of interest to private lenders. What terms and interest rate will you have to pay on the debt in order to attract private capital? The answer is specific to the individuals and firms who might entertain such an arrangement. The terms a lender might be willing to accept depend on a wide range of factors, such as how solid the deal is, how much the investors trust you personally, how much capital they are seeking to deploy, and what other investment options are available to them.

Hard-Money Lenders

Speaking of risk, you can also borrow from so-called hard-money lenders, which are people and firms who specialize in extending short-term debt to people or projects that are not able to secure funds from traditional sources due to the high levels of risk involved, a lack of qualifications, or a project's timeline.

Hard-money loans are usually put in place with the intent that they will have shorter terms, with repayment periods ranging from six to twenty-four months. Hard money is typically considered a debt of last resort for the borrower due to the generally unfavorable lending terms. Borrowers will typically have to pay "points" up front, which are based on a percentage of the debt being extended. Interest rates are usually high—often double the rate you'd expect from a conventional lender or more. Many hard-money lenders are "lend to own" operations, so it is extremely important to pick the lender carefully and fully understand the consequences if loan terms cannot be met.

Bridge, Construction, and Rehabilitation Financing

When you are planning to undertake a major turnaround project or otherwise make substantial improvements that will create significant value within a year or two, securing permanent financing at the time of acquisition can be a challenge. The problem is that most banks want to see enough in-place revenue to demonstrate that you can adequately cover the debt, and you may not have that until the work is complete. If you were to put long-term financing in place when you close, the size of the loan would be limited due to the lower cash flow. This means you'd have to come up with a lot more cash to close, and you'd be sitting on a lot of equity after the improvements are done, which lowers your cash-on-cash returns.

Wouldn't it be great if you could wait until after the work is done and the value has been created before putting permanent debt on the property? That's where bridge debt comes into play. Bridge debt provides you with a short-term loan, usually for one to three years, that is intended to carry you through until you are in a position to secure permanent financing.

Another scenario that lends itself well to bridge debt is the need to close faster than might be possible with permanent debt. A bridge lender might be able to close in as little as two or three weeks. This can be useful when time is of the essence, such as in an auction sale. It can also help when you're facing a normal timeline but can't wait for permanent financing from sources that take a notoriously long time to close, such as HUD loans.

The ability to secure short-term financing can be very valuable. However, it does come with some downsides. First, the loans are considered high risk, so interest rates are higher than for permanent debt and are often a floating rate. Second, if your project doesn't go as planned, you may find it challenging to secure the permanent debt as intended. Finally, other variables can come into play during the time you have the bridge debt: Interest rates could go way up, or the lending environment could deteriorate. A bridge lender may also require additional equity before funding additional rehab work. It is imperative that you fully understand all loan conditions and the potential risks they pose if things do not go as planned. As we'll discuss in Chapter Twenty-One, on recession resistance, putting yourself in a position to need debt in a few short years is always risky.

Master Lease with Option

While a master lease with option is not technically debt, it can sometimes be used as an alternative to bridge debt. A master lease basically gives you all the rights and responsibilities of an owner without actually transferring ownership. In exchange for getting the rights to the profits that are generated, the lessee will generally make a monthly lease payment to the owner to compensate them for the use of their investment property. The agreement usually includes an option to purchase that gives the lessee the option to acquire the property under defined terms and price at some point in the future.

This is how Brandon was able to acquire his first apartment building, a twenty-four-unit property in Aberdeen, Washington. He wasn't able to get a typical commercial loan, so initially he was aiming for seller financing. However, he didn't even have enough capital to cover the closing costs and have adequate reserves, so instead, he negotiated a master lease with option. For the first six months, the seller maintained ownership but Brandon collected all income and paid all bills, saving up the cash flow, which he later turned into a down payment so he could convert this deal into a seller-financed arrangement.

What is the appeal of a master lease? As with bridge debt, a master lease can provide a prospective buyer with time to make improvements to a property with the goal of increasing its value. The more you can increase the property's value, the higher it will appraise for when the time comes to buy.

For example, let's say you determine the value of a property to be $4.8 million. Instead of purchasing the property immediately, you propose to sign a master lease with an option to purchase the property in two years for a price of $5 million. In the meantime, you make all your planned improvements to the property, which raises its value by 25 percent, to

$6 million. With the work complete, you can exercise your option to buy the property for $5 million—a full $1 million below its current value.

Assuming a lender will allow you to borrow 75 percent, you would qualify for a loan of $4.5 million, meaning you need to come up with $500,000 to close, which is only 10 percent of the purchase price or 8.3 percent of the property value. If you managed to raise the value even higher, you might be able to close without any cash out of pocket. Alternatively, you could sell your option to purchase to a third party and pocket the equity you added as profit. That's a lot of cash—you might need bigger pockets.

Note that master leases are not very common, mainly because they can trigger a "due on sale" clause. This clause, which exists in most mortgages, states that if you convey full rights to a property to another party in a manner that substantially amounts to a sale, the bank can call the mortgage due. In practice, some parties elect to enter into a master lease despite the fact that it could trigger this clause. We have engaged in multiple master leases with option transactions, even though many property owners and buyers see the potential for it to trigger the due-on-sale clause as an unacceptable risk.

If you do enter into a master lease with option agreement, pay particular attention to how mortgage payments, property taxes, and insurance are paid. For example, if a seller states that they will pay all of these out of their monthly lease payments, you'll want to ensure there is a way to verify that on a monthly basis. Ideally, the money that goes toward these expenses will be deposited into an escrow account that is administered by a third party. This advice holds true whether you are the buyer or the seller. Don't take the other party's word that they're going to make the payments. Either make them yourself or put a foolproof process in place to ensure that their obligations are being fulfilled.

Refinancing

As you grow a large real estate portfolio, you'll find that refinancing becomes fairly routine. A variety of factors could prompt you to pursue this option. One of the most exciting scenarios is when you've added enough value to a property that you can safely do a cash-out refinance. Executing on value-add and accessing the equity created through cash-out refinances is a strategy Brandon and I have both employed successfully and repeatedly as we've grown our respective portfolios.

A cash-out refinance, as long as it's done without over-leveraging, can deliver some great benefits. For example:

- You can access the equity you built while retaining full ownership of the property. Instead of refinancing, many investors will build equity and then unlock that equity through a sale. While you can get access to more cash through a sale, you can't reap the rewards of a buy-and-hold strategy.
- The proceeds you receive from a cash-out refinance are not taxed as income, which gives you full freedom to invest these funds however you choose. If you want to defer taxes on the gains from a sale, you must follow the strict guidelines of a 1031 exchange (which we'll cover in a later chapter). However, a cash-out refinance avoids any of these restrictions.

In addition to the ability to pull out equity, there are several other reasons a multifamily investor may elect to refinance. The first is that refinancing can represent an opportunity to improve your lending terms. (We'll cover this in detail in Chapter Twenty-One.) You may also refinance out of necessity when you have an approaching term expiring or a balloon payment coming due.

KEY TAKEAWAYS

- The wise use of debt can help you succeed in multifamily investing by increasing your purchasing ability, but you must exercise caution to manage your risk exposure.
- There are many sources of debt for large multifamily properties, including portfolio lenders, agency lenders, CMBS lenders, and insurance companies. A mortgage broker or mortgage banker can help you evaluate the options and find the best solution for your needs.
- Creative financing options, such as mortgage assumptions and seller financing, offer an alternative to traditional lending. Other tools at your disposal include subordinated debt, private debt, hard money, bridge financing, and a master lease with option to purchase.

River Apartments: Part VI

After researching all things HUD, I decided to move forward with the deal to acquire River Apartments for two reasons: First, there was significant value in the HAP contract, and second, the deal we had negotiated was just too good to pass up. The combination of attractive subordinate financing and abundant value-add potential created the opportunity to achieve some pretty extraordinary returns, but there was one big complication: the HAP contract. I was really concerned about the prospect of dealing with HUD, so I decided to enlist some help.

After getting the purchase agreement extended, I hired a big law firm out of New York City that specializes in HUD to help me navigate the application and approval process. Despite the ridiculously high cost, bringing in the experts proved to be a good move. The process was too complex and relationship-based for me to handle on my own, and every bit as challenging and bureaucratic as I'd feared. But the attorneys were total rock stars and got the job done.

Meanwhile, I had to tackle an even bigger problem. During the course of my research and initial dealings with HUD, I developed an appreciation for the challenges of successfully managing a HUD housing project. It was a whole different world, with a different set of rules.

I'd lined up a strong property manager for the project, but they had no experience with subsidized housing, and I began to realize this project could bury them. Taking on a distressed hundred-plus unit property is difficult enough to begin with, but figuring out how to meet HUD requirements at the same time would be downright painful and a recipe for disaster. Instead, I would need to find a reliable third-party property manager that specialized in affordable housing.

From experience, I knew that getting a good property manager in place is essential to the success of any multifamily investment, but what property manager would want to take on a place like River Apartments? Property management margins are thin enough without having to fix all the problems left behind by an incompetent and criminal staff.

I had never owned a HUD property and had no idea where to find a property management firm with the appropriate expertise. There was no simple solution, other than to dig in, start calling people again, and try to find a great company that was willing to rise to the challenge of overhauling a distressed property's operations. Otherwise this wasn't going to work. I looked through my notes from my earlier HUD research and made a list of people who might be able to point me in the right direction. As I picked up the phone to make my first call, I thought I might have better chances of winning the lottery.

To be continued...

Chapter Six

THE LENDER'S PERSPECTIVE

The borrower is servant to the lender.

—PROVERBS 22:7

Anyone who has been through the commercial lending process will tell you that it involves a lot of information and many moving parts. Working through all the complexities with a lender can be challenging. While we may not want to admit it, much of what makes the process so frustrating and stressful is that we don't understand what is happening on the other end and why.

This is especially true when you're working with a lender for the first time. Each lender has a different process, a different way of underwriting, and a different set of criteria they consider important. Many borrowers will choose to go with a lender they have done business with before even if they could get better terms elsewhere, because they know the process and have more certainty of closing. However, new lenders are a big black box, and they're operating from an entirely different framework.

The good news is that at a high level, most lenders view multifamily assets favorably. Even though apartments have shorter leases and higher turnover than other types of commercial real estate, multifamily has proved to be a relatively stable investment, even in challenging economic times—and banks love stability. But even if a bank extends financing for multifamily deals, that doesn't mean they're going to want to finance *your* deal. Keep your expectations reasonable. Yes, banks want to extend loans, but they won't lend indiscriminately.

The best way to understand lenders is to hop into their shoes and look at things from their perspective. A bank is not handing out subsidies, and you are not entitled to a loan. They are a business entity striving to earn a return on their capital, just like you are. When a lender provides the debt capital in your deal, they are in partnership with you. They underwrite a deal and conduct due diligence, just as you do, to make sure they are comfortable with the risk involved—and just like you, they're weighing risk versus reward.

A lender will expect higher rates and more favorable terms (for them) when there are risk factors that increase the likelihood of an eventual default. And when they deem those factors to be at unacceptable levels, they're going to pass. They also might pass because they're too busy and your deal could be more confusing, require more time and effort, or entail marginally more risk than the other deals that they are currently working on.

For a real estate investor, hearing "no" might be frustrating, but you shouldn't take it personally. It's a business decision—and the lender could even be doing you a favor, because as hard as it might be to accept, a no is often based on a fundamental weakness in the deal or the borrower.

One of the advantages most banks have is an abundance of experience to draw on when evaluating a lending opportunity. Over the years, they will have seen which characteristics of a property and borrower bode well for an investment and which ones raise red flags. When lenders poke and prod at the soft spots of a deal, it is difficult not to get frustrated or defensive, but remember they're doing their job. The people you are dealing with have been entrusted to make wise decisions to safely deploy funds, and they would be remiss not to ask a lot of questions and look for problems. Frankly, the aspects of a deal that concern a lender often have substance.

Over time, Brandon and I have both learned to look at deals through the lens of a lender, and this shift in perspective has nudged us in the right direction in defining our respective investment criteria and deciding which properties to acquire. From a logistical standpoint, understanding a lender's process and point of view allows you to provide the right information, which makes a positive first impression and helps avoid the delays associated with much of the typical back-and-forth.

Lender Underwriting

What exactly are lenders looking for when they examine your deal? They want their capital to be safely deployed and, with the exception of a few bad apples with a "lend-to-own" mindset, they have no desire whatsoever to end up owning your property. As such, there are three primary things a lender will need to get comfortable with on a deal before agreeing to extend debt. We call these the BPM: the borrower, the property, and the market. The strength or weakness of the BPM will determine a project's chances for long-term success or failure.

B: The Borrower

When evaluating the borrower (also referred to as the sponsor), one of the most important things a lender will be looking for is experience. A successful track record with similar properties will go a long way toward putting a lender at ease. Some lenders will require you to have a minimum of two years of relevant experience with similarly sized properties in the same market. Others may be satisfied if you make a strong enough case or engage the services of a solid property management firm that brings such qualifications to the table.

As the deals get bigger and bigger, the bar gets higher in terms of a lender's expectations for experience. If you can't meet their expectations, you may need to partner with someone who can, or hire somebody. Why is this so important? Lenders know that the quality of asset management and property management are primary determinants of a project's outcome. Regardless of whether you intend to self-manage or use a third party, recognize that the borrower's experience, and that of their team, is likely to be closely scrutinized.

The second thing a lender will be looking for in a borrower is their personal financial strength. Whether a loan is full recourse or nonrecourse, if things ever go sideways with a project, lenders want to have an invested party who has the financial wherewithal to weather the storm. They also want to avoid personal financial distress situations that could end up spilling over to the property. If they lend to someone who ends up in dire financial straits, that borrower's personal situation could influence how a property is managed.

For example, the need for cash could prompt a borrower to curb spending on routine maintenance or take other detrimental actions designed to suck money out of a property. In some cases, this could result in long-term damage that reduces the property's value and causes the loan to go into default.

How much personal wealth is enough? As explained in Chapter Four, lenders will require that a borrower have a high enough net worth and enough liquidity to satisfy their lending guidelines. Specific requirements vary, but most banks will want to see a net worth equal to the size of the loan, and liquidity equal to 10 percent of the loan amount post-close. We say "post-close" because if part of the capital stack is equity coming out of your pocket, the lender will deduct that amount from your current liquid assets when determining whether you meet the liquidity requirement.

For example, let's say you are going to acquire a $10 million property and are hoping to borrow $8 million. The bank would expect you to have a net worth of at least $8 million and liquid assets of $800,000. If you were planning to put $200,000 into the deal out of your own pocket, then your current liquid assets would need to be valued at a minimum of $1 million.

Liquid assets include cash, money market funds, stocks, and any other financial instruments that can be quickly and easily converted to cash. Most lenders will not count retirement funds as liquid assets unless an individual has reached an age that allows a penalty-free withdrawal, nor are they likely to count whole life insurance cash values or lines of credit toward liquidity—you would have to draw from an available credit line and have it properly seasoned (typically two months or more).

In order to determine whether the borrower meets these criteria, you will be required to submit a personal financial statement (PFS) and schedule of real estate owned (SREO), also referred to as an REO schedule. Banks will typically have their own specific PFS and SREO forms, though most lenders will accept others as long as the version you submit has all the necessary information. When you get to full underwriting, you can also expect the lender to request copies of recent bank statements and sometimes tax returns that support the information in your PFS.

What should you do if you can't meet the net worth or liquidity requirement? Partner with someone who does. In syndication projects, this person is called the key principal (KP). Keep in mind that whoever satisfies the net worth and liquidity requirement will have to sign the loan documents, and there is some liability associated with that, even with nonrecourse debt. Therefore, most people who serve as KP will expect part of the equity. The amount of equity you give a KP can vary widely depending on their experience and reputation, the project risk, what other responsibilities the KP might have, whether the KP is also putting capital into the deal, and the KP's own requirements.

It's not unusual in multifamily deals for the person who brings the money to the table and signs the loan documents to get half of the project equity, while the other half goes to the partner who contributes "sweat equity" by doing the majority of the work. On the other end of the spectrum, I have met some large syndicators who were able to develop relationships with high net worth individuals who will sign loan documents for little to no equity. If you have this type of arrangement, you are very fortunate.

Some lenders, though, will want to see the signer have something meaningful at stake, and they may insist on a certain level of equity for the KP. Without meaningful ownership, the loan guarantor has little motivation to step up and help a project should that ever become necessary. In a syndication, it is more common for a KP to be granted between 5 and 15 percent of GP equity, an arrangement that is more apt to satisfy lenders.

P: The Property

When a lender evaluates the property, you can expect them to consider many of the same things you're considering as part of your own due diligence. The rent roll will be carefully scrutinized, as well as the historical income and operating expenses. If anything appears to be outside normal ranges, the lender will seek clarification. The lender may also want to see the lease form that is in place and the one you intend to use going forward. They will also look at things such as collection losses, rents versus market rents, criminal activity at the property, and occupancy history.

Many lenders will have minimum occupancy levels as part of their lending guidelines. For example, Fannie Mae and Freddie Mac currently require a minimum of 85 percent physical occupancy (90 percent for a refinance) and 70 percent economic occupancy at the time of the commitment and for the preceding quarter.

Economic occupancy is the percentage of the units that tenants are physically occupying and paying rent on. Furthermore, the tenants are expected to be under a lease agreement. When calculating occupancy, you can also count units that are occupied but not producing revenue, such as employee-occupied units or model units, as long as the number of these units doesn't exceed what is customary for stabilized properties in the market. In addition, the occupancy trend should look positive.

Finally, the lender will look at the physical condition of the property. Many lenders will require that a third party conduct an inspection and prepare a property condition assessment (PCA) and environmental report. The findings in a report can cause a lender to reevaluate the project, hold back proceeds from the loan at closing, or require a borrower to escrow funds for repairs.

Lenders will closely scrutinize the physical condition of the property and whether it provides safe housing to its tenants. Some lenders will not consider properties with significant deferred maintenance and will require repairs within three to twelve months after you acquire a property. Significant safety hazards may have to be fixed by the seller prior to the closing.

M: The Market

Just as important as the property itself is its location and what's going on in the environment around it. Even the most experienced and wealthy investor can have trouble keeping a property afloat if it's in a truly bad location. Operating a property in an area that is in rapid decline can be like swimming against a strong current. It's hard work. It's tiring. And even with the most valiant effort, it's difficult not to lose ground. On the other hand, being in a market with strong growth can be very forgiving. An investor can make plenty of mistakes, but with the current at their back, they'll still move in the right direction.

Lenders understand the importance of location, so they will analyze a market, taking into consideration the demographics and economic factors such as employment trends, housing prices, market rents, and even state and local laws that could affect your investment property. These kinds of high-level considerations will be factored into a lender's assessment of how desirable the project is, which can influence whether they decide to lend and, if they do, under what terms.

Lenders may avoid some markets entirely or just be leerier of deals in suspect areas. Within a given metropolitan area, a lender may also look at neighborhood-level information such as crime statistics, proximity to shopping, and employers. Even the best markets have bad neighborhoods, while even the worst cities have pockets of growth. You should be comfortable with a project's location for your own sake and share the story with your lender to help get them on board.

Underwriting Parameters

The property's income and expense information are used to determine the net operating income (NOI), which is calculated by taking the property's annual income and subtracting expenses. The NOI is the cash left over after paying all the bills, which is what the lender wants to see so they can ensure that a property is generating enough NOI for you to comfortably make your mortgage payments. Except for bridge and hard-money lenders, most lenders will not underwrite to your pro forma but to in-place collections (typically the last three months of rents and last twelve months of other income).

Furthermore, lenders will not underwrite to the in-place expenses but will "normalize" the expenses by estimating expenses under the new ownership (see Chapter Fourteen for more details). While not technically an expense, replacement reserves are also included. They are typically at least $250 per unit but can be as high as $600, depending on the property's condition and the loan program.

Once the NOI has been estimated, the lender can calculate the primary underwriting parameters that are taken into account in the loan analysis to determine the maximum amount of the loan they can extend to the borrower; the debt service coverage ratio, the loan-to-value ratio, and the debt yield.

Debt Service Coverage Ratio

The metric lenders use to determine whether the property generates sufficient cash flow to pay your mortgage is called the debt service coverage ratio (DSCR or DCR). The DSCR is calculated by taking a property's NOI and dividing it by the debt service. Note that in calculating your debt service, you should include principal, interest, and any required mezzanine financing.

$$DSCR = NOI \div Debt\ Service$$

When calculating DSCR, you should also include hard preferred equity payments, which would be funds you've secured by selling equity but are structured more like debt. A lender probably wouldn't be aware that you will be making hard preferred equity payments. While it's important for the borrower to make sure a deal can still cash flow, these payments won't likely be factored into the lender's initial underwriting or ongoing checks of DSCR after closing unless it is disclosed. Still, it is always better to avoid misrepresentations or omissions during the loan application process.

A DSCR below 1.0x means the property is not generating enough cash flow to cover debt payments. Obviously, this would not be acceptable for most traditional loan products. Instead, you will want to demonstrate a surplus of cash flow so you can weather the inevitable ups and downs you'll experience over time. Lenders typically like to see a DSCR of at least 1.2x, but it can range from 1.15x to 1.4x. With a DSCR of 1.2x you could lose 20 percent of your property-level cash flow and still fulfill your debt obligations.

Assuming each tenant pays the same amount of rent, that means you could lose 20 percent of your tenants, or reduce your monthly rents by 20 percent, or some combination of the two. Note that these numbers are the typical minimum criteria a lender will require. If you meet the bare minimum, other aspects of the underwriting will have to compensate for this, just as a higher DSCR may mitigate other concerns.

Finally, if you're undertaking a significant value-add project or rehab, you may be projecting a DSCR of less than 1.0x. This doesn't mean you have no options. There are loan products (bridge and hard-money loans and some bank loans) out there for which the lender will accept less than 1.0x, but they are generally shorter with less favorable terms.

Loan-to-Value Ratio (LTV)

The other critical underwriting parameter is the loan-to-value ratio, or LTV. The LTV is the ratio of the loan amount to a property's "as-is" value, expressed as a percentage. The maximum LTV for most traditional multifamily loans is usually no higher than 75 to 80 percent, though it can be as high as 90 percent. Some lenders may be willing to lend more than that under certain circumstances.

As a borrower, recognize that these LTVs are maximums, not standards. Borrowing less than the maximum will increase the overall loan profile and improve the terms of the loan. Beyond the syndication space, most loans aren't done at 75 to 80 percent LTV, and a surprising number of loans are done at LTVs as low as 40 to 55 percent. Many life insurance lenders set their maximum LTV at 65 to 70 percent.

While the default maximum loan amount is based on the LTV, note that if the NOI will not meet the lender's minimum DSCR with in-place income, the lender will usually reduce the loan amount until their lending criteria are satisfied. This DSCR constraint will come up more frequently when cap rates are low and you're trying to secure a full-leverage loan.

Say, for example, a bank will lend 75 percent of the purchase price and you are acquiring a property for $10 million. That means the loan amount would be $7.5 million based on the LTV. If the DSCR for a loan of $7.5 million is 1.0x and the minimum required DSCR is 1.2x, then the loan amount would have to be reduced by 20 percent to achieve the DSCR. The result is a maximum loan amount of $6 million.

While the value of the property is ultimately determined through a third-party appraisal, before the appraisal the lender will typically assume that the current value of the property is equal to the purchase price reflected in the purchase and sale agreement. This is what the property will cost but not necessarily what it is worth, so the ratio used is technically the lesser of the loan-to-cost ratio (LTC) and the LTV. Whether the cost and value are the same depends on the outcome of the appraisal. If the appraisal comes in lower than the purchase price, the lender is going to maintain their LTV, which means the loan amount will be reduced. If the appraisal comes in higher than the purchase price, the lender typically will not increase their loan amount, but that depends on the lender.

In addition to the appraisal, lenders will usually rely on third parties to assess the property's condition and determine whether there are any environmental risks, but third-party reports tend to be ordered later in the process. First a term sheet/loan application is issued, and that is followed by a commitment letter, usually a week or two prior to closing. We will delve into the entire process in the next chapter.

Debt Yield

While DSCR and LTV are widely used, they are not without their limitations. The DSCR can be over-inflated by low interest rates and long amortization periods, while the LTV is largely dependent on capitalization rates and market conditions, which can sometimes change rapidly.

For this reason, lenders—especially bridge debt and CMBS lenders—are placing an increasing emphasis on debt yield to measure their risk. Debt yield is expressed as a percentage and is calculated by dividing a property's NOI by the loan amount.

$$\text{Debt Yield} = \text{NOI} \div \text{Loan Amount}$$

Lenders value the debt yield as a metric because unlike LTV and DSCR, it is independent of capitalization rates, interest rates, or amortization. The debt yield is a metric that allows banks to better quantify their risk exposure, because it basically represents how much of a return the lender would make through a property's cash flow if the worst-case scenario unfolded and they had to foreclose on the property. For example, if a lender extends a $5 million loan on a property with a $450,000 per year NOI and it forecloses on that property, the annual return on the $5 million in capital would be: $450,000 ÷ $5,000,000 = 9 percent.

Banks want to avoid this scenario at all costs, but instituting minimum required debt yields mitigates their exposure. Debt yield thresholds vary depending on a wide range of factors but are typically between 7 and 10 percent for large multifamily properties. Just like DSCR, a lender's minimum required debt yield can be a constraint on loan proceeds.

KEY TAKEAWAYS

- Lenders need to make sure deals fit their criteria, just like investors do.
- Before extending debt, a lender will need to get comfortable with the BPM: the borrower, the property, and the market.
- When underwriting a project, lenders will typically evaluate the debt service coverage ratio, loan-to-value ratio, and debt yield.

River Apartments: Part VII

As I began my search for a property manager, I was both excited and relieved to get some fantastic news from the bank. The appraisal for River Apartments came back well above what we had the property under contact for and ensured that the proposed loan amount would not exceed the bank's maximum allowable LTV.

Even though the appraisal assumed the property would operate as market-rate housing, it was still encouraging. I discussed my change in plans with the lender and was grateful that they would not require the appraisal to be redone. The financing was all set, which was a huge relief! Now I just needed to secure the necessary HUD approvals and get someone to manage the property.

The prospect of finding a good property manager for River Apartments seemed bleak, but fortunately, a solution soon emerged. In my whirlwind of self-education on all things HUD, several of my contacts had mentioned the same expert. I gave him a call and quickly arranged to meet with him in person to discuss my situation. His company specialized in the acquisition, redevelopment, and long-term ownership of affordable rental housing. His firm was also successfully redeveloping another HUD project not far from River Apartments, demonstrating what they were capable of. I was impressed.

The owner of this company and I hit it off right away. He struck me as genuine and we saw things eye to eye. I considered myself fortunate to have found somebody who shared my values and supported my plans for turning around the property. He even reviewed my pro forma and offered feedback based on his vast experience with HUD properties.

We were in agreement regarding the significant upside potential, and together we came up with a plan. I would proceed with the acquisition, and he would help me navigate the HUD requirements in cooperation with my lawyers. Then, even though his company didn't normally do third-party management, he agreed that they would manage River Apartments after closing and we would work together to clean things up.

But he had a grander vision that could make this generous offer worthwhile for him in the long run, something that I could fully support. While they were managing River Apartments, his company would also investigate funding to complete a full restoration of the property, which was in severe need of an overhaul. This plan had the potential to dramatically enhance living conditions for the tenants as well as improve our local community. If everything fell into place, we would consider entering into a formal agreement to partner, or I could potentially sell him the property at a fair value. We shook hands and agreed to move ahead.

With the property management situation resolved, I was ready to close. Well, at least I hoped so. Last time I'd had an unpleasant surprise. Maybe this time things would proceed more smoothly, but I wasn't going to hold my breath.

To be continued...

Chapter Seven
THE LENDING PROCESS

> *If you would know the value of money, go and try
> to borrow some; for he that goes a borrowing goes
> a sorrowing.*
>
> —BENJAMIN FRANKLIN

The lending process can be long and arduous, but learning how to navigate it is helpful for any real estate transaction, especially as you get into large multifamily. To keep things simple, we've outlined seven basic steps to the lending process you'll follow as you secure your debt.

Step 1: Verbal Guidance
For large multifamily deals, some early lender guidance is often necessary in order to complete your preliminary underwriting. If you are an active borrower and highly experienced, you may be able to skip this

step. However, it's usually valuable to get insights from someone who specializes in multifamily lending, just to make sure you're not missing anything.

In order to see whether your project is likely to qualify for a loan and get some high-level, tentative feedback on terms, you should forward your mortgage broker the following basic information (or you can send it to the lender directly if you prefer):

- Brief project overview, including the purpose of the loan, a basic description of the property, and the location. A copy of the listing broker's offering memorandum (OM), if available, can be helpful at this stage. The OM includes most of the information a lender is seeking, conveniently packaged in one pretty document.
- Trailing twelve months (T-12) of income and expenses
- Most recent rent roll available
- Borrower qualifications, including experience, net worth, and liquidity
- Preliminary CapEx budget, if available
- Preliminary pro forma, if available

Based on this information, you should be able to get some indication of what lending terms you can expect. The preliminary guidance you receive can help you complete your pro forma and zero in on your maximum purchase price. While you can certainly come up with a valuation independent of debt, the quality of the debt you're able to secure will usually affect some of your purchasing criteria.

For example, let's say you are trying to determine how much you can pay for a property and still hit your minimum allowable cash-on-cash return. If you were able to secure debt that is interest-only for the first two years, it would improve your cash flow and allow you to pay a higher price. Your cash-on-cash return would also be affected by the interest rate, amortization period, and any other factor that affects the size of your mortgage payments, and thus your cash flow.

Step 2: The Loan Request Package

Once you have incorporated the preliminary feedback into your modeling, you are in a better position to determine whether the project is feasible. Assuming all signs are positive and you're ready to move forward, the next step is to get some more concrete lender quotes and validate your assumptions. If you are working with a broker, they may be able to assemble a quote matrix for you to compare options. Otherwise, you'll have to collect the quotes on your own.

Best practice for securing lending quotes is to put together a loan request package. Even if you have a mortgage broker to help you assemble this package, they will be relying on you to gather the necessary information. Again, if the property you are hoping to acquire is listed with a broker and they can provide the OM, that will make things easier, since it contains much of the information a lender will need. Listing brokers will do this work up front to help the process along, since it's in their best interest that the buyer be successful in securing debt for the transaction.

In order for the process to go as smoothly as possible, a loan request package should also include the following information:

- Two- to three-paragraph executive summary touching on the highlights of the project.
- The purpose of the loan request, and the sources and uses of capital in more detail. If the loan is a new purchase, you should describe the capital stack, noting exactly where the equity capital will come from and how that capital will be deployed. For example, if you are intending to make upgrades to the property, you should include a scope of work with a breakdown of projected costs. If you are applying for a cash-out refinance, you should state your intended use of the proceeds.
- More detailed description of the property, including the size, class, unit mix, floor plans, square footage, amenities, and parking.
- Information on the location, including population trends, major development projects, and proximity to major employers.
- Details of your business strategy, including any planned improvements, rent increases, or other strategies for value-add. If you plan to raise rents, you should include your analysis of comparable properties to support your rent projections.
- Profit-and-loss statements from the prior three years, if available.
- Your pro forma projections and property valuation.
- Detailed borrower information, including relevant experience, your personal financial statement, schedule of real estate owned, last two years of tax returns, and the past few months of supporting bank statements that corroborate your PFS.

Once you have provided this information, you can expect some back-and-forth as you answer questions and fill in any gaps. Each property may have some unique considerations that require a little more due diligence. The lender then uses the information to conduct a preliminary underwriting to determine whether they are interested in lending to you and, if so, what terms they can offer.

Step 3: The Term Sheet

When you receive a preliminary quote from a lender, it is delivered in the form of something called a term sheet, also sometimes referred to as a conditional commitment letter, loan proposal, loan application, or similar. A term sheet is a nonbinding quote that provides you with a high-level overview of the potential rates, business terms, and possible options you can expect for your loan, subject to all necessary underwriting and approvals.

Because the term sheet is provided prior to underwriting and credit approval, the terms are nonbinding and intended to be more of an expression of interest. That said, the stated terms are usually carried through to closing unless problems or concerns surface during the full underwriting. Be wary of lenders who are quick to issue term sheets and do their underwriting only after you've accepted them—they are the most likely to back out or change their terms later in the process.

The specific content of term sheets can vary, but many sections and terms are standard. As you might expect, a term sheet will specify basic information such as who the borrower is, the purpose of the loan, and the collateral, which in most cases will be the property you are acquiring. You can also expect to find the following important information.

The Loan Amount

The amount of the loan is typically constrained by the lender's underwriting criteria. Based on the specifics of the property, a bank will generally calculate the maximum loan amount initially based on the LTV and the DSCR, as covered earlier in this chapter. However, the loan amount could be further reduced depending on the outcome of the appraisal. As a result, the loan amount in the term sheet will frequently state that it is the lesser of the preliminary calculation or the amount calculated by applying the LTV to the appraised value.

For example, let's say that a lender is willing to extend a loan equal to 80 percent of the LTV on a property you are acquiring for $4 million, which would yield a loan amount of $3.2 million. The DSCR is solid, so this loan amount doesn't have to be reduced. In this circumstance, the term sheet would likely specify the loan amount as *the lesser of* $3.2 million or 80 percent of the property's appraised value. For example, if the appraisal comes back at $3.5 million, the loan amount would be reduced to $2.8 million.

Guarantors

The term sheet will specify who is going to guarantee the note. The lender will likely require the guarantee of any entities or individuals with significant ownership. What a lender considers "significant" may vary, but the threshold tends to be between 10 and 25 percent.

The liability associated with being a guarantor will vary depending on whether the loan is full recourse or nonrecourse. With a full-recourse loan, the guarantors are personally liable in the case of default. With a nonrecourse loan, the lender can foreclose on the property but not go after the guarantors personally, with limited exceptions.

A guarantor's liability for a nonrecourse loan is typically limited to "bad acts," such as negligence and fraud. In the industry this exception is referred to as a "bad boy" carve-out. Examples of conduct that could trigger such a clause are taking on additional debt when it is prohibited, falsifying financial statements or tax returns, causing a lapse in insurance or a reduction in coverage below the minimum lender requirements, or making misrepresentations during the application process.

Term and Amortization Period

The loan term is how long you have to pay back the remaining principal balance of the loan. For most multifamily loans, the term is between five and ten years with a balloon payment at the end. Note that the term is different from the amortization period, which is the period of time on which the loan payments are based. The amortization period is usually longer than the loan term and reflects the amount of time it would take to pay down the full loan principal balance. Loans where the term equals the amortization period are called fully amortizing.

Interest Rate and Rate Lock

Interest rates for most commercial loans are quoted based on a standard index, such as the ten-year United States Treasury bond, LIBOR, or prime rate, and then applying a margin on top of that, which is called the spread. Rates can be fixed or variable, though the unpredictability of variable-rate debt generally makes such loans undesirable for multifamily investors. The term sheet will also state when the rate will be "locked." Portfolio lenders may offer a rate in the term sheet that they will honor all the way through closing, but most lenders won't lock rates until right before closing.

The term sheet will also note whether there is an interest-only period, during which time you will not have to make principal payments. This feature can boost cash flow in the early years and be particularly appealing when you are turning a property around or otherwise executing on a plan to boost income or cut expenses. Interest-only periods can be as short as a few months or as long as the full term of the loan but are most commonly one to three years. Longer interest-only periods are typically associated with low LTVs.

There is a tendency for investors to fixate on the interest rate, even though it might not be as significant as other terms of the loan. It's important to understand that there are no standard "best terms." Neither a low interest rate nor a higher LTV, longer term, or longer amortization period *by itself* is necessarily better if the overall terms don't align with your investment strategy and business plan.

Prepayment Penalties and Lockout Provisions

The term sheet will also note whether there are any penalties associated with paying off the loan early and having it released from the mortgage lien prior to maturity. There may also be "lockout periods" during which you can't pay the loan off at all. Such provisions are particularly important to note if you anticipate a short hold period or may want to refinance.

The prepayment penalties are sometimes structured so as to decline each year, or "step down," and are typically stated as a percentage of the loan balance. For example, your penalty may be 5 percent of the principal balance in year one, 3 percent in year two, and 1 percent in years three, four, and five. A declining prepayment penalty can span as much as ten years depending on the loan product, although that is rare—most span five years or less.

Other loans will include a prepayment penalty in the form of "yield maintenance," which is based on a complex formula that is used to determine the current value of interest the bank would have received over the life of the loan. Some securitized loans require defeasance, in which the property is released in exchange for purchasing a security whose cash flow will match the remaining payment dates and amounts on the loan. Both yield maintenance and defeasance can be very costly—sometimes to the point of rendering prepayment unviable. If you search for "yield maintenance calculator" or "defeasance calculator" online, you can find plenty of free tools to estimate the cost.

If you have the option of yield maintenance or defeasance, the preferred choice will depend on the note rate and where rates move during the term of the loan. If rates have risen enough, not only can the cost of prepayment drop, but you can sometimes even be "in the money" and get a credit when you prepay.

Fees

Lenders can charge a wide range of fees, including an origination fee and an underwriting fee to cover the lender's costs. Some lenders charge a fee at closing that is calculated as a percentage of the loan amount and closing costs. Other lenders and loan programs require a "good faith deposit" at the time of the rate lock, which will be credited back at the time of the closing or shortly thereafter. Fees for third-party reports are also stated and usually must be paid at the time of the loan application. The amounts are typically presented as estimates, and the final fees will depend on actual costs.

Escrow and Reserve Requirements

A variety of escrow and reserve requirements may be specified in the term sheet, and monthly deposits into these accounts will be invoiced together with the loan payments. For example, most lenders will establish an escrow for property tax and insurance premiums. The lender will collect your monthly payments and set them aside to make these payments directly. This is a risk mitigation strategy for the lender, who doesn't want to entrust these critical payments to the borrower.

In terms of reserves, the most common requirement is a replacement reserve, which sets aside funds for future capital expenditures. Additional escrow or reserve accounts may also be required, depending on the specifics of the project and lender guidelines as well as the market environment.

Performance Covenants

The borrow will often have to meet certain performance requirements during the term of the loan. Common examples include the need to maintain a specific DSCR, financial reporting requirements, and mandatory annual inspections. Failure to meet performance requirements could trigger a "cash management" provision that would entitle the lender to collect all rental payments directly from the tenants. If certain performance requirements are not met, a lender may also require the escrowing of interest reserves, suspend the funding of rehab draws, or take some other remedy.

Additional Conditions

Some of the other conditions that might be specified in a term sheet include insurance requirements, escrow and reserve requirements, and necessary third-party reports. There may also be custom provisions to address any unique risks the lender identifies as being associated with the property. For example, a lender might require specific crime mitigation measures for a property with a history of high crime.

The term sheet will likely have an expiration date and a variety of disclaimers to make it subject to approval based on the lender's complete underwriting, including any third-party reports. It will also outline what documentation you will be required to submit and whether you need to open any accounts, such as a checking or savings account, with the lender or a servicer.

Finally, a term sheet/loan application will state the next steps for moving forward, which typically entail signing and returning the letter as an expression of interest. Some lenders will also require a good faith deposit before proceeding to full underwriting.

One of the most important things to know about term sheets is that they are negotiable—especially if you have a project that is appealing to multiple lenders. Not attempting to negotiate a term sheet is a common mistake made by less experienced borrowers. Almost any aspect of a term sheet is negotiable, and you can usually get a lender to improve their terms in at least one area. Part of the challenge here is knowing what to ask for, since the flexibility of the loan terms can vary from lender to lender and deal to deal.

If you have term sheets from more than one lender, compare them side by side to see where there might room for improvement. This is where a good mortgage broker can really earn their fees. An experienced mortgage broker will know which levers can be pulled and which are less flexible, and help guide you through the process of negotiating the best possible terms. If you're able to successfully negotiate a change in the loan terms, the lender will issue an updated term sheet/loan application and return it for your signature.

Step 4: The Commitment Letter

Once you sign and return a finalized version of the term sheet, the deal proceeds to full underwriting. At this point, the lender will begin a thorough review and analysis of all the information in your loan package while further vetting the project through other sources. This will invariably trigger many requests for information and documentation, which you should do your best to promptly supply. Patience and responsiveness are important. By this time it's also possible that some of the information in your original loan package will need to be updated, such as the rent roll and trailing twelve-month financials, so be prepared or, better yet, proactively secure and deliver the updated information as soon as it's available.

If the underwriting goes smoothly and the lender is satisfied with everything they find, they will issue a commitment letter. The commitment letter outlines the specific lending terms, which are often identical to those in the term sheet. However, there is one major difference: The commitment letter is a legally binding document for both the lender and the borrower.

The lender is committing to make a loan on the stated terms, and if any issues arise from this point forward, they are obliged to make a good faith effort to resolve them. The borrower, on the other hand, is committing to pay any specified fees or expense reimbursements, even if the loan doesn't close. It's at this stage that the borrower will often need to make a good faith deposit.

In addition to stating the terms of the loan and any borrower obligations, the commitment letter will list any conditions that must be satisfied for closing. These conditions typically include the completion and approval of third-party reports, that there be no material adverse changes to the property or the borrower's and guarantor(s)' finances prior to the closing of the loan, and that the loan close by the date specified.

Step 5: The Third-Party Reports

Once the term sheet/loan application is executed and any application fees are paid, most lenders will promptly order third-party reports. Because these are a crucial part of the lender's underwriting, they will not generally issue a commitment prior to receipt, review, and approval of third-party reports.

Note that if you have a tight deadline to close or other extenuating circumstances, smaller lenders like local banks and credit unions may have more flexibility in the lending process. For example, they may be willing to order third-party reports prior to the issuance of a commitment letter and require payment for the reports in advance or otherwise obligate you to reimburse the costs. They may also make an exception and issue a commitment prior to completion of the third-party reports, making the commitment subject to review. It is important to recognize that such practices would require special exceptions and are requests that most lenders will not accommodate.

The three third-party reports that are most critical to loan approval include the appraisal, the property condition assessment, and the environmental assessment.

Appraisal

The appraisal is probably the single most important third-party report because it directly affects the size of the loan a lender is willing to extend. When an appraisal comes in low, the loan size is likely to be reduced accordingly, and many times that is enough to kill a deal. Is there anything you can do to make sure you get the results you want? I think the best opportunity to influence an appraisal is through the loan application package, though many times a lender will not or cannot share details on the loan request with the appraiser. In that case, the borrower or mortgage broker should be prepared with a detailed package of information to share with the appraiser to help get a full understanding of the deal.

This is your opportunity to make your strongest argument for the value of the property. As such, the package you provide to the lender and appraiser is not the place to be overly conservative in your assumptions. Save that for your internal stress tests. The loan application package should be neither conservative nor aggressive, but prepared honestly and objectively with assumptions substantiated by data wherever possible. Do you have some great comparables for market rents, occupancy, and sales, for example? Include them in your loan application package. Appraisers are busy people, and if your data is solid enough, they will use it.

The second opportunity to influence an appraisal is during the appraiser's physical inspection of the property. If possible, you or your mortgage broker should accompany the appraiser, explain anything requiring elaboration, answer any questions, and promptly follow up on anything you can't answer on the spot.

It's not obvious to most borrowers, but the appraisal will often impact how a lender must underwrite expenses. As an example, if the lender initially underwrote payroll at $1,100 per unit and the appraiser insists on $1,200 per unit based on their view of how the comps operate, the underwriter will in most cases be required to use the higher number. This would reduce the NOI and in turn not only negatively affect the property's valuation but also lower the DSCR and debt yield. A good mortgage broker will work with the appraiser and underwriter to get the best expense comps possible, another of the many areas in which a mortgage broker can add a ton of value.

Property Condition Assessment

A property condition assessment (PCA) is an evaluation of the multifamily asset based on a thorough inspection that includes all property improvements and building systems. The product of this inspection is a detailed report that identifies "priority" or "critical" repairs and includes a replacement reserve table. Cost estimates are included for the immediate repair work, and lenders will frequently require that this work be completed before closing or, more likely, that funds be set aside at closing and held until the work is complete. Either option will increase the amount of capital you'll need to close on a property.

The replacement reserve table inventories the longer-term capital expenditure requirements. It includes the expected useful life of every major system and the associated capital costs. Many lenders then use these projections as the basis for establishing replacement reserve requirements, which affect the property's cash flow. Also, going forward, only work done on the items specifically identified in lender documents will qualify for reimbursement from the replacement reserve.

Environmental Assessment

Most lenders will require some level of environmental investigation for the purpose of identifying any existing or potential environmental contamination liabilities. While some lenders may be satisfied with the completion of a questionnaire, the industry standard is to conduct a Phase I environmental site assessment (ESA), which involves a physical inspection and reviews the history of the property and neighboring lands to assess the level of environmental risk. In the rare instance where there is deemed to be a significant likelihood of contamination, a more expensive and involved Phase II ESA may be conducted in which actual samples are taken.

While the bank is responsible for ordering these third-party reports, there are other third parties that you will need to engage. You'll want to secure an insurance binder for the property and coordinate with your attorney to ensure that the survey and title are ordered so that when the loan is approved you can move quickly toward closing. Getting accurate and binding insurance quotes typically takes weeks for multifamily properties, so you should get that ball rolling with an insurance broker experienced in multifamily as early in the process as possible.

You'll need to order a title search and examination. After these are completed, the title insurance company will issue a preliminary title report that will show any liens or other encumbrances against the title to the property. Your attorney and the lender's counsel will review the report to make sure they are comfortable with everything and ensure that any issues are resolved to everyone's satisfaction prior to closing.

Step 6: Final Approval

Once all third-party reports and full underwriting have been successfully completed, the lender's loan committee reviews the final loan package for approval. For some loan programs, the lender does not have approval authority and is required to submit the package for approval to another party (e.g., Freddie Mac). Then, when approval is granted, closing documents will be prepared. These loan documents should be carefully reviewed to ensure they are consistent with the terms in the commitment letter. Your attorney can ask for drafts of the closing documents early in the process to pre-negotiate any points important to the borrower. However, this can get expensive so it's generally appropriate only for reasons such as a partner buyout or estate planning. If you have a specific need, you'll want to negotiate it early—even as early as on the term sheet—before going all the way through the lending process only to realize you can't come to terms on a deal-breaking item.

If you object to any of the terms in the loan documents and have a sound basis for those objections, negotiation regarding certain terms and language might be possible. However, for some loan programs, loan documents are not negotiable.

Step 7: Closing

Many of the terms, customs, and procedures surrounding closing and titles vary from state to state and can even vary among regions within a specific state, so it's a good idea to make sure your attorney has local experience. For example, in some states an escrow agent or title agent will drive much of the closing process, while in other states the attorneys will handle everything.

There is usually a flurry of activity in the days leading up to closing and on closing day. The attorneys will develop a closing checklist showing all that needs to be done and who is responsible for what in order to keep everything organized. Even with the benefit of a list, the process can get chaotic. It's not unusual for issues to arise, and when they are related to the mortgage, your mortgage broker can often be of assistance. There are many moving parts to a closing, and unfortunately, delays are not unusual. But once you've come this far, most problems that arise can be resolved. (We will cover closing in much more detail in Chapter Seventeen.)

KEY TAKEAWAYS

- The lending process can be long and arduous, but learning how to navigate it is critical for successfully financing your large multi-family acquisitions.
- The seven-step lending process generally starts with verbal guidance, followed by a loan package, term sheet, commitment letter, third-party reports, final approval, and then closing.

River Apartments: Part VIII

When we finally secured all the necessary HUD approvals for River Apartments and closing day was approaching (again), I got some more great news. As I reviewed the closing statement, I learned that the credit for the seller's replacement reserve balance was more than I had dared hope for. I would be getting a credit of $140,000.

The combination of bank and seller financing that I had secured was only $100,000 short of the purchase price. The credit of $140,000 was enough to cover not only the $100,000 but my closing costs as well. I couldn't believe I was going to close on a 115-unit property with no cash out of pocket. After paying for the property and closing costs, I actually walked out of closing with a check for a little over $1,000.

Apart from paying for the property and closing costs, I knew I would also need to deposit funds in the property's operating account in order to pay the expenses we would start to incur immediately after closing. I further bolstered my cash position by employing one more simple strategy, which was to schedule my closing early in the month. The purchase agreement included a standard provision for crediting the buyer for prorated rents at closing. I had scheduled the closing for the first week of the month, and as a result, I got a rent credit of about $80,000, which was deposited directly into our operating account. Now I was primed and ready to go!

Or at least that's what I thought. In fact, I had crested a peak on the multifamily roller coaster and was about to take a precipitous dive.

To be continued...

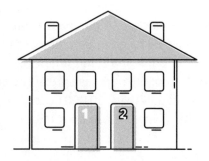

Chapter Eight
BUILDING YOUR TEAM

Great things in business are never done by one person. They're done by a team of people.

—STEVE JOBS

I was filled with gratitude. It was January, and my wife and I had left cold and snowy New York behind and flown to Hawaii to attend Open Door Capital's first annual company meeting. The team was getting together in Maui to have fun and do some strategic planning for the coming year—it was time to put our heads together and set some big goals.

Looking around the table, I realized that I was in the company of six rock stars. I would have felt blessed just to share coffee with these high performers, but knowing that these were my teammates seemed too good to be true. How was this possible? Well, it wasn't luck, that's for sure. It was a situation created through intention and deliberate action.

Brandon Turner had crafted a vivid vision and then carefully sought out the people who could bring it to fruition. Some of the people he'd known for years, while others had started off in lesser roles and proved themselves to be extraordinary. Brandon plucked people from Maine to New York to Atlanta to Hawaii, and assembled the perfect team for a common purpose.

Each person at that table had their own unique strengths and had been carefully selected for a role that would leverage their abilities to maximum effect. Combined, we had everything we needed to achieve the loftiest of goals—goals that none of us could have hoped to achieve on our own. We had the leadership, the skills, the experience, the drive, the resources, and the shared values. What's more, these were genuinely good people. We'd been working together for less than six months, but I already knew these things to be true.

It's rare that everything aligns and a high-functioning team is brought together to achieve a clear and common goal, but when it happens, it's magical. Brandon's vision was to own a $50 million portfolio in mobile home parks within three years—in a fulfilling way that created value for everyone involved, including the investors who entrusted us with their money. Now, sitting around the table with this team, the energy was palpable and I knew we could do more. This was a team that wouldn't be satisfied with just meeting a goal. This was a team that would need to blow it out of the water.

"I think we should consider adding a zero to our number," I told the group. "Let's see if we can grow the portfolio to $500 million."

Why Teams Are Important

People are often surprised to learn that both Brandon and I started investing in real estate without mentors, training, or experience, and yet we thrived. Well, the explanation is pretty simple. We didn't do it alone. We had a lot of help from a lot of people, and that's how it is for most investors. Even if you're investing in smaller properties, you'll need help. Sometimes you'll need legal advice. Or a tax accountant. Occasionally a plumber, electrician, or exterminator. It all depends on where your competencies lie and the challenges you face along the way. Unless you're flying around in the sky wearing tights and a cape, you're probably not going it alone. None of us are. Well, at least nobody who is successful. Sometimes their team is at the forefront, and sometimes they're in the background—but the team is always there, whether you can see them or not.

If you think you have the knowledge and ability to do everything, or even most things by yourself—and at the level necessary to achieve great things—you're deluded. Time to awaken your dormant humility and take a harder look. In the words of spiritualist Anthony de Mello, "Wisdom tends to grow in proportion to one's awareness of one's ignorance." With experience we learn that in order to thrive, it's imperative to recognize our weaknesses, and then compensate for them by leveraging the skills and knowledge of others.

As your real estate portfolio grows, your daily roles and responsibilities will need to change, and you'll have to expand your team. For example, when I had one property, I was shoveling snow and mowing lawns. When I had five properties, that didn't make sense anymore. It was time to hand things over to a property manager. As your portfolio grows and you buy larger multifamily properties, you'll have to get comfortable handing more things off and learning to rely more on team members. Delegating isn't easy, but it's necessary. If you try to do too much yourself, you'll miss things, your growth will slow down, and you'll risk burning out.

Every time your investing reaches a new level, you'll have to narrow your personal focus even further and revamp your team. Investing on a large scale and competing at a higher level takes a different set of skills than smaller-scale investing, and so will frequently require a different team too.

Identifying Your Needs

The question isn't whether you need a team to go big in multifamily. The question is, *what do you want your team to look like?* What roles and responsibilities do you want to fill with team members? What characteristics are you looking for in these individuals, and how do you want to structure those relationships? With some team members you'll have a contractual or vendor type of relationship, while others might be employees. You could have full-blown partners who share ownership in your deals or in your company. To further complicate things, you can have hybrid arrangements with team members who don't fall neatly into any one of these buckets.

Complementary Skills and Experience

A variety of factors will affect how you decide to structure your team, but the first step is an objective self-assessment. You need to identify your greatest strengths and determine how you can add the most value toward achieving your goals. What do you do that really moves the needle? What's your superpower? Sit down and make an inventory of what you bring to the table, including what you're good at, what you're great at, what you enjoy, and how to best leverage those things. Then take a look at your weaknesses and the tasks that make you miserable. Once you've done this, overlay it with the skill sets, competencies, and resources necessary to achieve your goals. It's your team that's going to fill in the gaps. It's your team that can take those weaknesses and make them strengths. Because in the end, what's going to determine your success or failure isn't your own skills. It's the team's skills.

For example, let's say you hate math, computers make you anxious, and formulas make your head hurt. If you partner with a computer geek who reads math books for fun and gets jazzed up about complicated formulas and spreadsheets, you've just turned a liability into a strength, because your partner will now be handling these things, not you. The same logic applies if your knowledge of real estate law is limited, but you find a great real estate attorney to handle any legal issues that arise. As the legendary basketball coach Phil Jackson once said, "The strength of the team is each individual member. The strength of each member is the team."

Intangibles

Beyond the concrete need for skill sets, competencies, and resources, there are a variety of less tangible things you should consider when selecting team members—things that can be more important than someone's talents and experience. Examples of some of the factors you may want to consider include the following:

- **Ethics:** Be uncompromising when it comes to ethics. As you get to know someone, listen for suggestions or comments that might be indicative of questionable integrity, such as a propensity for discounting legal requirements, deceptiveness, or a disregard for others. Another red flag is when someone discusses information that was shared with them in confidence or openly bashes former employers or colleagues. The person who does this is likely to do the same to you someday. Watch for telltale signs of questionable ethics such as frequent exaggerations, half-truths, and omissions.

You should only engage in business with someone honest you feel confident you can trust. Trust is the cornerstone of any good working relationship. Without it, your team is destined to fail.

- **Values:** Working with people who share common values is essential. Examples of some values you may find important include dependability, commitment, positivity, entrepreneurial spirit, perseverance, respect, and a strong work ethic. It's hard to overestimate the power of values; whether good or bad, they tend to be contagious. Drop an openly positive person in a group, for example, and they can lift everyone's spirits and create energy. On the other hand, undesirable values such as negativity and laziness can spread like a disease.

- **Baggage:** Someone who brings significant drama or challenges from outside of work into your business and investments can be a distraction and affect the outcome of your projects. Make sure that any trials or tribulations someone is dealing with won't trickle over into the workplace or prohibit them from fulfilling their professional obligations.

- **Resources:** A team member who brings financial strength, an extensive professional network, credibility, or other resources to the table can add value beyond their skills. On the flip side, be wary of bringing someone into the fold who is in financial distress or has a lot of contentious business relationships or a bad reputation.

- **Vision:** If you're going to partner with someone, make sure you're on the same page insofar as the future direction of the venture. That doesn't mean there shouldn't be discussion and flexibility along the way. In fact, a partner who is willing to ask the hard questions and challenge you can be tremendously valuable—provided your long-term goals are in alignment.

- **Niceness:** Personally, if we could only pick one attribute in a team member, we would ask that they be nice. You need to work with these team members, which means interacting and spending time with them. Whether the team member is a full-blown partner or just a vendor, they will be associated with you and their conduct will reflect on you. Regardless of how talented someone is, we don't advise hiring them (and certainly not partnering with them) if they are rude, arrogant, pretentious, or inconsiderate. Instead, seek out people who demonstrate humility, courtesy, and consideration. Meet them at a restaurant and see how they treat the waitstaff. Do they look the waiter in the eye, smile, and engage warmly and politely? Do they show respect? Or are they brusque and condescending? If the latter, keep looking and find a more decent human being.

Yes, those are a lot of things to consider, but they're all important when creating a team to take your multifamily investing to the next level(s). You assemble the right people, align their superpowers with their roles and responsibilities, get them all working in concert, and then get out of their way and let them do their thing. The famed industrialist Andrew Carnegie once said that "teamwork is the ability to work together toward a common vision. The ability to direct individual accomplishments toward organizational objectives. It is the fuel that allows common people to attain uncommon results."

Types of Team Members

As you prepare to take things to the next level, you'll also be faced with the challenge of figuring out what types of relationships you should establish with team members. Should they be third parties, freelance contractors, employees, or equity partners—or should you come up with some other kind of arrangement? When weighing such decisions, identify what's most important to you at this stage of your investing career, and what resources you have at your disposal.

For example, if being in full control and retaining ownership are top priorities, you might want to avoid taking on partners and try to fulfill your needs by contracting with third parties, since going solo preserves your equity and puts you in the driver's seat. That said, employees and contract services may not be feasible because they can be costly. If your resources are limited, you may need to look for partners who are willing to work at your side for the shared promise of future rewards.

In the end, there is no one right way to build and structure your team. Everyone's priorities, circumstances, and interests are unique. You need to weigh the pros and cons of the different types of relationships and figure out what will work best for you.

Third Parties

The larger your investment portfolio grows, the harder it becomes to scale operations and the more you'll need to rely on third parties. Therefore, you'll have to decide what business you want to be in. What do we mean by that? Although you are a multifamily investor, you may be filling other roles as well. Are you also managing your own properties? If so, you're gaining valuable knowledge and saving money, which can be great for a small investor, but you're actually in two businesses—investment and property management.

In that case, you need to ask yourself if you want to scale up and grow a property management business alongside your investment business. If so, you will be growing two businesses at the same time—and you may be in other businesses as well. We've watched plenty of people grow multiple businesses simultaneously and do so successfully, but it can take a toll. The workload will be mammoth and you're going to need a lot of good help.

In addition to considering what's beyond your core focus, be aware that some roles and responsibilities are just more practical to outsource to third parties. This is especially true of functions that require highly specialized knowledge or skills and tend to have irregular work demands. For example, when we started syndicating and realized we needed to fill the gap in our knowledge of securities law, it quickly became clear that we should engage the services of an experienced attorney to handle all the paperwork and help us ensure compliance. Of course we'd still have to learn the basics in order to stay compliant, but we would need someone who specialized in securities law whenever we put together a new deal. Even though we'd have to pay a high hourly rate, it was far more cost effective to engage a professional firm than to hire in-house counsel or give away equity in exchange for legal services.

One of the primary benefits of outsourcing is that you can have access to someone with specialized skills on an as-needed basis. Another advantage is that you're not responsible for managing them on a day-to-day basis or dealing with the headaches of recruiting, hiring, training, and payroll.

The following are some of the more common roles filled by third parties for the large multifamily investor:

- **Brokers:** Yes, you can find off-market deals, but building and maintaining relationships with some of the key brokers in your target market is important. As we'll discuss in Chapter Nine, broker listings tend to be one of the primary sources of deals, and some of those properties are offered to only a select group of buyers.

- **Attorney(s):** A good real estate attorney who has experience with properties on the scale you're targeting is essential. Small multifamily experience is not adequate. There are more complexities with larger multifamily deals and financing. If you're syndicating, you'll also need a securities attorney.
- **Tax Accountant:** A tax accountant with deep multifamily experience can save you far more money than you'll pay in accounting fees. You'll also want to develop relationships with companies that specialize in cost segregation studies, which will be covered in Chapter Twenty.
- **Insurance Broker:** Insurance is important for a variety of reasons. First, you want to be protected and manage your risk. Second, it's a significant cost in multifamily, sometimes accounting for 10 percent of a property's expenses. Therefore, you need just the right policy to satisfy your lenders and provide you with adequate coverage without over-insuring or over-paying.
- **Mortgage Broker:** As explained in Chapter Five, a mortgage broker can help you navigate the lending process, matching you with the right debt product and securing the best rates.

In addition to the above third parties, the larger you scale, the more common it is to outsource property management. Your property manager is arguably your single most important partner, because how a property is managed determines how well your investments will perform.

Property Management

As discussed in Volume I, managing your own multifamily property has many advantages. There's no substitute for getting some hands-on operating experience under your belt, but there are obvious tradeoffs, since property management isn't easy and can be time-consuming.

Once you graduate to large multifamily properties and begin to build a portfolio in the hundreds or even thousands of units, property management is no joke. Your first business, which is your multifamily investment firm, is going to be demanding on its own, so growing a large property management company on the side is a bigger endeavor than most investors are capable of pursuing. It can be a huge distraction. That's not to say it can't be done, just that it's a monumental undertaking and one that shouldn't be embarked on without careful consideration. Property management is labor-intensive: For a portfolio of, say, 1,000 units, you'll likely have thirty to forty employees, including on-site personnel, management, and support staff. Building and managing an operation of this scale can be great for people with the bandwidth who are so inclined, but for most large investors it's neither practical nor appealing.

Instead of owning and operating a property management company, most large multifamily investors will outsource this function to a third party. The downside of outsourcing property management for large multifamily assets is the same as for smaller properties—a management company is unlikely to care as much or give a property as much attention as you would yourself, and the service they provide comes at a price. However, for most of us, the trade-off is both necessary and worthwhile once you reach a certain size. If you can find the right property management company, the benefits of outsourcing can be substantial, including the ability to:

- Apply experience and systems that have been built and refined over a long period of time. They will have learned a lot of lessons along the way and made a lot of improvements in their operations during their time managing other people's properties. You're now in a position to benefit from that experience.
- Leverage in-depth knowledge of local market dynamics, including supply-and-demand issues. They will know what rents are reasonable, what is generally included or not included, what concessions are common, what unit types are most in demand, what specific areas are good or bad, and more. All of this will come in handy not only when operating the property but during underwriting and due diligence.
- Draw on established relationships with all kinds of vendors and professionals. They will know which contractors and suppliers to avoid, and which will do quality work at a fair price. If they have a lot of properties nearby, they may also be in a position to secure better prices due to the volume of business they conduct.
- Help find deals and provide valuable input and feedback during underwriting and due diligence. A good property management firm will be able to review your underwriting and help validate

assumptions on all aspects of income, expenses, and capital expenditure plans. They can sometimes even help collect comps, perform inspections, develop pro formas, estimate staffing requirements, identify value-add opportunities, and secure quotes from contractors.

When considering property management companies, most investors are focused on operations post-closing. While those are, of course, critical, a good property management partner can also be invaluable when you are identifying and evaluating potential acquisitions.

How do you locate and hire a good property management firm? Fortunately, there are usually plenty of options, particularly in larger metropolitan areas. You should be able to find a competent firm with experience operating similar properties and knowledge of the local market. A good place to start is with referrals. Brokers, lenders, and fellow investors who are active in your target market should all know who the most reputable property management firms are. That should give you a place to start.

Every investor has their own ideas of what they think will make a property management firm ideal for them, but once you get into large multifamily properties, the selection criteria get a lot clearer. You're primarily looking for qualifications and experience that will allow you to reap the benefits of third-party property management that we just outlined. This means you're looking for a firm that has a successful track record managing property of a similar size in the same market. Should you make exceptions to these criteria? It depends. Other factors can be just as important, such as a firm's integrity, customer service, cultural fit, and your own experience with and level of trust in the firm you're considering.

For example, if you have an established relationship with a fantastic property management company and your property is outside the area that the firm currently operates in, should you give them a chance? How about if they've only managed properties up to 200 units and you're acquiring a complex with 350 units? In either case, your established relationship and trust in this company might make these other factors non-issues. You may have found a partner company to grow with you— one that will always make you the highest priority. In fact, some investors avoid property management companies that are too large out of concern that their property will be a low priority. The point is that there is no formula for choosing your ideal property management firm. It's about exercising judgment. You have to weigh all factors and make the best decision you can.

Note that the services provided by the best property management firms are likely to be in demand. Therefore, you'll need to do everything possible to sell yourself as a serious investor and a quality partner, somebody who will be good to work with and somebody they can grow with. Let them know what you bring to the table other than just the management fees you'll be paying them. It's not all about you selecting them. You're entering into a serious relationship, and those don't tend to end well if they're one-sided. If you want a healthy relationship, both parties need to be excited about their future together and willing to be there for each other in good times and bad.

Employees

When there is sufficient work to keep someone busy over the long term, hiring an employee can make sense. This will depend in large part on what kind of resources you have available and your capacity to manage others. Yes, the administrative side of having employees can be a burden and the drama can be draining, but salaried or hourly employees can sometimes be a good solution for getting work done at a better rate than you'd have to pay someone on a contractual basis. Another advantage of hiring employees is that you don't need to give up equity in your company or deals. However, structuring a way for some key employees to share in the upside of your projects can attract better people, align your interests, provide motivation, and foster loyalty.

Partners

The more valuable the skill set and person you're hoping to attract, the more difficult it becomes to entice that individual to come on board without giving up some equity. The best of the best in the real estate investing world are often entrepreneurial at heart and will be motivated by ownership.

Doing large multifamily deals results in more equity to go around, and few investors have the resources to hire staff of the caliber you need to operate at a high level. As a result, partnering with others is a very common approach for large multifamily investors.

Partnering obviously comes with a broad range of risks and rewards. If hiring a property manager is like entering a relationship, bringing on partners is more like entering a marriage, with much more commitment. Like a marriage, partnerships can go in almost any direction. They can be contentious or loving, exhilarating or tedious, successful or devastating. The world is full of traumatized investors who are suffering from failed partnerships, but for every partnership gone bad there is one that is wildly successful.

If you decide to partner, go in with eyes wide open and realistic expectations. You need to give a lot up, and you hope to get a lot in return. It all hinges on getting the right partner and being a good partner yourself. It takes two committed people to make a marriage work.

Partnership Agreements

One of the keys to a successful partnership is clear and open communication, and that should start from the very beginning. Make sure you've talked everything through so that you're on the same page and expectations are clear. Best practice is to memorialize your mutual understanding by putting it in writing. A partnership agreement is a contract between you and your partner(s) that defines the terms of the partnership, including the duties, obligations, and responsibilities of each partner. The agreement will also define the percentages of ownership, how decisions will be made, division of profits and losses, capital contributions, and how disputes will be handled.

The goal is to define everything in advance, so a good partnership agreement will go further and consider a multitude of possible scenarios. It will outline what steps will be taken if a partner wants out or is no longer able to fulfill their duties for any reason, including major events such as death or divorce. These types of situations are usually addressed with a buyout provision that is agreed to ahead of time, when things are good, which should avoid or minimize disputes if things go awry.

Partnerships agreements are legal documents and can get pretty complicated. We highly recommend that you have an attorney help you draft an agreement that is clear and complete to avoid ambiguity and ensure it will stand up in court or, better yet, keep you out of court to begin with.

How to Find Ideal Partners

Investors who are open to partnering usually struggle with how to find the right people. While there is no single best approach, if you're looking for a partner or key employee, we would encourage you to ramp up your networking and attend meetups, masterminds, and industry events. Go out of your way to meet people and build relationships. Make the extra effort to not just gain contacts but really get to know people. In doing so, you are planting seeds. Once those seeds start to sprout, figure out which show the most promise, tend to those carefully, and watch the relationships blossom.

In my case, attending masterminds yielded breakthroughs. In fact, it was at a mastermind in Maui that I told Brandon about my plans to take my multifamily investing to the next level by assembling a team to do larger syndications, and I learned that he was planning to do the same at Open Door Capital. After spending a few days together and speaking at length, we realized that if we partnered, we could achieve more than either of us could on our own.

Brandon had already brought aboard Ryan Murdock, whom I also met at the mastermind. Ryan and I connected right away, and I was impressed with him. Feeling good about both Brandon and Ryan, I decided to join the partnership as the asset manager. We all jumped in with both feet, and working together cemented our relationships. I knew I had made the right decision, and I never looked back.

There is a common misconception that relationships will just come to you like moths to a flame. As convenient as that would be, it doesn't usually work that way. You might meet a limited number of people without venturing too far off your usual path—maybe in the workplace, in a class, or at another structured activity where your routine puts you in contact with the same people repeatedly over long periods of time. In these types of circumstances, you tend to have shared experiences and come to know other people without much effort. They're just there. However, just being there isn't necessarily the best criterion for deciding who to build business relationships with. To find the best partners, you should cast a broader net. Convenience can take you only so far, and making the effort to grow is worthwhile.

Relationships take work. You have to step beyond your comfort zone and go out of your way to meet people. As you build these relationships, you'll want to constantly assess and reassess them to determine whether someone is the right fit. Just as partnerships are like marriages, finding those business partners is like dating. Set high standards for who you're going to ask on a date, and higher standards for who you're going to continue seeing.

When you're ready to take the next step, make it a trial run. In other words, do a project together before you make a longer-term commitment. Depending on a person's role and their level of experience, you could offer them an internship, hire them on a contract basis, or partner with them on a single deal. The traditional ways of hiring people are flawed. Résumés, recommendations, interviews, and even referrals are often poor indicators of what kind of employee someone will be. The truth is, you never know what somebody will be like until you work with them. Therefore, find a way to work with somebody before you fully bring them into your life.

Another tool you can use to evaluate candidates are tests such as personality profiles and skill assessments. At Open Door Capital, we had prospective partners and key hires take a DISC personality test. The DISC factors, which are dominance, influence, steadiness, and compliance, are assessed in order to understand what motivates someone's actions and behaviors and to predict their behavior toward others. We would also give some intern or job candidates test assignments to see how they performed, which gave us a way to see them in action and effectively narrow down a large pool of candidates. Invariably, someone will set themselves apart and rise to the top. In our case, some of these people eventually ended up joining our partnership.

KEY TAKEAWAYS

- Nobody can do it alone—there is always a team behind people in the spotlight, whether you can see them or not. In order to thrive, it's imperative to recognize your weaknesses, and then compensate for them by leveraging the skills and knowledge of third parties, employees, or equity partners.

- Third parties, especially property managers, play an important role in building your multifamily investing team. Other important relationships to establish include those with brokers, attorneys, tax accountants, and insurance and mortgage brokers.

- Intangibles such as ethics, values, baggage, resources, vision, and niceness are arguably more important than a person's résumé. It can take a concerted effort to find the right people and maintain those relationships.

- When you're ready for a partnership, as opposed to hiring employees or third parties, take it as seriously as you would a marriage. It is a big commitment with a written contract, so make sure you find a good fit and are a good partner in return.

River Apartments: Part IX

Closing day had finally arrived, our cash position was strong, and we felt confident we had the right team in place to hit the ground running. The property management company we were partnering with for River Apartments had impressed us so far, but they were about to be put to the test. We were inheriting a project in complete disarray.

Due to our concerns about how the property was being managed, our new property management company agreed that we should not retain any of the seller's staff. On the morning of closing, the seller stopped by the management office and notified his employees that it was their last day. After we closed later that afternoon, we headed over to the management office to find it had been stripped bare. *Everything* was gone: computers, tenants' files, furniture, all the tools and equipment, and all the inventory. There was literally nothing left but debris from the frantic raid that had obviously taken place earlier in the day.

The former employees had stolen everything, confirming all our suspicions about how they had been conducting themselves up to that point. They even took larger items, including appliances, snow blowers, and a new washer and dryer. Setting my shock aside, I had to admit that hauling away all that stuff so quickly was pretty impressive. Based on what I had seen during due diligence, I wouldn't have thought they had that much energy in them. It was probably the hardest they had ever worked. Hopefully some of them strained themselves in the process, or would at least be sore the next day.

When I called the seller and told him what had happened, he was mortified, though I don't think he was that surprised. In fact, it probably made him glad the deal was done. They spent the next couple of days trying to figure out what exactly had been taken and track down the missing items. In the end, they were able to locate and return only a handful of items. I was impressed when they offered to compensate us to replace everything else. This was a show of integrity and good faith, and we agreed not to involve the authorities.

Wow, I never imagined this was how we'd start off. It's hard enough to transition a property, but this made the challenge much more difficult. I hoped this incident wasn't an indication of things to come. I couldn't help but second-guess myself and wonder if I'd made a huge mistake.

To be continued...

Chapter Nine
FINDING DEALS

*To find something you dreamed of, searching is
not enough! You must make the universe sense
how badly you want your dream!*

—MEHMET MURAT

It was eight o'clock on a Wednesday morning and I was looking across my desk at a multifamily investor who I had agreed to meet. She had accumulated a portfolio of about fifty units and was anxious to take her investing to the next level. Her goal was consistent with The Stack method we introduced in Volume I—she wanted to acquire a hundred-unit property in the coming year, and she wanted to pick my brain. After a few minutes of small talk, she jumped right in and threw out the question she really wanted to ask.

"If you had to pick just *one* thing I could do to reach my goal, what would it be? I know what I'm looking for, but it still seems like a big leap. I feel like I have a lot to figure out."

I thought for a moment before responding, then said, "Go out and find a *really* good deal. And I don't mean something you find online that thousands of other people have already seen. I mean an off-market deal. Figure out what properties you'd like to own, go directly to the owners, and find somebody who will sell. Get something under contract at a great price."

"Okay..." she responded tentatively. "But I don't know how I'd pay for it. I could refinance my portfolio, but that's not going to be enough. I don't have any partners either."

"You can work on those things too," I said. "Maybe start the refi process now while you're looking. But you asked me to name *one* thing. If you find a smoking-hot deal and get it locked up, everything else will fall into place. You'll have something incredibly valuable to bring to the table. Doors will open, people are going to want to partner with you, and it will be a whole lot easier to raise the cash you need to close. If you want to catapult your investing forward, finding a great deal can do that."

I could see her wheels turning as she processed what I was telling her. "Well, if it's really that easy, why doesn't everyone do it?" she asked.

"I think you may have misunderstood me. I never said it would be easy. In fact, if you decide to do this, I think it will be super hard, and I'm not sure you'll be able to find anything."

"Why do you say that? I'm pretty motivated. And I've found off-market properties before," she responded.

"I'm sure you are motivated, and I know you've found plenty of deals, but you're playing at a whole different level now and the competition is fierce. It can take a ridiculous amount of time and effort to find off-market deals this big, with absolutely no guarantee of any return whatsoever. I've met people who've spent thousands of hours trying to find a great off-market multifamily deal before finally landing one. And I've met people who've spent even longer than that only to give up out of frustration, which, frankly, is completely understandable. We only have a finite amount of time, and there's a limit to how much of it any of us can dedicate to sourcing deals. That's why we tend to rely on brokers. It's a lot easier. Most people don't see what goes into it, but what brokers do is really valuable."

"Yeah," she said. "I never thought of it that way, but I guess it makes sense." She paused for a moment. Then came the follow-up question: "If I find a great deal, will you partner with me and help me buy it?"

"If you find a good enough deal," I said, "you can let me know. But you're not going to need me."

Brokers

Building good working relationships with multifamily brokers is an important part of your journey into large multifamily investing. Brokers are on the front lines of the battle to unearth multifamily property owners interested in selling, and they are highly incentivized to bring deals to market. Given the effort involved, they deserve to be.

To get a better idea of what's at stake for brokers relative to smaller multifamily properties, let's say you're in a market where apartments are selling for an average of $100,000 per unit. A duplex might go for $200,000, while a 400-unit apartment community could sell for $40 million. For selling the duplex, a broker makes a 6 percent commission, or $12,000. On the 400-unit property, a broker earns only 3 percent commission, but that's $1.2 million. In other words, a broker makes as much on one 400-unit complex as they would on 100 duplexes. Does it take 100 times as much work to close the larger property? Certainly not. The real work is on the front end—finding owners interested in selling, packaging the property in a way that will fetch the best price, marketing it, and then guiding the buyers and seller through the sales process to secure the best price for the seller.

While $1.2 million at closing sounds like a pretty solid motivator, it's usually split multiple ways. More important, brokers put in lots of effort up front with no guarantee of ever getting paid. They do tons of preliminary work on properties that never get brought to market, and even when a broker gets a listing, the deals can get derailed along the way for a multitude of reasons. There could be a shooting at the property, or a fire, or a plague of locusts. The owner could die, go bankrupt, or just change their mind. There are a thousand reasons deals don't make it to closing. All this to say that brokers have a very difficult job, competition is fierce, and it's not easy money.

If you recognize the challenges brokers face and respect the value they bring, you'll be in a better position to work with them. And you'll need to work with them or you're going to miss out on a lot of opportunities.

In addition to deals, brokers will also frequently have access to market data that isn't publicly available, such as rent and property comparables. They're usually in tune with cap rates and cap rate trends within the markets where they operate. Getting good cap rate information can be difficult, and brokers are one of the best sources.

Top multifamily brokers are also master networkers. They are well connected with property owners and buyers, developers, fellow brokers, and other players in the industry, such as lenders and attorneys. The result is that a broker can bring you deals in a variety of forms.

Marketed Listings

As you learn more about your target market, pay close attention to which multifamily brokers are most active there. Most markets tend to have one or two brokerages who get most of the listings, and they're the ones you'll want to reach out to and establish a rapport with. Depending on your level of experience, when approaching a brokerage firm, you may not always be best served by going straight to the top. Sometimes you'll get more attention and support from a hungry, junior-level person who is likely to be building their network, just as you are. Managing brokers tend to have their hands full maintaining established relationships, so it can be hard to get their attention unless you're already a heavy hitter.

When a broker gets a listing, they will prepare a sales package, commonly referred to as an offering memorandum (OM), which includes a complete overview of the property. If it's not already included in the OM, they will also assemble supporting documentation such as a rent roll, historical financials, and sometimes additional materials like photos, surveys, and third-party reports.

How and where these listings are promoted varies by broker. If you have an established relationship and are in regular communication with the broker, they may reach out to you directly to give you a heads-up that the offering is coming, sometimes even before getting a signed listing agreement. It's a good idea to get on every broker's email distribution list, which is typically the first place the deal will appear after direct, personal communications. A little while later, the deal will likely go up on the broker's website. Some brokers will also put their deals on larger sites such as LoopNet, CREXi, or ApartmentBuildings.com.

Since deals have usually been evaluated by numerous people by the time they appear on these websites, some investors don't value them. However, good deals occasionally show up, so you shouldn't discount them entirely. Besides, there's educational value in seeing as many deals as possible that fall within your buying criteria.

Pocket Listings

A pocket listing is a property a broker has a listing agreement for but is not marketing publicly. There are a variety of good reasons why multifamily property owners may prefer that a broker shop their property around privately. For example, the seller may not want to alarm their employees, or they may have concerns about disrupting their tenants. In such circumstances, having brokers quietly shop the property to a select group of the most qualified buyers can be appealing. Such an arrangement is usually attractive to the broker as well, because it lessens their workload and ensures that they won't have to split their commission with another broker.

While pocket listings aren't always bargains, the fact that fewer people know about them means less competition, which frequently translates to a lower price. How good a deal they are depends on several factors, including the seller's motivation and how many people are given the opportunity to review the deal and make offers. Some brokers will distribute a pocket listing to dozens of prospective buyers, still calling it "off-market" because they didn't post it publicly. Then, if a good enough offer doesn't come through, they will advertise it, assuming the seller agrees.

If you can build your relationship with a broker to the point that you are privy to deals that are offered only to select parties, it can reap great rewards. If your relationship grows stronger, a broker may even bring you an exclusive private listing and give you a chance to put it under contract before they take it to anyone else. However, this kind of preferential treatment is usually reserved for a client who has already closed multiple deals with the broker or referred people to them.

Nonexclusive Listings

Sometimes a seller is willing to work with brokers but doesn't want to limit themselves to any one firm. In that case, the seller will open the property to offers from multiple brokers. If you have a good working relationship with a broker, they may occasionally present you with this type of opportunity. The likelihood of getting a good deal will depend in part on the breadth of exposure of the listing. The downside of nonexclusive properties is that no one broker has insights into other offers or what's going on, which can make it more difficult for them to provide feedback or guide you through the process.

Broker Off-Market Leads

Brokers have lots of connections with property owners and can sometimes bring you deals that are completely off-market. This usually happens when a seller rebuffs a broker's attempt to get them to sign a listing agreement but concedes that they would be willing to entertain the right offer. However, the seller may refuse to pay a broker fee, which would shift that burden to the buyer. You'll want to clarify how your broker prefers to handle these situations and factor that information into your underwriting.

Off-Market Deals

If you want to find really great deals, off-market properties might be the answer. An off-market deal is basically any property that isn't listed with a broker or otherwise publicly listed for sale. There are many pros and cons to off-market transactions, but the biggest positive is that the pricing is sometimes below market. Working directly with a seller can avoid the competition that sometimes drives up prices. This doesn't mean you're trying to take advantage of the seller, because just eliminating the broker's commission can translate into a significant discount without affecting the net proceeds that would go to the seller.

Off-market deals can also be beneficial to the seller. Some sellers may be in need of a quick sale. Others may not want to go through the disruption and drama of a drawn-out listing process, or maybe they have an aversion to brokers. Still others may be emotionally invested in the property and want to be comfortable with the person they sell it to. This is particularly true of mom-and-pop owners who may have invested a lot of sweat equity in their property. Going through a broker might feel too transactional, and they fear a new owner might do things they wouldn't support. In a situation like this, working directly with you could make them feel better about what kind of owner you'll be. Sometimes that's just as important to them as the final price, if not more so.

Often a seller will have a specific number in mind that will make them happy. It could be above market and it could be below. You won't know until you ask—and you won't be able to ask until you find them.

One of the better ways to get off-market deals is through referrals, and the best way to get referrals is by putting the word out: Let everyone know you're looking for real estate, and educate them about your buying criteria. Property managers are a great source of leads, as are attorneys, banks, and contractors. Anyone working in the industry or providing services may know of an owner who's motivated to sell. Referrals can even come from people who aren't in the industry but have some personal connection to a property owner. One way to really motivate people to make these introductions is by offering either equity in the deal or a referral fee to anyone who brings you a property you end up purchasing. Establishing an online presence and driving traffic using social media or marketing tools such as Google AdWords can be an effective way to initiate referrals and even reach owners directly.

Although reaching owners directly is ideal, tracking down the owner of a property, much less getting them to speak with you and convincing them to sell, can be challenging. Tax records will often list the property management company as the point of contact, and property managers are generally not interested in connecting you with the owner since you may not elect to keep them on if you were to acquire the property. Paid services such as CoStar and Reonomy can sometimes be good sources of data, but subscriptions can be costly, and based on our experience you will still have to contend with inaccuracies. That said, these types of services do provide value and they have plenty of happy users.

The difficulty of getting solid information is just one reason why the mass-communication methods used for smaller properties aren't as effective for reaching large multifamily owners. The bigger challenge is the fact that there are far fewer large properties than small ones, and there is a lot more at stake. As a result, the competition to get an off-market deal can be fierce, especially in major metropolitan areas.

If you're trying to find property owners who are willing to sell, remember that brokers are out there doing the same. When you have charismatic brokers knocking on doors, working the phones, and getting the ear of owners, something like a postcard isn't usually going to have much impact. In addition to all the brokers out there trying to get listing agreements, don't forget about all the other buyers like yourself trying to find off-market deals.

Another significant difference between small and large multifamily properties is that bigger deals tend to require a correspondingly larger amount of relationship building and personal selling. This is the nature of sales in general. Consider how consumer products are sold: Lower-priced items rarely involve much personal interaction. When you visit a convenience store, for example, nobody walks up to greet you and guide you through your snack choices. With larger purchases, such as a car or a house, there is a lot more at stake, and thus a higher level of personal involvement and selling. Bigger transactions represent a more significant commitment on behalf of both buyer and seller. Getting an owner to sell you their apartment community will likely involve building a relationship with them over time until they feel comfortable enough with you and decide they're ready to move forward.

While the effectiveness of direct-mail campaigns is limited, they occasionally yield results. To improve your odds, anything you mail to an owner should be personalized as much as possible, with the goal being to get them on the phone. Speaking with a prospective seller is much more effective than communicating in writing, and meeting with them face-to-face is even better. It's all about comfort and trust, which is generated through effective communication.

Once you find a property owner who's willing to sell, be prepared for a frustrating experience, especially if you're accustomed to buying listed deals, where everything is nicely packaged and the process is profession-ally shepherded along by a broker. Without a broker's involvement, you may have to deal with missing records, indecisive or combative sellers, third-party interference, and any number of other wrenches that can get thrown into the works.

On numerous occasions we've had off-market deals fall through after we'd agreed on terms with sellers, who then changed their mind. Maybe their accountant told them there would be tax consequences. Or their best friend, Bubba, convinced them to keep their property. Or maybe they just woke up with doubts and decided to pull the plug. Off-market deals are highly unpredictable—especially if you have an inexperienced or unsophisticated seller. The entire process of buying large multifamily properties is complicated enough, and without a broker to smooth things out, it can be even more of a quagmire.

Residential Brokers

The larger the multifamily property, the less likely it will be listed by a residential broker or show up on the Multiple Listing Service (MLS). However, there are exceptions, especially for properties with fewer than forty units. When a residential broker does list a larger multifamily property, it's usually because there's a pre-existing relationship with the owner or the property is in a rural area that doesn't have much of a commercial broker presence. As a result, fewer large investors will be aware of the deal, so there should be less competition.

Multifamily properties that get listed on the MLS are also not always priced properly, because residential brokers who have limited experience with multifamily will rely solely on comps, instead of doing a proper income-based valuation. As a result, a multifamily listing on the MLS can sometimes be a good deal. Finding a 200-unit deal there is highly unlikely, but if you're looking for properties of fifty units or fewer, setting up an alert to monitor your target market could be worthwhile.

Wholesalers

Brokers and investors aren't the only ones out there beating the bushes trying to find owners who want to sell—wholesalers are also part of the mix. Wholesalers are experts at finding properties with potential and putting them under contract for the purpose of selling that contract to a third party. The good news is that if you can develop some good working relationships with wholesalers, they're another potential source for deals. The logistics involve either an assignment of contract or a double closing.

When considering a property from a wholesaler, you should carefully review the terms of the contract that's in place so you know what your obligations would be if you move forward. You'll want to confirm that there is an "assignment clause," which permits the wholesaler to assign the contract to you in exchange for a fee. Otherwise, you would need to do a more costly "double close," which involves a simultaneous sale from the seller to the wholesaler, and the wholesaler to the end buyer—which can add significant expense and complication to the transaction.

You can expect to pay a fair amount for a deal you secure through a wholesaler, in the form of either a flat fee or a percentage of the purchase price. Before balking at the high cost, understand that the money is well earned. Making a living by wholesaling large multifamily properties requires good systems, a lot of networking, expansive knowledge, and a boatload of hard work. For people with the right skill set and mental fortitude, it can be lucrative, with a low cost of entry, and can serve as an excellent stepping stone into the investment world.

Online Listings

It's rare for large multifamily sellers to list their properties for sale online, but it does happen. Occasionally a deal might pop up on a classified site, such as Craigslist, or an industry-specific website, such as MobileHomeParkStore.com.

Auctions

Multifamily property auctions are less common than traditionally listed offerings, but there are enough of them to be worth keeping an eye on. Foreclosure auctions are commonly done old-school, right on the courthouse steps, but the largest properties are more apt to end up on one of the larger auction platforms, such as Ten-X or CREXi. Some multifamily brokerages may also host auctions on their own platform.

Probably the biggest challenge with buying properties at auction is the terms of the sale, which you should always review very carefully, together with the details of the bidding process. There are also usually bidder qualification requirements that must be met in advance. The most problematic term of sale for most buyers is the timeline for closing, which is usually thirty days. This requirement tends to limit the bidders to cash buyers or buyers who have the relationships in place to access large amounts of cash or debt in a short time frame. On a positive note, this time constraint limits the competition and can help you get a better deal if you're in a position to pull it off.

KEY TAKEAWAYS

- Brokers provide a valuable service and can be an excellent source for deals, including marketed deals, pocket listings, nonexclusive listings, and off-market properties. Building good relationships with multifamily brokers is important.
- Off-market properties are challenging to find but can present excellent opportunities to acquire large multifamily assets at below-market prices.
- Other possible deal sources include wholesalers, residential brokers, online listings, and auctions.

River Apartments: Part X

By the time we closed on River Apartments and got through our dramatic first day, memories of how the deal was originally sourced had long since faded away. But as a large multifamily investor, even though I had just closed on a large deal, I was already on the lookout for new opportunities every day, both through brokers and off-market. Searching for deals constantly and creatively is one of the most important keys to success. I never would have had the opportunity to purchase River Apartments to begin with if I weren't continuously planting seeds by tracking down the owners of off-market properties and reaching out to build relationships with them.

Of course, at this stage in our story, you might think this particular seed is one I may have been better off not planting, and I wouldn't blame you. Our ownership of River Apartments was off to a dreadful start. While we had been sitting around the closing table, the former employees had stolen everything that wasn't nailed down, and the management office now looked like a hurricane had blown through.

Fortunately, that first-day robbery was not a sign of things to come. The unsavory event was quickly overshadowed by something more encouraging: The new property management staff were clearly experienced and set high standards. The trust I had invested in the property management company's owner had been well placed. The new staff weren't deterred by the theft. They quickly cleaned things up, outfitted the office, and began to put new processes in place. Then they methodically began to turn the property around, even though we discovered lots of issues, as you'd expect from a property that had operated for years under poor management.

My role as asset manager was to oversee the property manager, and while this was time-consuming early on, that was primarily a result of my desire to keep a close eye on things. Asset management got easier after the first few months as I became more comfortable with the direction things were going. The property management company's demonstrated competence made it easier for me to begin delegating and step back. The staff worked through challenge after challenge, and the progress was tangible. By the end of the year, we were hitting the numbers in the property's budget, and the investment started to generate a healthy cash flow.

Less than a year after we had closed, the property was stabilized, and I sat back down with the property management company's owner to discuss next steps. He wanted to move forward on his earlier plan to do a full-scale renovation and suggested that I sell them the property. I was grateful for all the work they had done turning the project around and agreed to his proposal. We quickly settled on a value we were both comfortable with, shook hands, and let the lawyers draw up the paperwork. The property ended up being under contract for more than a year while the buyer secured funding for not only the acquisition but also a $17 million rehab.

While River Apartments was under contract, I was approached by multiple buyers with higher offers. But I stuck with the property management company because they had been an excellent partner from the beginning and were diligently making progress to line up a project that would dramatically change the community for the better. As things stood, I would make more than enough profit anyway, and I believed that following through on the original deal was the right thing to do.

Approximately two years after the original acquisition, we finally closed and sold the property at a price that resulted in a profit of $800,000. In addition, the property's operations generated more than $200,000 in cash during the period we held ownership, so our total profit exceeded $1 million.

The proceeds of the sale were deposited with a qualified 1031 exchange intermediary and later reinvested in other properties to avoid taxes and grow my portfolio. The plan was to hold these replacement properties long term, but then again, I had learned to be flexible and take advantage of unforeseen opportunities under the right circumstances.

River Apartments was quite the roller-coaster ride. We had plenty of scares and plenty of excitement—enough to make me scream a few times. Fortunately, when all was said and done, we could look back and say it was worth it. Things could have gone in a less desirable direction, but we persisted and stayed on track with lots of help. I am grateful for the many people who played a role in the final outcome.

You might be wondering whether after such an experience we would ever take on a project with so much drama again. In the next chapter, we'll introduce you to the Apartments at Madison Barracks, a project that would give River Apartments a run for its money in terms of entertainment value.

Stay tuned for the next adventure!

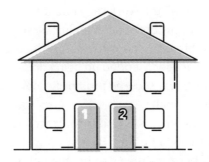

Chapter Ten
SCREENING DEALS

*If you want to make good use of your time, you've
got to know what's most important and then give
it all you've got.*

—LEE IACOCCA

After about nine months of efforts to build our deal pipeline at Open Door
Capital, we were really starting to see results. We built a lot of sources
that were trickling leads, and together they formed a more substantial
stream of leads that would sometimes surge into a full-blown river. While
that was exciting, we had created a new problem for ourselves—a pile
of work that was growing larger by the day and threatening to bury our
partner Walker Meadows, who was doing all our underwriting at the
time, before taking on broader responsibilities.

Normally, we would hear from Walker routinely, so when he started
going radio silent for longer and longer stretches, we grew increasingly

concerned. His wife had recently had twins, and he was burning the candle at both ends trying to keep up with everything. Walker is an exceptional underwriter, but there is a limit to what any one person can do. We knew this kind of thing wasn't sustainable, so we reached out and began working on solutions.

To start, we recognized that even with other partners helping, we couldn't get through all the underwriting in a timely manner. The first step was to prioritize every deal that came in, making sure the most promising and time-sensitive opportunities were underwritten first. Our stack of leads had to be continually shuffled so that the most important lead was always on top. Though this was a start, as the deals continued to flow in, we recognized this wasn't a sustainable solution.

The long-term solution was twofold: First, we had to tweak our investment criteria, and second, we had to implement a more refined and accurate screening process for vetting leads before subjecting them to the full-blown underwriting process. Every time we underwrote a deal, we learned a little more about what to look out for and what would indicate a deal was more suitable for our investment strategy. We made it a higher priority to capture those insights and incorporate them into a screening process that would give us a more accurate and faster indication of a deal's potential. This way we could dramatically reduce the number of prospective deals that would need to go through the full underwriting process.

In Chapter One, we covered the rationale and process for setting your investment criteria. We reviewed the many advantages of being focused and the rationale for narrowing your search to specific property types and markets, including the practical need to bring the number of opportunities down to a manageable level. We also touched on the need to strike the right balance between staying focused and getting enough deal flow. It's not easy to consistently find that balance. If your investment criteria are too open-ended, you'll have too many properties to underwrite, which is a time-consuming process for large multifamily deals. On the other hand, if your investment criteria are too stringent, you'll pass on deals that fall shy of your criteria but might have been strong enough to merit further consideration. You'll miss opportunities, you won't see enough deals, and ultimately, you won't close on anything.

Many large multifamily investors have addressed this concern by implementing an initial screening process for the properties that meet their investment criteria. This is the approach we took at Open Door Capital, and it has proven highly effective.

Why You Should Screen Deals

Creating a screening process allows you to keep your investment criteria open enough to mitigate the risk of missing something of potential interest while still giving you the opportunity to further narrow down leads before initiating the underwriting process. The screening process is fairly simple and involves taking all the leads that meet your investment criteria and then passing them through a second, slightly more detailed set of filters before you take the time to fully underwrite them.

Think of it this way: You're in the kitchen whipping up a delicious spaghetti dinner. After boiling the noodles, you want to drain the water while still preserving the noodles; otherwise you'll be stuck with an unappetizing water-logged meal. However, if your colander's holes are too big, the noodles could slip through and go straight down the drain, leaving you with no meal at all. Developing a screening process is about finding the right size colander for the right pasta.

While the idea of adding another step to the process might not be appealing initially, this approach has several long-term practical advantages:

- A screening process cuts down on the amount of time spent to determine whether deals are appropriate by eliminating investment criteria that are too extensive or deep.
- By keeping your investment criteria a little more open, you reduce the chances of missing a good deal without being overwhelmed by underwriting.
- Screening will allow you to dig a little bit deeper into any potential areas of concern and rule out properties before you waste time underwriting them.
- For those deals that aren't discarded, screening provides you with a basis to prioritize deals in your underwriting queue so you invest your time and effort in the most qualified leads first.

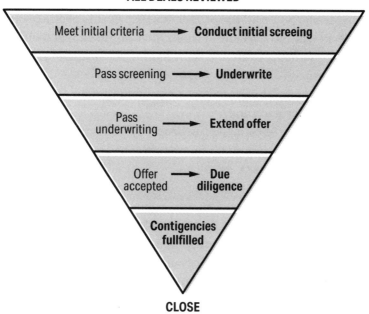

ALL DEALS REVIEWED

Meet initial criteria ⟶ **Conduct initial screeing**

Pass screening ⟶ **Underwrite**

Pass underwriting ⟶ **Extend offer**

Offer accepted ⟶ **Due diligence**

Contigencies fullfilled

CLOSE

In terms of how this initial screening falls into the overall process, visualize it as a series of filters that deals pass through before getting to closing. Each filter eliminates more properties, until you're left with those you actually acquire. The process filters out some of the deals passing from the investment criteria to underwriting. Getting to a "no" quickly is just as important as getting to a "yes."

How to Set Up the Screening Process

Investment criteria are usually kept fairly limited and straightforward so that they can be quickly and readily applied to a high volume of deals. For example, your investment criteria could be Class C apartment communities with a minimum of 100 units that were built in the 1980s or 1990s, priced between $8 million and $15 million, and located either in the Tampa–St. Petersburg–Clearwater metropolitan statistical area (MSA) or within thirty miles of this MSA.

These investment criteria define the class, size, age, price, and location, all of which can be quickly and easily determined. Any property you find that meets these investment criteria is then going to be further analyzed. However, if you were to jump in without screening and then thoroughly underwrite all the properties that fit this profile, you would probably find that 90 percent of them have some characteristics that don't fit your goals and preferences. What might those be? Here are just a few possibilities:

- Undesirable nearby properties or neighborhood
- Location in a flood zone
- History of violent crime at the property
- Odd floor plans
- Lack of adequate parking
- Rents at or above market

The Tampa area is a pretty strong market (at least as of publication), but many suburbs and communities outside the MSA vary in terms of their overall desirability. Regardless of what your target market is, you might find that a particular town or municipality is problematic due to things such as:

- Declining population
- Lack of job growth
- Onerous landlord-tenant laws
- Low household income
- High crime rates
- Poor school districts
- Low home prices

These are just some of the many factors that could be legitimate causes for concern, but everyone's preferences are different. Factors that could be deal breakers for one investor might not bother another; there are no inherently right or wrong screening criteria. The best thing to do is to prepare a list of criteria based on your personal judgment, preferences, and experience that you think will help you evaluate the quality or suitability of a deal. Then revisit and refine the list periodically, because the more deals you underwrite, the more easily you'll identify the factors that routinely make a deal a go or a no-go. Eventually, you'll want to consider adding these factors to your initial screening criteria so you can avoid subjecting inappropriate deals to full underwriting.

Your list of screening criteria should include information that can be determined or looked up relatively easily. Research may involve checking websites or running some back-of-the-envelope calculations. At this stage, it should not involve in-depth evaluation.

At Open Door Capital, we sometimes refer to this screening process as a sniff test. It involves some initial research into information about the property and market that we think is important. Most of the data can be collected from free online resources. Here are a few specific examples:

- We check a city's population trend at www.worldpopulationreview. com. We like to see a positive trend over the past decade, and especially over the past three to five years. We also like to see a healthy population—ideally an MSA with more than 200,000 residents or 100,000 people within a fifteen-mile radius. A good place to check the population within a specific radius of the property is www. freemaptools.com.

- We check for crime at the property and in the area by searching Google News and online resources that offer crime maps, such as LexisNexis and Trulia Neighborhoods. We are particularly concerned with recent violent crimes that might affect our ability to secure financing or increasing levels of criminal activity.

- We typically use Google Street View and Google Maps to "walk" the perimeter of the property and the immediate vicinity. We will continue outward and view the streets for several blocks in each direction in order to get a better feel for the surrounding area to see proximity to travel arteries, attractions, schools, major employers, and more. We try to avoid properties in neighborhoods that show evidence of neglect or appear to be in decline.

- We look at all nearby school district ratings at (www.niche.com, www.greatschools.org).

- We look at economic and demographic data on Data USA (www. datausa.io) and BestPlaces (www.bestplaces.net). BestPlaces includes data on job growth and market rents. We will check income and median home prices at www.city-data.com. We also like to use Zillow to zoom in and look at home prices in close proximity to the subject property.

- We check FEMA flood maps to determine whether the property is within a flood zone by visiting the FEMA website (www.msc.fema. gov/portal/search).

- Perhaps most importantly, we run a very quick back-of-the-envelope valuation of the property based on the property's financials, some basic value-add and debt assumptions, and the market cap rate. We'll also approximate an exit value and project returns. The idea is to get a rough feel for how reasonable the asking price is and a deal's potential to hit our target returns. In our experience this last step will filter out about 50 percent of the deals that clear all the other criteria.

In addition to the above, we check a few other items. The entire screening may take thirty to forty-five minutes per property, but it gives us a much better picture of how attractive an investment is and allows us to determine whether to proceed to underwriting. Thirty to forty-five minutes might seem like a long time, but that's just a fraction of the six to eight hours required for full underwriting. It just doesn't make sense to go through all that if we can establish whether the property is potentially viable or not with much less effort.

The goal as you set up this process is to identify the factors, or combination of factors, that would allow you to prioritize a deal or know quickly that the deal is a no-go. Screening for these factors requires a modest amount of time up front but avoids wasting significantly more time on underwriting.

Note that the data sources mentioned in the Open Door Capital process are just examples; many other options are available. Also be aware that the best resources tend to change over time. Data companies and their websites are frequently acquired, cease operations, or change their business model. Some will charge fees and others will be free. It's up to you to decide whether the quality and convenience of paid data sources offer enough value to make them worthwhile.

How to Screen Properties Using the 4C Process

While there are many different ways you can screen properties that meet your investment criteria, they are all likely to include the same fundamental steps. Implementing these steps using the 4C process will help ensure you're effectively managing leads that meet your investment criteria.

Step 1: Check Your Deal-Breakers

The first C in the 4C process is to check the deal to see whether there are any deal-breakers, meaning characteristics of the investment or market that will result in a hard "no" and prompt you to discard the deal and move on. How do you do this? You'll have to decide what you can live with in an investment property and what you can't. Everybody's deal breakers are different. To determine what yours are, go through your list of screening criteria and determine how much flexibility you have. If the answer is zero for any of them, those are your deal breakers.

Referring back to the Open Door Capital screening factors, one example of a deal breaker could be criminal activity at the subject property. We are particularly concerned about major crime, so if there have been a couple of recent shootings near the property, that would be a deal breaker. We don't want to place our staff in dangerous situations, so we'd drop this deal and move on to the next one.

Another deal breaker would be if the property is shown on the FEMA maps to be located in a Special Flood Hazard Area (SFHA), which is defined as an area with a 1 percent chance of experiencing a flood in any given year, also known as a hundred-year flood zone. Even though we could get flood insurance, this is going to be an issue for lenders and is not a risk we're willing to take.

For other factors, whether a deal is a no-go may not be so black and white. For example, let's say you're screening for population trends. "Population trends" is a general term and less objective than a property being in a particular flood zone. The question to ask yourself is whether there is a specific, quantifiable number that would make population trends a deal breaker. For example, you may decide that any market that has experienced a 5 percent or greater population drop over the past decade is a hard no. Nailing this down ahead of time makes the screening process more efficient, and can help eliminate much of the hemming and hawing that will inevitably occur as you screen properties.

As a multifamily investor, you want to clearly specify what your deal breakers are and, if possible, apply those criteria first in your screening process. In the words of the preeminent German writer Johann Wolfgang von Goethe, "Things which matter most must never be at the mercy of things which matter least."

Step 2: Consider Secondary Factors

Most of your screening process criteria are not likely to be deal breakers. Instead, they will be attributes you weigh to varying degrees that, in conjunction with one another, allow you to get a good feel for the overall desirability of the property. That's why the second C in the 4C process is to consider the not-so-black-and-white secondary factors—those that don't immediately take an investment out of the running.

The subjective aspect of this second step can be a challenge. The approach I have found most useful is to take the time to fully consider each factor in advance and determine how to prioritize it as you weigh everything in aggregate. Think through the possible scenarios, and if you have partners, discuss them in advance. What are you comfortable with, and what are you not?

Let's again use some of the Open Door Capital screening factors as an example, starting with population. Yes, we'd like our property to be in an MSA of 200,000-plus, but is that a deal breaker? Absolutely not. If the property is in an MSA that hits our target, that certainly weighs in the property's favor. However, if it isn't and the property checks most of the other boxes, we're still good to go—especially if it has a lower population but shows strong growth.

In Step 1 we shared that a property in a 1 percent, or hundred-year, flood zone is a no-go, but what if it's in a less-risky flood zone? If the property is in a zone with minimal flood risk, we are happy. If it's in a moderate flood zone, which has somewhere between a 0.2 percent and 1 percent annual chance of a flood, this is of concern to us, but it's not a deal-breaker. Whether to move forward would depend on how everything else looked—whether the positives outweighed the negatives. If nearly everything else checked out, we would proceed with underwriting, get a solid quote on flood insurance, and make sure we included the associated cost in our expense projections.

As you can tell from these examples, Step 2 is not formulaic. It relies on a subjective analysis of all the factors involved, weighing them against one another and in aggregate. How far you bend in any one area is likely to be dependent on the overall quality of the deal. The idea here isn't to use an equation. It is to use some preliminary data to form a rough assessment of the overall desirability of a property. You should be left with a positive or negative feeling, and you'll use your good judgment to determine whether the potential deal merits the further time and effort of putting it through a thorough underwriting.

Step 3: Calculate a Value

Assuming a property has survived Step 1 and Step 2, it's time for the third C: Calculate some quick numbers on the property to get a rough idea of what it might be worth. If the property has an asking price, this will also help you determine whether it's even feasible for you to get anywhere close to that price. If there is no asking price, which has become more common for large multifamily offerings, you'll usually have some pricing guidance from the broker, and at least get a better feel for whether the price is within the range defined in your investment criteria. That said, valuation at this stage is going to be a rough estimate, so don't place a tremendous amount of weight on any numbers you come up with. Remember, at this stage we're trying to answer only one question—*is the deal worth taking through the entire underwriting process?*

The easiest way to do a rough valuation is to take the current rent roll and annualize it to approximate income. For expenses, you can use the T-12 actuals, if available, and make any preliminary adjustments to the T-12 numbers you think are appropriate to account for any obvious anomalies or expenses you don't expect to incur during your ownership. For example, if the current owner has season tickets for the Los Angeles Lakers listed as an operating expense, you can probably take that out. Then subtract those adjusted expenses from the income to get an NOI. Divide the NOI by the market cap rate in order to get an approximate valuation (see Chapter Fourteen for more details).

Again, if the income or expense numbers appear to be off, you can "normalize" them to get a rough idea of a pro forma valuation. (We'll discuss normalizing data in more detail in a later chapter, but it basically involves adjusting data to make it more realistic.) For example, if a seller is charging rents that are 50 percent below market, it wouldn't make sense to value a property based solely on that income because rents can obviously be raised, so you may elect to use rents closer to market. To estimate expenses, you can adjust individual line items (like deleting the cost of those season tickets) or simply apply an expense ratio that is typical in that marketplace for properties of that class and condition.

This very basic valuation process will serve as an effective back-of-the-envelope estimate. As you invest more and learn your market, coming up with a rough valuation will become easier and you might not even have to do much math. Active multifamily investors who really know their market are often able to quickly estimate what a specific class of property might command in terms of rent and purchase price.

Let's say you're looking for Class C properties in a specific metropolitan area. You are screening a hundred-unit property that is all two-bedrooms. Because you analyze a lot of deals and are active in that market, you know that market rent in that part of the city is around $800 per month for two-bedroom apartments of that class. Since you've done so many valuations, you know you can expect to pay about $75,000 per unit and operate it in as-is condition. However, you also know from experience that you could probably upgrade the units for about $5,000 each, which would help you command closer to $950 per month in rent. This value-add approach might allow you to achieve your target returns with a purchase price closer to $90,000 per unit. Of course, you're making a lot of assumptions here, but you're doing rough approximations so that's okay at this early stage. The more experience you have, the quicker and more accurate your initial estimates will be.

Finally, you should design the quick financial analysis to match your investment strategy. If you're buying a stabilized property, the analysis will focus more on a property's current value. If you're planning to do a significant value-add project, you'll be more concerned with what you can pay today relative to what the value will be after the update is complete.

Step 4: Communicate

Regardless of who brought you the deal, if you've been communicating with them or imposing on them in any way to provide you with information, it's important that you keep them posted and fulfill any promises you've made. Communication and follow-through will go a long way toward maintaining and improving relationships.

Once you've run a property through a screening process, it's a good idea to share the outcome. This is particularly important if you're setting the property aside and will not be doing due diligence. Reach out to the broker, owner, or whomever you've been in contact with and let them know how much you appreciate the information they've shared and the opportunity to take a look. If you've decided not to move forward, kindly explain why. If they're a broker or a wholesaler, that feedback will help them get a better understanding of what you're looking for so they'll know what to bring you in the future. This can also enhance your credibility, since they should respect that you've done your homework, be impressed that you know exactly what you're looking for, and appreciate your professionalism in communicating with them. If you promised feedback within a specific time frame, always meet that deadline. Brokers value responsiveness and quick feedback on deals they send out. You might be shocked by how few potential buyers follow up on deals they elect not to pursue. By always closing the loop, you can stand out from the competition, gain credibility, and build relationships.

If the deal survives your screening process, you should inform the person who brought it to you that based on your preliminary research and analysis, you are going to proceed with a full underwriting. This lets them know that you're working on it and are still interested. It can also impress them with your thoroughness and professionalism.

A Living Process

Once you create your screening process, it needs to be continually revisited and refined. Consider it a living process and not carved in stone. Adjust your criteria based on what you learn through experience. Periodically go back and compare your quick analyses to your full-blown underwriting. If things are way off, make adjustments. Tweak things, add things, and remove things that will allow you to be as effective as possible.

KEY TAKEAWAYS

- A screening process allows you to keep your investment criteria simple and open enough to mitigate the risk of missing something while still giving you the opportunity to further narrow down leads before initiating the underwriting process.
- Your screening criteria should be composed of factors that will help you evaluate the quality or suitability of a deal based on your judgment, preferences, and experience.
- A good screening process lets you to prioritize a deal or know up front that a deal is a no-go by checking it against your deal breakers, considering secondary factors, and calculating a value. You should then communicate your decision to all involved parties.
- Consider your screening system a living process. Continually revisit and refine it in order to make better decisions more quickly.

Madison Barracks: Part I

With multifamily valuations near all-time highs, finding properties that met our investment criteria and survived our screening process was becoming increasingly difficult. In this challenging climate, the value-add strategy was more important than ever. In light of this, I found myself reconsidering properties that had previously been rejected through our screening process, either because they were overpriced or because they were too heavy a lift in terms of the work they would require. One of these properties was a historic community called the Apartments at Madison Barracks, which includes 126 units spread across seventeen former military housing structures dating back to the 1800s.

The property had been on the market a few years earlier with an asking price of $7.5 million but never sold, primarily due to an excessive amount of deferred maintenance and struggles with occupancy, both of which made the asking price too high. Despite these very real issues, the property was intriguing enough for me to take another look. It's located on the fringe of a quaint village along the shores of Lake Ontario. Many of the units have lake views and are quite spacious, averaging over 1,200 square feet.

Madison Barracks also had an impressive history. It was originally established in 1816 as a United States Army installation and named in honor of President James Madison, who visited the property to view the construction. Additional U.S. presidents would visit over the years, and in 1906, its commander established a new training ground that would eventually become Fort Drum.

Another reason the property intrigued me is that about ten years prior I had been a tenant there. The idea of owning an apartment complex where I had once been a renter was appealing on a personal level. I had always loved the property and the village. In fact, I still lived nearby; Madison Barracks was only a couple of miles from my house. Because I was a local, I saw the property often, and I couldn't help but take note of what was going on. After more than a decade of investing, I found myself looking at all properties with a new eye, always sizing them up—gauging things like their condition and how they were being managed.

When I'm outside an apartment complex, I'm scrutinizing the grounds, windows, and roof. I'll look at the quality of the vehicles and the presence of window treatments for clues about the tenants and occupancy levels. I'll take note of the signage, landscaping, and amenities. Of course, as a value-add investor, I'm always ticking off a mental list of potential improvements and looking for untapped potential.

At Madison Barracks, I saw how the condition of the property steadily deteriorated and occupancy dropped over the years. I'd heard that multiple pipes had frozen the prior winter, resulting in significant water damage. From the exterior I could see that routine maintenance was being neglected and many of the units were vacant. While I didn't know the specifics, the property was obviously spiraling downward. You can never be certain what this says about the seller, but the condition of the property was indicative of an owner who had checked out and was ready to move on—potentially someone highly motivated to sell.

As a former resident and a member of the community, I was saddened and frustrated that such a vital and historically significant property had fallen into decline. As an investor, I had seen this type of situation many times before and knew where it was likely headed. Things were about to get really bad, but in my opinion, it wasn't too late. If action was taken soon, the downward spiral could still be reversed and a lot of value could be created.

After much careful consideration—and despite a nagging feeling that I could be making a huge mistake—I decided to reach out to the owner to see whether they would be willing to sell. I told myself I was just making an inquiry, and what harm was there in that? Only time would tell.

To be continued...

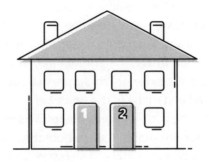

Chapter Eleven

SIX KEY COMPONENTS OF GOOD UNDERWRITING

*If I were a professional wrestler, I'd want a name
that strikes fear in most people. Something like
"The Underwriter."*

—LIGHTER SIDE OF REAL ESTATE WEBSITE

Once you've determined that a property meets your investment criteria and it has passed your screening process, it's time to begin the full underwriting. Solid underwriting is a critical part of investing in large multifamily properties. There are several reasons for this, the first being that selecting the right deal and paying the right price will ultimately play a large role in determining how successful you are in your investing.

To avoid overpaying and achieve your projected returns, you must do your homework on the front end. The larger the property, the more you have at stake, so the level of scrutiny you should apply increases in proportion to the deal size. This is particularly true if you're raising money from investors, who will be counting on you to adequately vet deals before you move forward.

The other reason underwriting is so important is that it plays a large role in determining how smoothly things will go later in the process. Because problems that arise later can be contentious, the quality of your underwriting also affects your reputation.

When you're operating at a high level in the multifamily world, competition for the best properties can be fierce, and brokers and sellers are constantly trying to assess your ability to close a deal at the contracted price. Brokers and sellers want to work with a buyer who will follow through on their commitments after a property is put under contract. If at all possible, you want to avoid retrading a deal (negotiating to get the price changed after the contract is signed) because it can tarnish your reputation. The best way to avoid retrading is to do a thorough job underwriting a property before submitting an offer to begin with. If you end up seeking a price change for something that arguably should or could have been discernable during the underwriting process, that reflects poorly on you. The goal of underwriting is to do a thorough enough job that due diligence is little more than a formality.

From the broker's and seller's standpoint, expectations around the underwriting of large multifamily deals differ significantly from those for smaller deals. On smaller multifamily deals, the brokers tend to be active in residential real estate and therefore accustomed to practices more common to single-family home sales. These brokers and sellers may be more accepting of a quick offer with heavier dependence on due diligence and inspections *after* the contract is in place.

For large multifamily deals, expectations are usually different. Most large multifamily deals are handled by seasoned commercial brokers who assume a certain level of sophistication and professionalism on the part of buyers. You're playing in the big leagues now, so they will expect you to do your homework up front and know what you're getting yourself into before making an offer. This means a detailed underwriting process that, depending on the size and nature of the deal, may even include steps that are sometimes reserved for the due diligence phase. Although savvy buyers at this level are thorough, they also know it's impossible to catch absolutely everything during underwriting. They assume they will find some things during due diligence they missed, and factor this into their purchase offer. Retrading is reserved for major problems the buyer could not reasonably have been expected to find during underwriting, or the discovery during due diligence that information originally provided by the seller grossly misrepresented the facts.

When there are multiple offers on a property, the buyer's perceived ability to follow through and promptly close without retrading is weighed heavily when selecting which offer to go with. When there is intense competition, buyers will sometimes demonstrate their confidence and reassure sellers with a deposit that goes "hard" on contract execution. A hard deposit is one that is nonrefundable. That means if the buyer tries to retrade or back out of the deal or otherwise fails to follow through on their commitments, the seller can keep the deposit even if the contingencies aren't satisfied. (Hard deposits and other negotiation strategies that are designed to provide confidence in your ability to close will be covered more extensively in Chapter Fifteen.)

The use of hard deposits has grown more commonplace for big multifamily deals—especially in highly competitive markets. The net effect has been to make underwriting even more important, because as a buyer, you don't want to lose your deposit. You know going in that if you miss something of significance and have to back out of the deal, your mistake will be costly. As a result, due diligence tasks, which had historically been performed after the execution of a purchase agreement, are being pulled forward and done earlier in the process.

Since thorough underwriting is so critical, you'll want to approach it systematically. Once a property passes your initial screening process, you should complete the six key components of good underwriting: documentation, location, tour, property management, value-add, and the model. Each of these components is important in its own way and should either precede or be completed in parallel with the underwriting of the property's income and expenses, which will be covered in the next two chapters.

Key Component No. 1: Documentation

By the time you get to underwriting, you should have the basics of a property, including the address, unit count, year the property was built, size of units and parcel, and amenities. If a broker is involved, this information and much more can be found in the offering memorandum (OM). Most OMs contain lots of valuable information, and when one is available, you should read through it carefully and thoroughly, including all footnotes and assumptions.

In addition to the basics above, the OM will sometimes include information such as financing options, recent improvements, and potential value-add strategies. It will also include a financial analysis, which, though it can be interesting, should never be taken at face value. While the OM is helpful for familiarizing yourself with a project, never forget that it is not an objective document. An OM is a sales tool, designed to portray things in the best light with the most favorable assumptions. Some buyers will skip entire steps of due diligence by using only the OM. This can be a huge mistake. You should approach every piece of documentation and every conversation with a seller or broker with a healthy dose of skepticism. In many ways, their interests are at odds with yours. In the end, your best bet is to independently verify everything you can.

Whether through an OM or conversations with the broker, it can also be helpful to get general background information, or the overall "story" of the property, to help put everything that follows in context. For example, how long has the seller owned the property? Why did they originally buy, and what were their plans? Did they implement them? How did it go? What trends has the property experienced? Is the property in distress? If so, why? Who is managing it, and how is that going? What financing is in place, and is it assumable? What prompted the owners to sell? This type of information is particularly important when the historical financials show significant changes or abnormalities in income and expenses. Your lender will notice these as well and expect an explanation.

There is much additional documentation and information that can be helpful in completing your underwriting. The basic things you should be looking for are listed below. Some of these items are more important than the rest and are listed as "high priority" and "medium priority." While the lower-priority items can be useful and are sometimes necessary at this stage, in many instances they can be provided during due diligence or might not be needed at all.

High Priority

It would be difficult (but not impossible) to complete an underwriting without these items:

- Basic rent roll information (number of units; types of units, including number of beds and baths; current rents; and unit vacancies)

- Trailing twelve months (T-12) of income and expenses
- Broker's OM when available

Medium Priority

These items can be helpful for underwriting and are sometimes important for getting financing quotes or if your offer will include a hard deposit:

- Floor plans and square footage for each unit type
- Complete rent roll with all tenant and lease details
- Copy of most recent survey and title insurance
- Income and operating expenses for the current year and the most recent two to three years
- Representative lease or lease form
- Photos or video (if a property tour is not possible)

Low Priority

These items can be useful if readily available but are not always necessary:

- Copies of all leases and rental applications
- Copies of any existing architectural, engineering, and/or feasibility studies
- Copies of any existing environmental reports
- Active service agreements and all contracts with service providers
- Copy of property insurance policies and loss runs for the past five years from the seller's insurance carrier
- Schedule of capital improvements made to the property over the past two to four years
- Schedule of rent increases over the past two to three years
- Most recent six months of certified bank deposits

While these priorities and items are generally appropriate, you may have to make adjustments depending on your specific situation. For example, if you have reason to suspect environmental contamination, getting a copy of previous environmental reports would be critical. If you're considering assuming the seller's mortgage, you would need to get a copy of the mortgage documents. If there are subsidized residents, you'll want to get copies of documents relating to the most recent government agency inspections.

A word of caution with regard to collecting this information: Don't go overboard. Asking for things you don't really need at this stage serves no purpose and is a common mistake. This is particularly true when dealing directly with a mom-and-pop seller who is operating their own property and could get overwhelmed by an expansive document request. Make too many demands on their time and they could get discouraged and start to second-guess their choice to sell. If you really do need extensive documentation, consider asking for the most critical items up front and requesting additional information as necessary so as not to overburden anyone.

Think carefully about what information the seller could provide that is likely to make a material difference in your underwriting. Remember that in the end, you're going to do your own projections, get your own quotes, and not rely heavily on *anything* the seller gives you. A massive list of requests is rarely justified, plus you'll come across as annoying. However, if you can get the basic information necessary, you're ready to dive in and do the financial analysis that will serve as the basis of your valuation and purchase offer. You can get more detailed information after you have the property under contract.

Key Component No. 2: Location

The location of a property—from a market, submarket, and micro perspective—is one of the most important considerations when making a purchase. By the time you get to underwriting, your screening process should already have provided most of the necessary information about a location's suitability. On a macro level, that means the location is within the target market defined in your investment criteria. Presumably you considered all relevant economic and demographic factors before settling on the market to begin with, though within larger target markets the dynamics can vary as you drill down into specific submarkets. Depending on your screening process, you may have also evaluated the submarket prior to underwriting.

Once underwriting is under way, you'll want to analyze any aspects of a property's location that have not already been evaluated. This should include a careful review of the market, submarket, neighborhood, and nearby properties.

To get a complete picture, you should look at not just the local municipality but any nearby major metropolitan areas, and examine neighborhood-level data where available. We listed out some resources in the previous chapter, if you need a quick refresher. Remember, information resources change regularly as sites are acquired, cease operations, or change their business model. There are many other resources out there, some of which may be specific to a property's location. You can find valuable data on the U.S. Census Bureau and U.S. Bureau of Labor Statistics websites, or on local government, chamber of commerce, and economic development sites. Some investors also like to use sources that rank the desirability or general economic health of a city, such as POLICOM's annual metropolitan and micropolitan statistical area rankings (available at www.policom.com). That said, keep in mind that there are limitations to what location data can tell you.

Key Component No. 3: Tour

To fully understand what an area is like, you have to visit in person. Even investors with deep experience can find it hard to gauge the true feel of an apartment unit or community without going there. Do the signage and landscaping make a good first impression? Does the neighborhood feel safe? I like to see who's out walking and whether kids are running around playing. I also like to enter an apartment community at night to see what kind of activity is going on. Evening is also the best time to check whether there is adequate parking.

Being there in person makes it far easier to identify issues and potential opportunities. For example, is there any excess land? If so, what is the terrain like and what could it be used for? Do the unit floor plans feel right? What is the state of the fixtures and finishes? Are there logical ways to improve the units that will make a significant difference? How do the buildings look? Does anything jump out at you that detracts from their appearance or needs updating? How do the roofs look? What about the balconies, patios, siding, railings, windows, doors, and paint? How about the parking lot? Sometimes a seller's or broker's property description doesn't capture what you see in person, and ideas that seem good on paper no longer appear feasible when you're standing there.

Finally, be hyper aware of everything around you. Are there bad odors in the buildings or outside? Are there any disturbingly loud sounds coming from nearby properties, roads, trains, airports, fire stations? The list of things you can readily observe in person that don't come across in photos or satellite images is practically endless.

The second reason to visit the property is that it gives you a chance to gather some additional intelligence from the staff, residents, and others in the area. For example, on a recent site visit, I was approached by a maintenance technician working outside and had a long discussion about the history of the property, challenges they were facing, and opportunities they saw for improvements. When I noticed a police cruiser passing by, I flagged it down and spoke with the officer about what kinds of criminal activity were going on in the community and how it had changed over time. I engaged multiple residents to ask them what they liked and didn't like about their apartments and the community as a whole. This kind of firsthand information is guaranteed to uncover issues or opportunities that wouldn't otherwise be discernible.

The final reason to schedule a property tour is that brokers and sellers will factor in a site visit when they are evaluating offers. Sellers want to make sure a buyer is actually going to close based on their "demonstrated interest" in the property. Brokers and sellers are monitoring demonstrated interest, and buyers who demonstrate interest, through property tours and frequent communication, are considered more serious. Brokers also know from experience that if you haven't visited a property, when you eventually show up, you're more likely to change your mind than someone who has already been there and knows exactly what they're buying. They realize that nice photos and videos just don't fully capture what a property is really like. Given the importance of visiting a property, if you drive by on your own and the broker or seller isn't aware of this, you'll want to share that information.

Underwriting Component No. 4: Property Management

There is a tendency to think of property management's role as not kicking in until after closing. That's understandable, considering that 99 percent of their work will be completed under your ownership over the lifetime of a project. However, the 1 percent that happens prior to closing can be just as valuable—if not more so—because a good property manager can help ensure you invest in the right project to begin with.

Savvy investors get reputable property management firms with local operating experience involved in underwriting and due diligence. In fact, if you don't have extensive and ongoing operating experience in the market where you're buying, getting a property management firm's input during underwriting is crucial. If you get a property under contract, they can also help with due diligence.

Whether or not you have a pre-existing relationship with a property management firm in the market doesn't really matter. Obviously, it's more convenient if you do, but if you don't, engaging with a property management company, or even several, is a chance to get a feel for what it's like to work with them. From their perspective, it's an opportunity to impress you and win a contract on the property if you close.

The areas of underwriting where a property management firm's input can be most valuable include the following:

- Weighing the pros and cons of the property location
- Touring the property and sharing their assessment
- Identifying and touring good market comps
- Validating your rent, other income, and loss projections
- Assessing the feasibility of your construction timelines and identifying any logistical concerns for work completion
- Assisting with securing any necessary quotes from contractors and vendors
- Confirming appropriate staffing and compensation projections
- Reviewing all your expense projections
- Quoting their property management fees
- Determining what repairs and upgrades should be completed and how much they will cost
- Weighing in on how the property should be operated

The amount of up-front work a property management firm is willing to do to help you during underwriting will vary. If you already have a relationship with them, they are likely to help in any way they can. If you don't, their assistance will depend in large part on how badly they want to win the contract for the property, and how legitimate a prospective buyer they think you are. Obviously, a property management company's incentive also increases in proportion to the size of the property. They are more likely to help with your evaluation of a 300-unit property than a 30-unit one.

In most cases, you shouldn't have to pay for a property management firm to provide the above input during underwriting. The potential to win the management contract if you close is usually enough incentive.

However, if you ask for something more involved, such as a detailed property inspection, you'll probably have to compensate them.

Finally, recognize that if a large property is being broadly marketed, there is a good chance that the leading property management firms in the area are being simultaneously approached by multiple prospective buyers, and may have more allegiance to some of them.

On one occasion while touring a 200-unit property in a hot market, I arranged to have a representative from a property management company accompany me. The woman who met me demonstrated a ton of knowledge of the property and submarket. Then she mentioned the high level of interest in the property and confided that she had already toured it with at least a dozen other prospective buyers who were planning to submit an offer. I had been super impressed with all the detailed info she sent me on the comps and her value-add recommendations—but I now realized that this analysis had originally been prepared for other buyers and was recycled! The information was still valuable, but I felt a little less privileged.

Key Component No. 5: Value-Add

At this stage in the underwriting process you should be starting to formulate any value-add strategies that might be appropriate for a property. Value-add boils down to steps you might be able to take to drive up revenue through rent or ancillary income, and ways to reduce expenses. You may decide to reposition the property or upgrade units.

A comprehensive overview of proven strategies for adding value is included in Chapter Nineteen. You'll want to familiarize yourself with the various approaches for adding value and determine which are suitable for the properties you underwrite.

As you progress through underwriting, you'll understand the property and market better, and these ideas can be further refined. The entire underwriting process is iterative, so you can continually refine assumptions as you move forward—but a path forward should start to take shape early on. As you gain more experience, you'll get better at nailing it down up front.

Key Component No. 6: The Model

The last key component for underwriting is a good software program or spreadsheet model. In the next three chapters we're going to take a deep dive into the financial aspects of underwriting a large multifamily property. We'll cover the underwriting of income and expenses, which are the basis for creating a pro forma that projects future cash flows. Then we'll review project return metrics and how to determine a purchase price. These financial gymnastics are intricate, can take a lot of time and effort to master, and frankly aren't for everyone. That's why one of the most important keys to good underwriting is to have a model you can use for financial analysis. You can develop a model yourself using spreadsheet software such as Microsoft Excel or Google Sheets, or you can buy a professional one that somebody else developed.

Commercially available underwriting tools can save you a ton of time, improve the accuracy of your underwriting, and simplify the entire process. Examples include Michael Blank's Syndicated Deal Analyzer, REIA Pro, redIQ, David Toupin's Multifamily Deal Analyzer, and Valuate. Most of these underwriting tools come with access to instructional videos, training, and support.

Multifamily underwriting software can be particularly helpful if you're syndicating and have to measure returns not only at the project level but also for GPs and LPs, which adds multiple layers of complexity to your financial analysis. Yes, there are educational benefits to building your own model for analyzing deals, but unless you're a freak in the spreadsheets, creating your own underwriting tools can be a rigorous exercise with lots of room for error. It can also take years of tweaking and refining to perfect your model.

Does this mean you can just go buy some software and skip the next three chapters? Well, I suppose you could, but we wouldn't advise it. A model is only as good as the information that goes into it, so you should do your best to understand the process and underlying concepts. If you know that financial analysis isn't your thing, you might want to consider outsourcing this part of your underwriting or partnering with someone with the appropriate skill set. Even then, we still recommend studying financial underwriting in order to be able to review the model and understand the basic principles.

KEY TAKEAWAYS

- Solid underwriting is critical because selecting the right deal and paying the right price plays a large role in determining how successful you are in your investing.
- The quality of your underwriting can affect your credibility and reputation. It plays a large role in determining how you are viewed by brokers and sellers, as well as whether you can follow through on your offers.
- When underwriting a property, you'll want to gather the appropriate documentation, research and visit the location, enlist the aid of a property manager, identify value-add opportunities, and develop or purchase a good multifamily financial analysis model.

Madison Barracks: Part II

The Apartments at Madison Barracks were falling into decline, and I had decided to reach out to the owner to find out whether they had any interest in selling. While the property had not made it through our initial screening process a few years ago, our situation had changed. We had adjusted our screening criteria in response to current market conditions, and I suspected the property could be acquired at a lower price than when we first looked at it. To confirm this, I first needed to determine who the owner was and whether they were still interested in selling. If they were, we would commence our underwriting.

The only contact information I could find was for the management office, so I had to dig a little deeper. With some online research, I uncovered the LLC that owned the property, and eventually the LLC's parent company, which was located 1,500 miles away. I found a company phone number, but it went straight to a generic voicemail, and repeated calls and messages over the course of the next two weeks went unanswered. Next, I turned to social media, and a search on LinkedIn helped me find the parent company's CEO. I crafted a message to send through LinkedIn:

> "Hello. One of the brokers I work with approached me a few years ago about the possibility of acquiring Madison Barracks. If you

are still open to selling this project, I might have an interest. If so, please let me know what your asking price is and if possible, forward me T-12 financials and a current rent roll. Thank you very much and have a great day."

I also provided my email address and cell phone number. The next day, I received a one-line reply: "We will do so, thanks for reaching out."

I promptly responded, "Perfect—I look forward to hearing from someone. Hopefully we can work something out."

While it may have been premature, I was excited by this development. Just tracking down an owner can be difficult enough, but actually connecting with them and getting an indication that they are willing to explore a sale is rare enough to feel like a small win, even if the deal doesn't pan out.

Even though it was early in the process, I started digging into the property's ownership history. There was no broker involved, so I knew I'd have to get the property's story on my own. From the property tax report available on the county's website, I was able to see what the taxes were, and discovered that the owner had purchased the property thirteen years ago for $4.8 million. From a local newspaper article, I learned more about when their pipes had frozen, and also that they were severely delinquent on their water/sewer bills.

All this was interesting, but I was curious about the owner's debt. If I could find out what kind of equity they had, I'd know whether a creative financing strategy might be possible. Two sources proved valuable. One was a service available through a research company called Real Capital Analytics. Their report showed that the seller had secured a $5 million Freddie Mac mortgage back in 2015 and that the property had appraised for $7.4 million at that time. Next, I called my mortgage broker because I wanted to hear his thoughts on the debt. While he didn't have access to the loan documents, he told me that the loan should be past any kind of lockout period and that such loans typically carry a 1 percent prepayment penalty. He looked up the property in the Trepp database of securitized mortgages and was able to confirm the monthly payment, interest rate, and principal balance, which was $4.7 million. He also noted that the property had been placed on the lender's "watchlist" because the DSCR had fallen below 1.0x. Properties are placed on a watchlist and given closer scrutiny when the mortgages or assets exhibit signs of heightened credit risk.

Obviously when a property is no longer able to cover its mortgage payments, things can get pretty dicey—especially when a project was syndicated or there are multiple investors involved. Those people aren't going to be very excited at the prospect of capital calls, in which investors are asked to send in more money to bridge shortfalls. After making their initial investment, most passive investors are expecting to get checks in the mail, not send more checks out!

These situations can devolve rapidly. Units don't get turned, replacement parts are raided from other equipment on-site, utilities are turned off in units that aren't occupied, and so on. I realized this was most likely what resulted in all the frozen pipes over the previous winter.

The property's story was now coming into focus. It was clearly in some level of distress, but at the same time there was a ton of underlying potential. I suspected the seller would be motivated, but there was plenty of work to be done. I would need to acquire the property at the right price for the investment to make sense.

To get a head start, I discreetly walked the property on my own and started gathering as much information as I could for my underwriting so that I'd be prepared to move quickly if the opportunity progressed. If I were to acquire this property, it would be my biggest project to date, but it had enough hair on it that it could sink me if I missed something or paid too much. No one wants to get sunk. I would need to do my homework. The underwriting would be critical.

To be continued...

Chapter Twelve
UNDERWRITING INCOME

*The difference between a calculated risk and rolling
the dice can be expressed in one word: homework.*

—GEORGETTE MOSBACHER

Once you've completed the six key components of good underwriting, it's time to underwrite a property's income. In this chapter, you'll learn how to verify exactly how much the property is currently earning and, more importantly, how much it *could* generate. While underwriting income is not particularly complicated, there are many steps involved and it can get confusing. In order to better illustrate the process, as an example, we're going to use actual underwriting that was done for a property we will call Park Place Apartments, which was an off-market 120-unit, Class C property located in an area that was trending in the right direction.

We completed the six key components of good underwriting for Park Place Apartments, and the results were encouraging. After going through the OM, rent roll, and all other documentation, we toured the property and liked what we saw. Our property management company agreed that this could be a great opportunity. We decided to proceed with the financial underwriting and began digging into the property's income.

Rent Roll

When underwriting a multifamily property's income, the first step is to review the rent roll in detail, then transfer all the information to a spreadsheet (or underwriting model) for further analysis. A typical rent roll will include the tenant name, identifying unit number, unit type (usually the number of bedrooms and baths, and sometimes whether it is a premium or upgraded unit), square footage, market rent, contract rent, vacancy loss, other charges or income, current balance, security deposit, move-in date, date of last rent increase, and lease end date.

For the purposes of your underwriting, you will need to transcribe the unit number, type, square footage, current rent, and other income. You'll make your own determination of market rent, vacancy loss, and any other income losses.

Once you have this information in a spreadsheet and are able to manipulate it a little better, you'll want to sort by unit type and get counts, totals, and averages for each unit type. This tabulation is called the unit mix and will allow you to get a clearer understanding of the current income situation at the property, which will be the basis for the remainder of your income analysis.

To illustrate, let's look at a unit mix from the actual underwriting for Park Place Apartments.

TYPE	UNITS	SF	AVERAGE RENT	RENT/SF	APPROXIMATE ANNUAL RENT
1BR/1BA	48	650	$747	$1.15	$430,356
2BR/1BA	33	855	$802	$0.94	$317,484
2BR/1BA—PREM	7	855	$965	$1.13	$81,060
2BR/1.5BA	26	855	$826	$0.97	$257,796
3BR/2BA	6	1,000	$882	$0.88	$63,504
	120	780	$799	$1.02	$1,150,200

Table 12-1 Unit Mix for Park Place Apartments

From the above example, you can readily see how Park Place's units are broken down in terms of type, square footage, asking rents, and rent per square foot. The unit mix is generally classified by the number of bedrooms and bathrooms, with seven of the two-bedroom units also being designated as "premium" units due to a range of upgrades. The rationale for breaking out the upgraded units separately is that they are likely to command a higher rent, and in order to determine market rent for these units, you will want to identify comps with a similar level of improvements.

Your rent roll represents the subject property's most recent scheduled rental income. You should also consider looking at the historical rental income to put the rent roll in context and see whether any trends jump out at you. You should approach this exercise from an investigative and skeptical perspective. Yes, you want to evaluate the magnitude of the numbers, but you're also looking for trends and anomalies. You can analyze the trailing three months (T-3), trailing six months (T-6), and trailing twelve months (T-12) to see how things have changed over the past year, as well as prior years. Then compare these to the annualized rent roll. If you see significant trends or irregularities, you should ask the broker or seller for an explanation. Find out why the income has increased or decreased. You have to understand what is happening at the property in order to model it accurately and make projections.

In general, when underwriting a property you should weigh recent data more heavily, as it is more likely to be representative of the current state of a property. Older income data may not reflect recent property improvements or changes in market conditions. Of course, you should always exercise judgment. Sometimes there's a good reason not to use the current rent roll in your analysis. For example, some units may have been taken offline temporarily in order to complete repairs. In that case, a T-6 or T-12 might be a more accurate representation of the property's anticipated state at closing. Sound judgment and critical thinking should always prevail, and if there are compelling reasons to base further analysis on a T-3, T-6, or T-12, you should do so.

Once you've entered the data into your spreadsheet and examined the historical income, you're ready to dig in a little deeper. Now it's time to determine gross potential income, effective rental income, other income, and effective gross income.

Gross Potential Rent

When underwriting a multifamily property's income, the first step is to determine the gross potential rent (GPR). The GPR is the maximum rental income that a property has the capacity to generate based on the current market rent. To calculate the GPR, you must determine the market rent for each type of unit at the property, which involves looking at comparable units (comps) to determine the average amount of rent being charged. A property's GPR is an idealistic number because it assumes 100 percent occupancy and no collection losses.

$$\text{GPR} = \begin{array}{c} \text{Number of} \\ \text{Units} \end{array} \times \begin{array}{c} \text{Market Rent} \\ \text{per Month} \end{array} \times \begin{array}{c} \text{12 Months} \\ \text{per Year} \end{array}$$

For example, let's say a property has 200 identical units and the average market rent for similar units is \$1,000 per month. Your annual GPR would be:

$$\text{GPR} = 200 \times \$1{,}000 \times 12 = \$2{,}400{,}000$$

How to Determine Market Rents

The formula to calculate GPR is straightforward. The trickier question is how to determine the average market rent. As a starting point, you would typically look for nearby properties with similar units and see what they are charging. However, it's usually not quite that simple. Most large multifamily properties have different unit types and sizes. Some properties may also have a mix of "traditional" or "classic" units, with original finishes, and "premium" units, which have been improved in some fashion, as Park Place Apartments does in our example. To account for these variations, you will make sure they are reflected in the unit mix for the subject property, just as we did for Park Place Apartments.

Note that when lenders calculate GPR they typically limit the income to market rent for traditional one-year leases and not include premiums that might be collected for things like furnished units, short-term leases, or the inclusion of extra services such as housekeeping. If you expect to garner higher rents from these types of premiums, you can include that information in your analysis for the purpose of projecting your returns, but be aware that a lender may treat this differently.

The next step is to identify the rent comps—a basket of properties that are as similar as possible to the subject property in terms of location, age, condition, and amenities. Once you locate the comps, you'll create a unit breakdown similar to the one we did in our example. As long as the comps are similar in nature to the subject property, you don't necessarily need to determine the exact unit mix, but you should try to determine the rent they are charging for each unit type and, if possible, the square footage. You'll also want to determine exactly what's included in the rent to make sure you're looking at fair comps. For example, if the subject property rent doesn't include utilities, you can't use a comp whose rent includes gas and electric unless you make an adjustment to account for the discrepancy.

Note that the OM will usually list comps, but while these can sometimes be a helpful starting point, you should be cautious about using them. Remember that an OM is a marketing tool and its primary purpose is to present the property in its most favorable light—including its potential for adding value through rent increases. You can't assume the comps in an OM were arrived at objectively, so do your own homework to independently verify them.

Free sources for rent comps include websites such as Apartment Finder, Apartments.com, Craigslist, Trulia, Zillow, and even individual property websites. Paid subscription-based services such as CoStar, Reonomy, and Yardi Matrix as well as local property management firms can also be excellent resources. Another option is to just pick up the phone and call the leasing office for each of the comps.

However, the best way to get quality comps is to visit the competition in person. Posing as a prospective renter is called mystery shopping and is a fairly common practice in the industry. The benefit of mystery shopping is that it will help you get a better feel for the competition and exactly what features and amenities are associated with market rents. Sometimes a property looks like a good comp on paper, but when you actually walk it you realize it is far worse or better than the subject property.

Ideally, you'll be able to collect data from at least three or four good comps, preferably more, and then average the rents for each unit type, both on a monthly basis. If you can collect square footage information, you can also calculate the rents per square foot. If you have enough comps, you can drop the highest and lowest as outliers. If you have a particularly close comp, you could weigh it more heavily when calculating the average, by counting it twice, for example. The same approach can also be used to reduce the weight of comps that aren't quite as good—maybe they are on the fringe in terms of location, class, or some other attribute. The table below shows the comps that were used for Park Place Apartments.

Comp Property	Year Built	Units	Distance (miles)	Occ	Unit Size 1BR	2BR	3BR	Rent 1BR	2BR	3BR	Rent/SF 1BR	2BR	3BR
Traditional style													
Butter Lake Apartments	1988	160	1.2	96%	725	880	995	$825	$1,010	$1,040	1.14	1.15	1.05
The Village Apartments	1978	90	2.0	97%	675	865	995	$800	$950	$990	1.19	1.10	0.99
Apple Tree Apartments	1976	180	2.1	93%	690	800	1,002	$795	$970	$1,033	1.15	1.21	1.03
The Commons	1992	150	1.0	96%	650	850	1,021	$804	$965	$1,024	1.24	1.14	1.00
Excaliber Apartments	1983	105	3.0	100%	620	825	935	$775	$920	$970	1.25	1.12	1.04
Premium style													
Butter Lake Apartments	1988	160	1.2	96%	725	880	995	$860	$1,045	$1,085	1.19	1.19	1.09
The Village Apartments	1978	90	2.0	97%	675	865	995	$850	$990	$1,035	1.26	1.14	1.04
The Commons	1992	150	1.0	96%	650	850	1,021	$875	$990	$1,079	1.35	1.16	1.06
Tailwind Place	1985	220	0.7	95%	625	835	990	$835	$925	$1,040	1.34	1.11	1.05
Total Averages	**1984**	**145**	**1.6**	**96%**	**671**	**850**	**994**	**$824**	**$974**	**$1,033**	**1.23**	**1.15**	**1.04**
Classic Averages	**1983**	**137**	**1.9**	**96%**	**672**	**844**	**990**	**$800**	**$963**	**$1,011**	**1.19**	**1.14**	**1.02**
Premium Averages	**1986**	**155**	**1.2**	**96%**	**669**	**858**	**1,000**	**$855**	**$988**	**$1,060**	**1.28**	**1.15**	**1.06**
Traditional style													
Market Averages	1983	137	1.86	96%	672	844	990	$800	$963	$1,011	1.19	1.14	1.02
Subject Property	1982	120		98%	650	855	1,000	$747	$813	$882	1.15	0.95	0.88
Difference					(22)	11	10	$(53)	$(150)	$(129)	(0.04)	(0.19)	(0.14)
Premium													
Market Averages	1986	155	1.23	96%	669	858	1,000	$855	$988	$1,060	1.28	1.15	1.06
Subject Property	1982	120		98%	650	855	1,000	$855	$965	$1,025	1.32	1.13	1.03
Difference					(19)	(3)	(0)	$—	$(23)	$(35)	0.04	(0.02)	(0.03)

Table 12-2 Comps for Park Place Apartments

You are now in a position to determine the average market rent for each unit type of the subject property. If the comps are somewhat similar in size and age to the subject property, you can use the average monthly rent directly. However, if there is a significant variation in the size of the units and you were able to determine square footage for the comps, it would be more accurate to multiply the market price per square foot for each unit type by the size of each unit at the subject property.

$$\text{Market Rent} = \frac{\text{Market Price per}}{\text{Square Foot}} \times \frac{\text{Square Footage of}}{\text{Subject Property}}$$

For example, if the average price per square foot for the market is $1.08 for two-bedroom/one-bathroom units, and these units are 855 square feet at the subject property, the market rent would be calculated as follows:

$$\$1.08/\text{SF} \times 855\ \text{SF} = \$923\ \text{per Month}$$

Here is what the actual unit breakdown for Park Place Apartments looked like after we completed our research into market rents.

TYPE	Units	SF	Average Leased Rent	Rent/SF	Annual Rent	Scheduled Market Rents	Market Rent/SF	Market Rent Based on $/SF	GPR Annually
1BR/1BA	48	650	$747	$1.15	$430,356	$747	$1.23	$800	$460,512
2BR/1BA	33	855	$802	$0.94	$317,484	$878	$1.08	$923	$365,666
2BR/1BA—PREM	7	855	$965	$1.13	$81,060	$965	$1.14	$975	$81,875
2BR/1.5BA	26	855	$826	$0.97	$257,796	$884	$1.17	$1,000	$312,109
3BR/2BA	6	1,000	$882	$0.88	$63,504	$950	$1.06	$1,060	$76,320
	120	780	$799	$1.02	$1,150,200	$836	$1.15	$900	$1,296,482

Table 12-3 Unit Breakdown with Market Rents for Park Place Apartments

Effective Rental Income

As mentioned earlier, GPR is an overly idealistic number. It would certainly be a lot easier if investment properties were always 100 percent full, commanded market rents, and everyone paid. Unfortunately, that's rare. Therefore, the next step in underwriting income is to subtract the economic losses you can reasonably expect to result from loss to lease (LTL), vacancy loss, bad debt, concessions, and any nonrevenue units.

Loss to Lease

LTL reflects the gap between the market rent and the rent that is currently being collected. The LTL can be measured for each individual unit or unit type or for the entire property. To calculate LTL, you simply subtract the current, in-place rent from the market rent.

$$LTL = Market\ Rent - Actual\ Rent$$

When evaluating a potential acquisition, investors often view LTL as an opportunity to add value. If a property is already at or near market rent, you don't need to be overly concerned with LTL. An LTL of 2 to 3 percent is normal, but if current rents are lagging behind the market by more than that, LTL should be a priority. For Park Place Apartments, the LTL for the entire property was calculated by subtracting the current, in-place rent from the GPR:

$$GPR - Current\ Rents = LTL$$
$$\$1,296,482 - \$1,150,200 = \$146,282$$

LTL can also be expressed as a percentage:

$$LTL\ (\$) \div GPR = LTL\ (\%)$$
$$\$146,282 \div \$1,296,482 = 11.28\%$$

TYPE	Units	SF	Market Rent Based on $/SF	Average Leased Rent	LTL	GPR	Average Leased Rent	LTL	LTL %
1BR/1BA	48	650	$800	$747	($52)	$460,512	$430,356	$30,156	6.55%
2BR/1BA	33	855	$923	$802	($122)	$365,666	$317,484	$48,182	13.18%
2BR/1BA - PREM	7	855	$975	$965	($10)	$81,875	$81,060	$815	1.00%
2BR/1.5BA	26	855	$1,000	$826	($174)	$312,109	$257,796	$54,313	17.40%
3BR/2BA	6	1,000	$1,060	$882	($178)	$76,320	$63,504	$12,816	16.79%
	120	780	$900	$799	($102)	$1,296,482	$1,150,200	$146,282	11.28%

Table 12-4 Park Place Unit Mix with Market Rents and LTL. Any small numerical variances on this table are due to rounding.

When acquiring a property with significant LTL, you can raise rents to market rate when they are available to lease, but you should be more methodical about addressing LTL for units that are occupied. Develop a plan to close the gap over time. For example, if existing rents are $120 per month below market, the gap for occupied units might be closed by $40 per year over the course of three to four years. If you were to raise the rents by $40 each year, your monthly LTL would be reduced from $120 to $80 per unit in the first year, assuming you increase the rent immediately after closing. More likely, you would implement the rent bumps as existing leases come up for renewal, meaning that you would average only six months at the higher rent. In this case, your monthly LTL in the first year would be $120 − $20 ($40 ÷ 2 = average 6 months higher rent), or $100 per unit. Another $40 rent bump in year two would drop the LTL to $60 per unit, then to $20 per unit in year three, and zero in year four. This scenario is a slight oversimplification, because market rents aren't static and are likely to rise during those four years, but as long as your annual rent bumps remain higher than the annual market increases, you will continue to close the gap over time.

The $40 annual bump cited in this scenario is just an example and not intended to be a guideline. You need to decide what's appropriate and ethical for your property and market. There are several factors to consider. For example, higher annual rent bumps might be justified if you will be making substantial improvements to the units and the property as a whole.

While eliminating LTL is a solid way to add value, it is not considered good practice to come in as a new owner and immediately eliminate a large LTL for occupied units because of the financial strain it can create for residents. Some occupants could be on fixed incomes or under other financial constraints. If you're not concerned about the ethical and humane aspects of jacking up rents with little notice, consider the fact that you may end up inciting organized resistance, retaliation, or bad press that could cause you more economic harm than implementing more modest rent bumps.

While it is far less common, if you're underwriting a property with rents that are actually higher than market rate, you'll end up with a negative LTL. This situation is a red flag and should be investigated to determine the cause. The two most common reasons why you might end up with a negative LTL are:

- The property is offering excessive concessions to boost occupancy. This is not a good practice because it will ultimately result in higher turnover. You're going to be saddled with a property that is charging higher rents than the competition and have to figure out how to retain the tenants when their leases come up for renewal.

- The market rent you calculated is not accurate. The competition may be charging less than market conditions will support, while the subject property is already charging market rent. In this case there is not likely to be any value to add in the near term by raising rents—at least not with the apartments in their current condition.

By themselves, high rents aren't usually enough to rule out a property, but they could make an investment less attractive. You might want to buy the comps instead!

Vacancy Loss

Vacancy loss occurs when the physical occupancy of a property drops below 100 percent. The loss results from rent not being collected on the vacant units and is calculated by adding up the scheduled rent for the units that are unoccupied.

For a large property, vacancy loss is nearly impossible to avoid. Even in the best markets, where properties may have a waiting list of prospective residents, units will usually need to come offline after a move-out in order to make them ready for the next resident.

In reality, an apartment's downtime isn't usually associated just with turning the unit over but also with getting it re-leased, which can take time. Since you only have downtime when a resident moves out, your loss is also affected by the retention rate. If you are doing a refinance or have operating data for a property, you can estimate the lost rent from unit turnover as follows:

$$\frac{\text{Vacancy}}{\text{Loss}} = \frac{\text{Number of Weeks}}{\text{Unit Is Down}} \div \frac{\text{52 Weeks}}{\text{per Year}} \times (1 - \text{Retention Rate})$$

For example, let's say your retention rate is 50 percent and it takes a property an average of six weeks from the time a tenant moves out until the time a new tenant moves in. That includes turning the units, marketing them, getting a lease signed, and then the time until the new lease starts. Your loss would be:

$$\text{Vacancy Loss} = 6 \div 52 \times (1 - 0.5) = 5.77\%$$

For the underwriting of a new property acquisition, however, you should use a vacancy loss that is consistent with the market average. Property managers, appraisers, brokers, other investors, and published market surveys are all good sources for average occupancy levels in a particular market. Note that even in the hottest markets, most underwriting standards will allocate a minimum of 5 percent of gross income for vacancy loss. In markets that are less healthy, this number should be increased to reflect the market norms. You should also assume a higher vacancy loss if you are going to be renovating units, which can be disruptive. The combination of moving tenants, higher rents, and construction activity is likely to result in a vacancy loss significantly above stabilized levels.

Collection Loss

Multifamily investors need to be concerned with both physical and economic occupancy. Economic occupancy is calculated by dividing the amount of rent collected from tenants by the gross scheduled rent (GSR).

$$\text{Economic Occupancy} = \text{Actual Collections} \div \text{GSR}$$

GSR is how much total rent would come in at the current rents if all units were filled with paying tenants and you didn't have any losses. To calculate the GSR, subtract the LTL from the GPR.

$$\text{GPR} - \text{LTL} = \text{GSR}$$

The difference between physical occupancy and economic occupancy is attributable to units that are occupied but not paying. This portion of missing income that results from the tenants' failure to pay is called collection loss, which is also known as credit loss.

$$\left(\begin{array}{c} \text{GSR} \times \\ \text{Physical Occupancy} \end{array} \right) - \left(\begin{array}{c} \text{GSR} \times \\ \text{Economic Occupancy} \end{array} \right) = \text{Collection Loss}$$

Obviously, it doesn't do a whole lot of good to keep a property full if the residents aren't paying. These nonpaying units will result in collection losses, which are accounted for as a type of bad debt.

Your default assumption should be that collection losses will remain at the level reflected in the T-12 provided by the sellers. If they are outside the normal range, you should dig into it a little deeper and adjust your projections if you have cause to believe the underlying reason can be addressed.

The 2019 National Apartment Association Income and Expense Survey found that the average collection loss is $92 per year for each apartment unit. Collection loss tends to be higher for lower-class properties and those in distress. For stabilized Class A and B properties, you can expect collection loss of no more than 1 to 2 percent of gross income, though it can sometimes run below 1 percent in well-managed properties. Collection losses above 3 percent at Class A and B properties usually indicate that something is awry. Similar levels of bad debt can sometimes occur at Class C properties with excellent management. If a property is less well managed, collection losses of 5 percent or higher are not unusual in these communities—especially for properties in distress.

Concessions

Depending on supply and demand in a given market, you may find that properties are offering temporary financial incentives to help attract or retain residents. These concessions represent value to the tenant that detracts from rent, and they need to be factored into your income projections. Common examples of concessions include:

- Move-in specials offering one or more months of free rent or a period of reduced rent
- Lower rents for tenants who agree to sign a longer-term lease, say, for eighteen months or two years
- Referral programs offering current residents a rent credit in exchange for their recruiting a new resident
- Gift cards, televisions, or other bonus items awarded for lease signings

To determine what is normal in your market, keep track of specials that are being promoted as you are documenting rent comps. Then calculate what percentage of rent would be lost to concessions. For example, if most comps are offering half off the first month's rent, the loss to concessions will be 1/24th of the annual rental income for that unit, or 4.15 percent, during the first year of occupancy. Nationwide averages for resident turnover rates tend to hover around 50 percent, so in any given year, your move-in special would affect income for approximately half your units, resulting in a net loss to concessions of 2.08 percent.

Nonrevenue Units

Sometimes multifamily properties will repurpose units for non-revenue-generating functions. Examples include model units and units being used for storage or maintenance or as a rental office. Another example is a unit that is provided either free of charge or at a reduced rate to an employee. Since your GPR is based on 100 percent occupancy, you would need to reduce your income projections to reflect the associated loss in income.

Note that if the property has down units that are not inhabitable for some reason, these should be counted as non-revenue-generating until they are restored. If you plan to bring these back online, you should reduce your losses in line with the time period you are projecting them to be made available.

Calculating Effective Rental Income

Once you have determined all your rental losses, you're ready to apply them to the GPR and determine your effective rental income (ERI). To do this, first subtract your LTL from the GPR to get the GSR. Next, subtract your vacancy loss, collections loss, concessions, and nonrevenue units to arrive at the ERI for the property.

$$ERI = GPR - LTL - \frac{Vacancy}{Loss} - \frac{Collection}{Loss} - \frac{Concessions}{Loss} - \frac{Nonrevenue}{Loss}$$

Below are our actual calculations for Park Place Apartments:

		PER UNIT	ANNUALLY
Gross Potential Rent (GPR)		$900	$1,296,482
Loss to Lease (LTL)		($102)	($146,282)
Gross Scheduled Rent (GSR)		$799	$1,150,200
Less: Vacancy Loss	5.00%	($40)	($57,510)
Less: Collection Loss	1.50%	($12)	($17,253)
Less: Concessions Loss	4.15%	($33)	($47,733)
Less: Nonrevenue Loss	0.74%	($6)	($8,511)
Effective Rental Income		**$708**	**$1,019,192**

Table 12-5 Effective Rental Income for Park Place Apartments. Any small numerical variances on this table are due to rounding.

Other Income

Now that you have accounted for all the rental losses, you need to look at other sources of income besides rent and add those in. Ancillary income sources include utility reimbursement, pet fees, laundry, administrative fees, late fees, and the sale or rental of various products and services.

Some of these sources can be substantial, and it's not unusual for the various fees a property charges to add 5 percent to its income. To quantify other income, the best place to start is usually with historical actuals for the property. You'll want to look at other income over the T-12, and preceding years if possible. Sometimes seller financials don't include a breakdown of "other income." If there is no indication of the source of this income, you should request this information from the seller.

When reviewing the various sources of other income in the historical expenses, you should also identify which of them are directly correlated to occupancy. For example, if every tenant is charged $10 per month for trash, your trash income will increase proportionally as you fill vacant units. Therefore, when projecting future income, you'll want to make sure the appropriate "other income" line items are adjusted to reflect occupancy levels.

While your baseline for other income will be the actuals from the property, there is nothing preventing you from making changes if the market will support them. If you plan to implement any modifications to the fees being charged, you should estimate how much incremental revenue can reasonably be anticipated and add it to the other income. Before doing so, make sure you examine the comps and see what fees or ancillary charges they have in place.

Effective Gross Income

Once you have estimated your other income sources, you have everything you need to calculate your effective gross income (EGI), also known as effective gross revenue (EGR). To do this, simply add other income to effective rental income (ERI).

$$EGI = ERI + Other\ Income$$

Continuing with our Park Place Apartments example, our gross income projections for the first year looked like this:

INCOME		PER UNIT	ANNUALLY
Gross Potential Rent (GPR)		$900	$1,296,482
Loss to Lease (LTL)		($102)	($146,282)
Gross Scheduled Rent (GSR)		$799	$1,150,200
Less: Vacancy Loss	5.00%	($40)	($57,510)
Less: Collection Loss	1.50%	($12)	($17,253)
Less: Concessions Loss	4.15%	($33)	($47,733)
Less: Nonrevenue Loss	0.74%	($6)	($8,511)
Effective Rental Income		$708	$1,019,192
Plus: Fee Income		$27	$38,919
Plus: Utility Reimbursement		$18	$25,950
Plus: Misc. Income		$14	$20,243
Total Other Income		$59	$85,112
Effective Gross Income		**$767**	**$1,104,304**

Table 12-6 Effective Gross Income for Park Place Apartments. Any small numerical variances on this table are due to rounding.

Value-Add

There are many ways to boost a property's income by adding value. We'll cover value-add strategies in detail in Chapter Nineteen. For now, let's review the steps you need to take to ensure that your value-add strategies are captured in your underwriting.

First, you should come up with a budget for any projected capital expenditures. If you plan on making major improvements, you should enlist an experienced property management firm or contractor to help prepare or review these projections. For example, recall that at Park Place Apartments seven of the two-bedroom, one-bathroom units had already been upgraded to "premium" condition and were collecting an extra $163 in monthly rent. The "classic" units were getting $802 per month, while the premium units were getting $965, and market rent for premium units was $975. That's a healthy amount of potential additional income, so we collected information on what upgrades were done and the cost involved, and then had our property management firm review the projections. Given the numbers, we decided that after closing we would upgrade all the classic units. In addition, we decided to improve the exterior by upgrading the common areas and amenities in order to further support the higher rent and improve the quality of life for all residents. Our budget for the improvements was as follows:

CLASSIC UNIT UPGRADES	UNITS	COST/UNIT	COST
Washer/Dryer Connections	113	$800	$90,400
Black Kitchen Appliances	113	$1,200	$135,600
Vinyl Plank Flooring	113	$1,000	$113,000
Quartz Countertops	113	$875	$98,875
Plumbing Hardware	113	$325	$36,725
Modern Lighting	113	$300	$33,900
Paint Cabinets	113	$900	$101,700
New Cabinet Knobs	113	$150	$16,950
Contingency	113	$700	$79,100
Total Interior		**$6,250**	**$706,250**
Exterior/Common Area			
Parking Lot Repairs & Restripe			$19,500
Landscaping			$25,000
Common Area Hallways			$15,000
Covered Parking Repairs			$12,000
Amenity Improvements			
—New Playground			$6,500
—Bark Park			$5,000
—Outdoor Grill Area			$12,000
—Unit Patio Repairs			$28,000
Contingency			$40,000
Total Exterior			**$163,000**
Total Improvement Costs			**$869,250**

Table 12-7 Cost of Improvements for Park Place Apartments

Once you have the budget, you need to project how the value-add changes will affect the property's income going forward. If the change is going to be implemented incrementally, you'll need to decide on a feasible timeline and determine the net financial impact for each year. For Park Place Apartments, the projected value-add was significant. The affected units would receive major upgrades that would certainly merit an additional $163 per month for two-bedroom/one-bathroom units (which is what the property was already getting for units that had received the same improvements). At that rate, the updated apartments would still be almost $10 per month below market rent. Charging the current premium unit rent of $965 per month would result in a total increase in income of:

$163 per Month per Unit × 33 Units × 12 Months = $64,548 per Year

TYPE	UNITS	AVERAGE LEASED RENT	CURRENT PREMIUM RENT	RENT PREMIUM	INCREASE IN INCOME
2BR/1BA	33	$802	$965	$163	$64,548

If you were to raise these units from the current rent of $802 per month all the way up to the market premium rate of $975, the increase in income would be:

$173 per Month per Unit × 33 Units × 12 Months = $68,508 per Year

TYPE	UNITS	AVERAGE LEASED RENT	CURRENT PREMIUM RENT	RENT PREMIUM	INCREASE IN INCOME
2BR/1BA	33	$802	$975	$173	$68,508

It might be a challenge for some of the residents to pay an extra $173 per month, so jumping straight to that rent could result in a fair amount of drama. However, other tenants might be glad to pay the higher rent, given the breadth and quality of the proposed improvements to their units. As discussed earlier in this chapter, you will have to make a judgment call on how to manage this situation. Further complicating things from an operational perspective is the fact that performing work of this scope can be highly disruptive and may require temporarily relocating tenants or shuffling units as work is done. These considerations may seem premature at this stage, but they need to be weighed during the underwriting process in order to project a property's income as accurately as possible.

The last step is to make sure you have comps that reflect the end product and make any necessary adjustments to market rents. For Park Place Apartments, seven units had already been upgraded, so you would have identified the comps already. Sometimes, however, the upgrades will be entirely new to the property. For example, let's say you are underwriting a dated property with all original finishes and no amenities. After your initial analysis, you decide to upgrade all the units with new finishes, fixtures, and appliances—and add some nice amenities like a community room and dog park. If your original rent comps did not reflect this improved offering, you'll need to get another set of comps to help gauge what kinds of rents you can expect post-renovation. In cases where we don't have solid comps, we sometimes run test ads in order to determine market demand. That said, the fewer or weaker the comps, the more caution you should use with your projections. You don't want to push rents to new levels without comps to support the increase.

Deciding on value-add plans, adjusting your income and expense projections, and then completing a financial analysis is likely to be an iterative process as you strive to identify the improvements that offer the best return. To avoid an all-too-common mistake, be careful not to increase your income projections beyond a reasonable and attainable figure just to reach target returns. Overreaching on rents can be very costly to you and your investors. It's always best to maintain discipline and objectivity in your projections.

Pro Forma Income

Once you've settled on your plans for the property, you'll want to complete your pro forma income projections. This involves taking your assumptions and using them to extrapolate the income forward. If you haven't done so already, you will enter the T-12 income numbers, and then complete projections for each year that you plan to own the property. Most large multifamily investors will have hold periods of five to seven years, which gives them enough time to execute on any value-add strategies and fully realize the associated returns. Others will purchase a property with the intention of flipping it or holding it indefinitely, so there is no single correct approach. If you are unsure of your hold period or would like to evaluate the potential implications of holding the property longer than expected, you should model the income (and expenses) for ten years. Any projections beyond a decade would be too speculative to be of any value. Even looking five years out is challenging, given the breadth of variables and unknowns.

Once again, deciding on what assumptions to use for future income growth will involve some judgment. However, a good place to start is with the market rent data collected in the screening process and the first part of your underwriting. You'll want to pay particular attention to historical rent growth and use that as a starting point for future projections.

For Park Place Apartments, a five-year pro forma income would look something like the table below. Notice that in years one through three the rent growth is larger than in later years. Remember that implementing a value-add program to achieve premium rents doesn't happen overnight. It could take twelve to thirty-six months to complete the upgrades and renovations. This will spread out the premium income growth over the course of two to three years.

INCOME	T-12	YEAR 1	YEAR 2	YEAR 3	YEAR 4	YEAR 5
Gross Potential Rent (GPR)	$900	$900	$961	$990	$1,019	$1,050
Loss to Lease (LTL)	($102)	($48)	($14)	($10)	($10)	($11)
Gross Scheduled Rent (GSR)	$799	$852	$947	$980	$1,009	$1,039
GSR Rent Increase	—	$54	$94	$33	$29	$30
% GSR Growth	—	6.7%	11.1%	3.5%	3.0%	3.0%
Less: Vacancy Loss	4.99%	10.00%	8.00%	5.00%	5.00%	5.00%
Less: Collection Loss	1.50%	1.50%	1.50%	1.50%	1.50%	1.50%
Less: Concessions Loss	4.14%	4.15%	4.15%	4.15%	4.15%	4.15%
Less: Nonrevenue Loss	0.74%	0.74%	0.74%	0.74%	0.74%	0.74%

INCOME	T-12	YEAR 1	YEAR 2	YEAR 3	YEAR 4	YEAR 5
Gross Potential Rent (GPR)	$1,296,482	$1,296,482	$1,383,593	$1,425,101	$1,467,854	$1,511,889
Loss to Lease (LTL)	($146,282)	($69,001)	($20,284)	($14,511)	($14,946)	($15,395)
Gross Scheduled Rent (GSR)	$1,150,200	$1,227,482	$1,363,309	$1,410,590	$1,452,907	$1,496,494
Less: Vacancy Loss	($57,510)	($122,748)	($109,065)	($70,529)	($72,645)	($74,825)
Less: Collection Loss	($17,253)	($18,412)	($20,450)	($21,159)	($21,794)	($22,447)
Less: Concessions Loss	($47,733)	($50,940)	($56,577)	($58,539)	($60,296)	($62,105)
Less: Nonrevenue Loss	($8,511)	($9,083)	($10,088)	($10,438)	($10,752)	($11,074)
Effective Rental Income	$1,019,192	$1,026,297	$1,167,129	$1,249,923	$1,287,421	$1,326,044
Plus: Fee Income	$38,919	$38,919	$40,087	$41,089	$42,116	$43,169
Plus: Utility Reimbursement	$25,950	$25,950	$26,729	$27,397	$28,082	$28,784
Plus: Misc. Income	$20,243	$20,243	$20,850	$21,372	$21,906	$22,453
Total Other Income	$85,112	$85,112	$87,665	$89,857	$92,103	$94,406
Effective Gross Income	$1,104,304	$1,111,409	$1,254,794	$1,339,780	$1,379,525	$1,420,450

Table 12-8 Pro Forma Income for Park Place Apartments. Any small numerical variances on this table are due to rounding.

When estimating income for future years, it's important to recognize that real estate values and rent growth tend to go in cycles and are notoriously challenging to forecast. There's a reason why people say the only thing we know for certain about a forecast is that it will be wrong. Don't pretend you're the exception and know what the future holds, or that anyone else does either—and don't fall prey to your own biases and lose objectivity.

Regardless of how hot a market is, most investors won't assume a long-term rent growth of higher than 2.5 to 3 percent, with more conservative underwriters capping growth at 2 percent. In the end, it's best to weigh all the information at your disposal as objectively as possible and use your best judgment.

KEY TAKEAWAYS

- Underwriting income involves analyzing the information included in the rent roll and identifying comparable properties and market rents, followed by calculating the gross potential rent and effective rental income.
- Value-add can be achieved on the income side through the growth of ancillary income, upgrades, and eliminating LTL. You need to strike the optimal balance between the CapEx associated with improvements and the corresponding value added through income growth.
- Pro forma income should be projected for up to ten years based on the rent data and trends identified in the screening process and underwriting. Real estate is cyclical, and you should exercise caution when projecting long-term rent growth.

Madison Barracks: Part III

Three days after I got the one-line message from the CEO saying he might be willing to sell the Apartments at Madison Barracks, I got an email from somebody at his company with the historical financials and current rent roll. I thanked them and told them I'd respond shortly. Now I had what I needed to really dig in and start underwriting the property's income.

I began by reviewing the rent roll and was surprised to see that it showed occupancy above 80 percent. On my recent property visit it appeared that many of the units were vacant, so I thought the occupancy would be considerably lower. When I transferred the rent roll to my own spreadsheet and analyzed it, however, I discovered that the owner was excluding "down units" (units they deemed unsuitable for occupancy) from their occupancy calculations. Running my own numbers, I determined that the occupancy level was closer to 65 percent—a pretty big difference!

I also noticed that the rents looked higher than I had expected, so I decided to do a market survey. Identifying comparable properties was easier than usual because I already owned other properties in the area. In addition, there were two multifamily properties adjacent to this one, and I had recently completed underwriting and submitted an offer on one of them. I called the neighboring properties and found out they were both 100 percent full with waiting lists, which was encouraging.

Next, I contacted the seller and got permission to speak with the current property manager. When I got the property manager on the phone, we had a long talk and he was very open about what was going on. It turns out he was overseeing the property from 1,500 miles away and would visit whenever he could, though there apparently wasn't much of a budget for travel. The property manager clearly held the property in high regard and seemed to take a deep personal interest in its welfare. When he visited, he would sleep in the property management office since the owner was running out of cash. Even more surprising, he mentioned that he had paid to have some necessary work done on the property with his own personal funds. This seemed crazy to me, but he came across as authentic and caring.

When I asked him about the occupancy issues, the property manager seemed genuinely perplexed about why units weren't leasing, although the answer seemed obvious to me—the rents were way too high. My conversations with him about rents and market conditions revealed that the property manager was out of touch with local market conditions. Based on the results of my preliminary market survey, asking rents at Madison Barracks were anywhere from $100 to $300 per month above what the market would support, depending on the unit type. In fact, I felt confident that we could raise occupancy to 90 percent if rents were reduced to a level the market could support and enough of the down units were brought back online.

To estimate the cost of restoring the property's down units, I needed to get inside some of them. I contacted the seller and set up a property tour for the following Monday morning. I told them they could expect an offer within a week after the tour, so they knew it wouldn't be a waste of their time.

"I'd like to see every vacant unit, as well as at least one unit for each floor plan," I told them. "I'd rather not disturb all the tenants at this point," I added. "But I know you have a lot of down units and others that are in rough shape, so make sure you show me the worst of the worst. Otherwise, this will all end up being a waste of everyone's time. If we're able to reach an agreement on price, I'll be inspecting every single unit. So I'll know if I've been misled, and we'll have to renegotiate the deal, and that's a practice I try hard to avoid."

The seller agreed. The property manager would fly in and meet me on Monday at the leasing office before heading out for the tour. In the meantime, I needed to start underwriting the expenses, and I shuddered to imagine what those might look like at a property where some of the buildings were 200 years old. They might be bad, but I was starting to think this project could actually work. Unfortunately, the above-market rents weren't the only issue. There were a whole lot more problems than what met the eye.

To be continued...

Chapter Thirteen

UNDERWRITING EXPENSES

The buyer needs a hundred eyes, the seller not one.

—GEORGE HERBERT

In the last chapter, we walked you through the income underwriting process, aiming to determine exactly how much the property currently brings in each month and how much it might bring in in the future. We'll continue to use the Park Place Apartments as an example to find the other half of the NOI equation. We were pretty excited about projecting an increase in EGI of more than $300,000 over five years—but now it was time to lift up the hood and take a close look at the property expenses.

Historical Expenses

When underwriting expenses, the first thing to do is look closely at the actual, historical expenses. If possible, examine the trailing twelve-month (T-12) expenses side by side with those from the prior two calendar years. If you observe any trends or drastic differences or notice anything missing, you should speak with the seller or their broker to get some context and understand what's going on. The numbers and trends always tell a story, and you need to make sure you know what it is in order to do thorough underwriting.

Analyzing longer periods of time is more important for expenses than for income. Not only can expenses fluctuate more throughout the year, but they are easier for a seller to manipulate, especially in the short term. There is too much seasonality and irregularity associated with expenses such as snow removal, cooling, property taxes, and so on. Additionally, sellers will sometimes cut way back on staffing or routine maintenance in anticipation of a sale. While that can be sustained for a while, it will lead to deferred maintenance and eventually cause significant issues.

The second step when you're analyzing the historical expenses is to roll them up into standard categories. Seller financials can be provided in a myriad of different formats and can categorize things in all kinds of interesting ways. The exact expense categories you choose for your underwriting are not as important as the need to be consistent in your analyses. Still, there are industry-standard categories you may want to work from, particularly if you want to draw comparisons with industry averages. If the seller financials are not already organized in a manner consistent with industry standards, transfer them to your own spreadsheet, using your best judgment about what category each line item most closely aligns with. For example, if there are separate line items for electrical repairs and plumbing repairs, those would be rolled up under "repairs and maintenance." The main categories most commonly used in underwriting include:

- **Payroll:** salaries, benefits, workers' comp, and other associated payroll costs
- **Insurance:** property and liability insurance premiums, including flood insurance when appropriate
- **Property Taxes:** all property taxes imposed by local authorities
- **Utilities and Trash:** gas, electric, water, cable, and any other utility expenses; trash can be included in utilities or separated out
- **Property Management:** all fees charged by a property management firm, excluding payroll reimbursement
- **General and Administrative:** a catchall for a wide range of expenses, including permits, office supplies, computer and software expenses, travel, and training

- **Professional Fees:** accounting, legal, engineering, architectural, and any other type of charges incurred for consulting or professional services associated with property operations; sometimes combined with general and administrative
- **Marketing:** advertising, signage, brochures, community events, gifts, swag
- **Contract Services:** all general property maintenance, services, and operations provided by third parties, such as cleaning, landscaping, painting, snow removal, and pest control
- **Repairs and Maintenance:** materials and supplies associated with the ongoing operation of the property, including routine and preventive maintenance, as well as repairs and improvements
- **Turnover:** all costs associated with unit turns or otherwise making a unit rent-ready; sometimes combined with repairs and maintenance

As you roll historical expenses up into categories, be sure to make note of any common expense that appears to be missing and determine whether there is a plausible explanation.

The third thing you should do when reviewing historical expenses is to divide each of the annual expense numbers by the number of units so that you can see them all in terms of dollars per unit. Experienced multifamily investors learn over time what the normal ranges are for expenses in terms of price per unit, so presenting expenses in these terms also allows you to more easily compare any property you're analyzing to other properties and industry norms. Some investors will also quantify expenses as a percentage of gross income, which can be particularly helpful for things like property management, which is usually based on a percentage of the property's EGI.

Below you can see the before-and-after for the T-12 expenses at Park Place Apartments. It was an off-market deal, so expenses were delivered at a more granular level than they would have been if a broker had been involved, which is common. The first table shows what was reported by the seller, while the second shows the expenses recategorized and expressed in terms of dollars per unit and percent of gross income. You'll see how everything was rolled up. For example, all items that fell under "Painting & Decorating" are now captured in "Repairs & Maintenance" Also notice that the trash line item under "Contracted Services" has been rolled into "Utilities & Trash." With everything cleaned up, we're ready to move on to the next step, which is normalizing the expenses.

Management Fees

6225 - Management Fee	39,988
Total Management Fees	**39,988**

Administrative Expense

6002 - Bank Fees	1,512
6005 - Office Supplies	640
6007 - Copier Expense	420
6008 - Postage	664
6009 - Telephone	2,424
6013 - Internet Service	2,464
6014 - Answering Service	972
6016 - Alarm	(696)
6023 - Computer Software	11,472
6042 - Website	2,496
6057 - Uniforms- Maintenance	624
6060 - Legal & Professional Fees	6,712
6066 - Audit Expense	4,268
6071 - Cable TV Expense	128
6083 - Renters Protection Admin Fees	400
6085 - Credit Reports	1,452
6091 - Payroll Services	2,692
Total Administrative Expense	**38,644**

Utilities

6455 - Electricity - Common Area	25,144
6458 - Electricity-Vacants	3,064
6465 - Gas - Common Area	2,868
6481 - Gas - Vacants	2,688
6488 - Sewer	20,316
6493 - Water	48,908
Total Utilities	**102,988**

Painting & Decorating

6805 - Apartment Cleaning - Turnover	5,780
6811 - Carpet Cleaning-Occupied	560
6812 - Carpet Cleaning-Turnover	1,780
6817 - Carpet/Floor Repairs-Occupied	1,016
6823 - Carpet/Floor Repairs-Turnover	956
6826 - Tub Reglazing - Turnover	1,040
6836 - Painting Contract-Turnover	33,436
6845 - Painting Supplies	1,068
6855 - Drywall Patching	2,480
Total Painting & Decorating	**48,116**

Tax & Insurance Expense

6951 - Real Estate Taxes	76,180
6952 - Personal Property Taxes	3,912
6960 - Property & Liability Insurance	43,328
Total Tax & Insurance Expense	**123,420**

Salaries Expense

6100 - Community Manager	73,200
6101 - Assistant Manager	28,596
6102 - Leasing Payroll	11,780
6104 - Rental Incentives	14,504
6106 - Maintenance Supervisor	46,224
6107 - Maintenance Tech 1	10,200
6115 - Groundsman 1	180
6155 - Payroll Taxes	11,996
6156 - Workman's Comp. Insurance	2,256
6162 - Health Insurance/Employee Benefit	6,080
Total Salaries Expense	**205,016**

Maintenance & Repair

6507 - Tools & Supplies	380
6510 - Appliance Parts/Service	2,456
6519 - HVAC Repairs/Maintenance Supplies	(504)
6527 - Tub Repairs / Resurfacing	800
6530 - Electrical Supplies	(1,460)
6535 - Plumbing Supplies	1,188
6536 - Cleaning & Paper Supplies	1,536
6551 - Hardware	384
6554 - Keys & Locks	(444)
6555 - Lightbulbs	(96)
6559 - Doors	1,632
6560 - Common Area Cleaning	7,200
6575 - Windows & Screens	532
6603 - Pool Permits	1,240
6606 - Misc. Maintenance	676
Total Maintenance & Repair	**15,520**

Contracted Services

6700 - Repairs Contract	11,488
6701 - Plumbing Repairs	7,592
6705 - HVAC Repairs Contract	3,920
6710 - Fire Protection Contract	4,116
6741 - Exterminating Contract	340
6742 - Trash Removal	5,076
6760 - Mowing	25,856
6765 - Snow Removal	5,100
Total Contracted Services	**63,488**

Advertising & Promotion

6302 - Advertising-Apartment Guide	10,680
6303 - Advertising-For Rent	9,696
6304 - Advertising-Internet	10,452
6332 - Leasing Hospitality	64
6360 - Signage-Advertising	4,200
Total Advertising & Promotion	**35,092**

Total Expenses	**672,272**

Table 13-1 Park Place T-12 Expenses

EXPENSES	$/YEAR	%	$/UNIT
Payroll	205,016	18.6%	1,708
Property Insurance	43,328	3.9%	361
Property Taxes	80,092	7.3%	667
Utilities & Trash	108,064	9.8%	901
Property Management	39,988	3.6%	333
General & Admin	38,644	3.5%	322
Marketing	35,092	3.2%	292
Contract Services	58,412	5.3%	487
Repairs & Maintenance	63,636	5.8%	530
Total Expenses	**672,272**	**60.9%**	**5,602**

Table 13-2 Park Place T-12 Expenses. Any small numerical variances on this table are due to rounding.

Normalizing Expenses

While it's important to look at historical expenses as a starting point, it's not necessarily reasonable to expect that a property will or should continue to incur identical expenses moving forward. Therefore, one of the most important aspects of good underwriting is a process called normalizing expenses, which means taking the information you're given and making adjustments to bring them more in line with what's reasonable.

In order to normalize expenses, you'll want to go through the actuals line by line to determine whether any appear to be missing, unnecessary, underreported, or inflated. Next, you'll want to find out the reasoning behind each expense. Your goal shouldn't be to challenge a seller or make any accusations, just to understand their logic so you can complete your underwriting.

Once you've received explanations, you'll have to use your best judgment to determine whether they are logical and justify projecting similar expenses moving forward. Again, your property management firm can be a good resource here. For example, let's say you notice that expenses for contract services seem high. After investigating further, you realize that the property has consistently incurred unusually high groundskeeping and landscaping costs. The seller might explain that there are a lot of mature trees, shrubs, and other vegetation and they're important to the curb appeal of the property. You would look at the property and if the explanation has merit, you can reasonably expect this expense to run high going forward. If you still have doubts, you or your property management firm could get a quote from a local vendor for landscaping services to see whether it aligns with this logic.

Sometimes the reasons why expenses are significantly higher or lower than normal are logical, but you will still have to discard them and establish your own projections. Here are three such scenarios:

1. The property might be operated by an owner who does a lot of work themselves without collecting a salary or charging property management fees. If it is a husband-wife team or involves other family members, the result can be substantially underreported expenses. This is a common reason why the salary expense might be low while other expenses, such as property management, lawn care, or snow removal, might not show up at all. On the flip side, an owner-operator may also include expenses that are unnecessary, such as those for their personal vehicle or home office.

2. Properties that are poorly managed often have abnormally high expenses. They may be overstaffed, contract out too many services, not bother to get competitive bids from vendors, and otherwise spend indiscriminately. Routine maintenance might not get done, resulting in expensive repairs and replacements, while tenants might not get properly screened, which results in damage to the property. The costs of poor management can be high, as we saw in the River Apartments story. This might seem alarming, but for a value-add investor it can be exciting because it represents opportunity. We'll look at some of the most common areas where expenses can be trimmed later on.

3. Some property financials will include interest expense or capital expenditures, both of which can throw off your valuation and should be removed from your underwriting. (These items are not considered operating expenses and do not factor into a property's NOI.) If depreciation is included, that should be removed as well. For Park Place Apartments, we removed the interest expense from the T-12. We'll account for our own debt and capital expenditures later, as well

as their impact on cash flow, so no need to bother with a seller's debt or CapEx history. If a property is listed with an experienced broker, you're not likely to find these line items on the financials, but sellers will sometimes leave them in for off-market properties.

Typical Expenses

Normalizing expenses is logical but can be challenging, particularly for investors with little experience owning large multifamily properties. Once an investor becomes more familiar with what's normal, the process gets easier. Fortunately, in the meantime, there are resources that can be helpful.

As discussed in previous chapters, property management firms can be a huge asset when it comes to estimating staffing levels, compensation, and other expenses. There are also annual multifamily operating expense surveys conducted by the National Apartment Association (NAA) and Institute of Real Estate Management (IREM). Before purchasing one of these survey reports, be aware that while valuable, they are certainly not perfect and shouldn't be used blindly. Broad market surveys can't account for the unique aspects of individual properties, which need to be considered when arriving at your final expense projections. Also, be aware that each industry survey has its own unique way of classifying and calculating expenses, so if you decide to purchase one of these annual reports, be sure to review the methodologies and make sure your underwriting is in alignment before applying the numbers.

Part of the reason estimating expenses can be such a challenge is that they can be so location- and property-specific. Some examples of major factors that can influence expenses include:

- **Local Cost of Living:** Expenses are generally higher across the board in areas with a higher cost of living.
- **Climate and Weather:** Expenses such as including heating, cooling, landscaping, pool maintenance, snow removal, and property insurance will be higher or lower depending on the local climate and weather.
- **Tax and Regulatory Environment:** Property taxes are one of the largest expenses and can vary widely by location. Landlord-tenant laws and how business-friendly a location is can also significantly affect expense levels.

- **Age of Property:** Older properties are almost always costlier to maintain, particularly when measured relative to income. New properties tend to have significantly lower expense ratios.
- **Size of Property:** There are clear economies of scale in multifamily. The cost per unit to operate a property decreases as the number of units increases.
- **Tenancy:** Some types of tenants are harder on a property and more management-intensive.
- **Condition of the Property:** The better the condition of a property, the fewer problems you are likely to encounter, and the less it should cost to maintain.
- **Property Type:** Overall expenses tend to be lower for garden-style apartments than for mid-rise and high-rise buildings.
- **Utilities:** Whether any or all utilities are directly paid by tenants can have a significant influence on a property's expenses.
- **Location:** The submarket, neighborhood, and even specific location within a neighborhood can all affect expenses. For example, the tax burden of a Business Improvement District (BID) or a flood zone may affect only a very small section of a neighborhood.

Due to these factors and many others, you must be cautious about using "industry norms" or broader averages. There is certainly great value in understanding the norms for each operating expense because it helps you readily identify when something is off. Just make sure you're exercising sound judgment and not automatically plugging in a "typical" number without giving it careful consideration in the context of the specific property and location. The best approach is to get input from people with local, hands-on knowledge when possible, and do your homework. A property management firm that has nearby properties can be a great resource, but in some cases, you'll still need to secure actual property-specific quotes.

Below are the most common multifamily operating expenses, along with guidance on how to better understand typical ranges and estimate them.

Payroll

Payroll expenses are highly dependent on the specific property and market. Your best bet for accurately estimating payroll expenses is to consult with a local property management firm. On average a large multifamily property requires approximately one full-time employee for every forty-five to fifty units with an average fully loaded compensation of $45,000 to $50,000 per employee, depending on the market. The range per unit is typically somewhere between $900 and $1,300.

$$\frac{\text{Gross}}{\text{Pay}} + \text{Bonus} + \frac{\text{Payroll}}{\text{Taxes}} + \text{Benefits} + \text{Insurance} = \frac{\text{Fully Loaded}}{\text{Compensation}}$$

For Park Place Apartments, we determined that we could operate this size of property with one on-site property manager and one experienced maintenance technician. We determined, in consultation with a property management firm, that the fully loaded compensation should run $102,070 ($1,037 per unit) in annual payroll expense. The table below breaks down the payroll costs. We estimated that the total PTBI (Payroll Taxes + Benefits + Insurance) costs are 18 percent of gross pay and bonus for this market.

POSITION	GROSS PAY	BONUS	PTBI	TOTAL
Property Manager	45,000	4,000	8,820	57,820
Maintenance Tech	45,000	2,500	8,550	56,050
Total	90,000	6,500	17,370	113,870

Insurance

Beware of low historical insurance costs, which usually indicate that the seller is under-insured. You won't have that option because your insurance requirements will be specified by your lender and can vary significantly. Agency debt tends to have the most rigorous insurance requirements, which drives up the cost of insurance considerably. Properties located in a flood zone or other high-risk area are also more expensive to insure. Insurance costs generally range from $200 to $400 per unit per year. The best way to get a more accurate figure is to secure a term sheet and ask the lender to provide a copy of their insurance requirements. You can then take these to your insurance broker and get an actual quote.

For Park Place Apartments we contacted two insurance brokers, provided the property details, and received multiple quotes ranging from $340 to $350 per unit in insurance coverage.

Property Taxes

In most instances you should avoid using historical property taxes to project future taxes unless there is a strong rationale for doing so. In fact, assuming property taxes won't change after a sale is one of the most common and potentially disastrous errors made by inexperienced investors for large and small properties alike. Property taxes will almost always increase after a sale and sometimes by a significant amount. In fact, if a property hasn't changed ownership in a long time, it wouldn't be unusual for a sale to cause property taxes to double or even triple. That said, the amount of the increase and the time until reassessment can vary dramatically depending on the specific property and location.

You can usually look up tax information on the local tax authority's website. Many have public search portals where you can locate specific parcels and find property-specific tax information. In order to accurately forecast the timing and amount of future property taxes on a large multifamily project, you should also call the local tax assessor and ask for guidance. Given how large a percentage of a property's expenses are typically associated with property taxes, there is too much at stake to not make this effort.

If you are unable to reach the local assessor or they are not willing to help, you can reach out to a local tax attorney and get an opinion letter. Tax attorneys are typically willing to do this in hopes of gaining your future business. You could also review the sales histories and tax impacts for the subject property and comparable properties. Opinion letters and comparable property tax histories are inexact methods and should be taken with a grain of salt, but they are suitable backups.

As a last resort for cases where you have been unsuccessful in reaching anyone or finding guidance on the taxing jurisdiction's website, some underwriters will assume a reassessment of the property's full market value in the first year after a sale at 80 to 90 percent of the sale price. But recognize this for what it is—a wild guess that is moderately conservative at best.

After you estimate the reassessed value, there are two steps you need to take in order to calculate the property's future tax liability. First, you will determine the assessed value by multiplying the full market value by the assessment ratio, which is the ratio of a property's assessed value to its market value—in other words, the percentage of the property value subject to tax. For example, if a property's full market value is $8 million and the assessment ratio is 70 percent, the assessed value would be $5.6 million. In many jurisdictions, the tax authority will tax 100 percent of the full market value.

Full Market Value × Assessment Ratio = Assessed Value

FULL MARKET VALUE	ASSESSMENT RATIO	ASSESSED VALUE
$8,000,000	70.0%	$5,600,000

The second step is to multiply the assessed value by the "mill rate" or "millage rate," which is the tax rate used to calculate how much you are actually going to owe in property tax. One mill equals 1/1000th of a dollar. In other words, a mill equates to one dollar for every $1,000 of property value. A tax authority's mill rate is the amount of taxes they charge per every $1,000 of a property's assessed value.

(Assessed Value ÷ 1,000) × Mill Rate = Property Tax

FULL MARKET VALUE	ASSESSMENT RATIO	ASSESSED VALUE	MILL RATE	PROPERTY TAX
$8,000,000	70.0%	$5,600,000	21.0	$117,600

Continuing with our above example, if the assessed value of the property is $5.6 million and the mill rate is 21 mills, the property tax will be $117,600 per year.

Keep in mind that a property is frequently subject to multiple tax authorities, each with their own mill rates, so you'll want to make sure you're using a combined rate. The combined mill rates and assessment ratios can usually be found on the assessor's website, along with due dates and information on how frequently properties are reassessed.

For Park Place Apartments we contacted the county assessor and found that we should expect to see the tax assessed value to be reassessed at 70 percent of the purchase price and the mill rate to be 21.

Trash Removal and Utilities

Trash removal and utility expenses such as electric, gas, water/sewer, and cable are likely to stay consistent with actual historical expenses. Unless you are planning to implement conservation measures or take other steps to manage these expenses, it is probably okay to assume these expenses will remain the same after closing. If you will make property improvements that may increase or decrease utilities, you should factor the anticipated changes into your future projections. For the trash component, we will often get competitive quotes during due diligence to make sure we're not overpaying by staying with the current provider.

Utility expenses will vary widely depending on whether a property is master metered or individually metered, with utilities paid directly by the tenants. For master-metered properties, utilities average around $800 to $1,200 per unit per year, while direct-billed properties average around $200 to $400 per unit. However, a multitude of factors can render such averages worthless. For example, the water bill alone for one of my large multifamily properties runs about $1,000 per unit per year due to high local rates. When it comes to utilities, you're better served by avoiding industry averages entirely and getting actual historical numbers whenever possible. When available, data from a similar property in the same market can be helpful. If your property management firm has other projects nearby, they may be able to secure this information for you. This would give you a basis for comparison to validate the actual historical numbers. If the subject property's usage is unusually high, that may signal an opportunity to make improvements.

For Park Place Apartments we confirmed with the property management firm that the current utility costs on the T-12 fell in line with what you would expect for this size property in this market, so we used historical costs in our assumptions.

Property Management

Property management fees are almost always tied directly to the project's gross income and can vary depending on the market and the size of the property. Numerous factors can influence the property management fee, so rather rely on typical ranges, you should get a quote.

In general, the larger the property, the lower the fee. For properties with fifty to one-hundred units, you can expect the property management fee to be in the range of 4 to 6 percent of gross income, while for

100-plus units, you can expect 3 to 4 percent. For 200-plus units, you are likely to be on the lower end of that range. Lenders and appraisers will typically not use a property management fee below 3 percent of EGI for their underwriting and valuation, even if you get a quote from someone willing to do it for less. A property management firm that charges less than 3 percent may not be your best option anyway, as the low price is likely to affect the level of service you can expect to receive.

For Park Place Apartments we confirmed in our property management interviews that the 3.5 percent management fee was appropriate. And don't forget—this cost is in addition to the payroll costs of your on-site management team, which we just discussed.

General and Administrative

A wide range of items get rolled up into general and administrative (G&A) expenses. Examples include office supplies, communications, transportation, computers and software, training, postage, and security. G&A expenses typically run about $100 to $200 per unit per year.

Professional Fees

Professional fees for items like legal, bookkeeping, accounting, architectural, and engineering services will typically range between $50 and $75 per unit per year. These can be kept as a separate line item or rolled up into G&A. You may also want to budget for a one-time fee to have a cost segregation study, which would typically run between $3,000 and $8,000, completed after closing. (Cost segregation is covered in more detail in Chapter Twenty.)

For Park Place Apartments we estimated $215 per unit for professional fees and G&A combined.

Marketing

Marketing expenses for large multifamily properties will typically range from $75 to $150 per unit per year, depending on factors like the property location, occupancy level, turnover, and local supply and demand. There are also efficiencies of scale with advertising, so the cost per unit drops significantly as the number of units climbs.

For Park Place Apartments we confirmed with property management that $15,000 in annual advertising ($125 per unit) would be more than adequate to reach and maintain the occupancy goals in the business plan.

Contract Services

On average, contract services tend to run around $200 to $400 per unit per year. Contract services include any work completed by contractors instead of employees, so this expense tends to be inversely correlated with payroll costs. That's because a property that is understaffed will rely more heavily on contractors, while properties with excess personnel are more likely to perform additional tasks in-house. If both payroll and contract service expenses are running high, there are probably issues to be resolved.

For Park Place Apartments we found contract services in the T-12 were running high due to some abnormal work, such as tree removals. After discussing market expectations with property management firms for the work on this property, we assumed $250 per unit would be a reasonable amount.

Repairs and Maintenance

Repair and maintenance (R&M) expenses are highly dependent on the age and condition of the property and vary by market. Newer properties tend to have fewer maintenance problems, so R&M can be as low as $300 per unit per year, while for older properties with deferred maintenance you can expect $500 to $700 per unit. An analysis of historical R&M expenses can help you gauge where on this wide spectrum you can expect to fall. However, if you plan on an extensive renovation after closing, you should expect a reduction in R&M expenses moving forward. In the end, you need to weigh these factors and make a judgment call. Again, if you don't have the experience to project R&M with some confidence, your property management partner can provide input.

Turnover

Some investors include the cost of unit turns in R&M expense, while others keep it separate. If you consider unit turns a separate line-item expense, as we're doing here, you're looking at around $200 to $400 per unit per year. This assumes a 50 percent turnover rate and an average cost of $400 to $800 for each unit turn, not including capital expenditures, which are covered out of replacement reserves. The cost to make a unit ready for the next tenant is highly dependent on the age and condition of the property, how much deferred maintenance is present, and the scope of what you'd like to accomplish during your unit turns. If you are implementing interior upgrades and attracting better renters, you can expect the cost of turns to drop. As with R&M, the factors and typical ranges should be weighed, but your final projections are ultimately a judgment call.

For Park Place Apartments we assumed $700 per unit per year, which includes both R&M and turnover costs. We anticipated a modest amount of deferred maintenance from our initial investigations of the property and planned a renovation that would help reduce R&M expenses.

Replacement Reserves

While technically not an expense, since the funds are intended to be used for capital expenditures, replacement reserve contributions are a cash requirement that should be budgeted for during underwriting. Replacement reserves are often defined by the lender and are usually calculated based on the results of the property condition assessment (PCA). Fannie Mae sets the minimum reserve requirement at $200 per unit per year, but that is a floor; a range of $250 to $300 per unit per year is more common, depending on the property's condition and lender requirements. Replacement reserves above $300 per unit are typical only for aging properties with an excessive amount of deferred maintenance. In the next chapter, we will discuss how to consider nonexpense items that affect cash flow in your underwriting.

For Park Place Apartments we assumed $300 per unit based on the condition of the property and guidance from lenders.

Example

The table below shows T-12 expenses versus normalized expenses for Park Place Apartments.

EXPENSES	CURRENT T-12 $/YEAR	%	$/UNIT	NORMALIZED $/YEAR	%	$/UNIT
Payroll	205,016	18.6%	1,708	136,290	12.3%	1,136
Property Insurance	43,328	3.9%	361	36,000	3.2%	300
Property Taxes	80,092	7.3%	667	117,600	10.6%	980
Utilities & Trash	108,064	9.8%	901	108,064	9.7%	901
Property Management	39,988	3.6%	333	38,899	3.5%	324
General & Admin	38,644	3.5%	322	25,800	2.3%	215
Marketing	35,092	3.2%	292	15,000	1.3%	125
Contract Services	58,412	5.3%	487	30,000	2.7%	250
Repairs & Maintenance	63,636	5.8%	530	84,000	7.6%	700
Total Expenses	**672,272**	**60.9%**	**5,602**	**591,653**	**53.2%**	**4,930**

Table 13-3 Park Place T-12 and Normalized Expenses. Any small numerical variances on this table are due to rounding.

Expense Ratio

Once you've estimated all your expenses, you should total them up. For most properties, annual expenses should be between $4,000 and $6,000 per unit. You can then use your total income and expenses to calculate your expense ratio, which is simply your total expenses divided by your effective gross income (EGI).

$$\text{Total Expenses} \div \text{EGI} = \text{Expense Ratio}$$

	T-12
Effective Gross Income (EGI)	$1,104,668
Total Operating Expenses	$672,272
Expense Ratio	**60.86%**

At Park Place Apartments our T-12 expense ratio and normalized expense ratio are shown below. As you can see, we projected a 53.23 percent expense ratio in the first year of operation.

	T-12	YEAR 1
Effective Gross Income (EGI)	$1,104,668	$1,111,409
Total Operating Expenses	$672,272	$591,653
Expense Ratio	**60.86%**	**53.23%**

The expense ratio is an important metric that experienced investors will use to get a fast, high-level indication of how efficiently a property is operating and whether it might fit their investment criteria. When we first look at a property, we quickly run this metric. A high expense ratio might indicate that the property has value-add potential and, thus, will be a good candidate for acquisition. On the other hand, an unusually low expense ratio often indicates underreported expenses and limited value-add opportunities, so the property is less likely to meet our criteria.

A 50 percent expense ratio is the standard most frequently cited in the industry, but a newer, well-managed property may have lower repair costs and achieve an expense ratio of 40 percent, while an older, poorly managed property might operate at 60 percent. Investors will often establish their own benchmarks based on experience with a specific type of property in the market where they operate. Property tax rates alone can swing this number up or down, as can the age of the property, cost of living, market rents, and whether tenants are responsible for their own utilities. A larger, newer multifamily property of 300-plus units might be able to achieve an expense ratio 5 to 10 percent lower than that of a much smaller property based solely on efficiencies of scale.

While expense ratios are a widely used and convenient metric for multifamily investors, it's important to recognize that they are a fairly crude and broad-brush measure. They are valuable for getting a high-level picture and double-checking that your underwritten expenses are in the right general range, but they are no substitute for digging into specifics and making the most accurate projections you can manage.

The Most Important Part of Underwriting

The typical ranges, formulas, ratios, resources, and examples included here are in no way meant to be definitive or universal, and are certainly no substitute for the single most important element of underwriting: good judgment. While we might all be more comfortable with a plug-and-play approach to multifamily underwriting and valuation, that is unfortunately not how it works. It's always messier and murkier than one would like. Underwriting can be as much of an art as it is a science, so don't take anything at face value. Ask questions, look at things in context, and be prepared to tap into both sides of your brain to harness both logic and creativity.

Each property is unique, and every project you undertake will require you to use your intuition, imagination, and judgment to figure out what makes the most sense for that particular deal. Investors who are new to large multifamily can often do a passable job of underwriting by edu-cating themselves, gathering as much information as they can, being diligent, and making the best decisions possible, especially if they already have experience with smaller properties. As with most things in life, there is no substitute for actual experience. Seasoned investors will hone their intuition over time and can sometimes develop a sixth sense, espe-cially if they also have experience on the operating side.

Pro Forma Expenses

Now that you have used your best judgment to complete all your expense projections and checked your expense ratio, you need to project them forward on the same timeline as your income. Again, if you do not have a specific hold period determined, you should project forward for ten years. Unless you have another basis for adjustments over time, you should assume annual increases for each expense based on inflation. As with rents, most investors will model annual increases at 2 to 3 percent per year. For our expenses at Park Place Apartments we assumed 2.5 percent, with the exception of property taxes, which were based on historical mill rate changes and property assessments increasing at 3 percent per year.

You should align the current and future projected income and expenses in columns for further analysis. Below this you should also identify any recurring but nonoperating expenses, such as asset management fees, capital expenditures, and other escrow contributions. These nonoperational expenses are generally excluded when calculating a property's net operating income. However, they are a cash requirement, so they need to be factored in when running other financial analyses, which we will review in the following chapter.

Once you've completed your pro forma, you'll get a better picture of the property overall and the numbers will begin to tell a story. Below you can see our full expense projections for Park Place Apartments. If you look carefully, you will see that the property was overstaffed and not watching their expenses closely. This indicated that the property was being mismanaged, and we could add value here. With improved expenses and efficiencies resulting from better management and unit upgrades, we could reasonably expect to see a reduction in operating expenses.

EXPENSES	T-12/ UNIT	YR 1/ UNIT	T-12	YEAR 1	YEAR 2	YEAR 3	YEAR 4	YEAR 5
Payroll	$1,708	$1,136	$205,016	$136,290	$139,697	$143,190	$146,769	$150,439
Property Insurance	$361	$300	$43,328	$36,000	$36,900	$37,823	$38,768	$39,737
Property Taxes	$667	$980	$80,092	$117,600	$121,128	$124,762	$128,505	$132,360
Utilities & Trash	$901	$901	$108,064	$108,064	$110,766	$113,535	$116,373	$119,282
Property Management	$333	$324	$39,988	$38,899	$39,872	$40,869	$41,890	$42,938
General & Admin	$322	$215	$38,644	$25,800	$26,445	$27,106	$27,784	$28,478
Marketing	$292	$125	$35,092	$15,000	$15,375	$15,759	$16,153	$16,557
Contract Services	$487	$250	$58,412	$30,000	$30,750	$31,519	$32,307	$33,114
Repairs & Maintenance	$530	$700	$63,636	$84,000	$86,100	$88,253	$90,459	$92,720
Total Operating Expenses	**$5,602**	**$4,930**	**$672,272**	**$591,653**	**$607,033**	**$622,814**	**$639,008**	**$655,626**
Expense Ratio			60.86%	53.23%	48.38%	46.49%	46.32%	46.16%

Table 13-4 Park Place Pro Forma and Expense Ratios. Please refer to table 12-8 for the EGI calculation. Any small numerical variances on this table are due to rounding.

KEY TAKEAWAYS

- When underwriting expenses, it's important to closely analyze historical expenses and note any trends, omissions, or anomalies. The numbers and trends always tell a story, and you need to make sure you know what it is.
- One of the most important steps is to normalize expenses, which involves estimating what expenses are most likely to be post-acquisition. Your property manager can be a great asset when undertaking this exercise.
- Expense ratios are an important metric that experienced investors will use to get a quick, high-level indication of how efficiently a property is operating or to double-check the underwriting, but they are a fairly crude and broad-brush measure.
- The single most important element of underwriting is good judgment, because underwriting can be as much of an art as it is a science.

Madison Barracks: Part IV

After underwriting the income for the Apartments at Madison Barracks, it was time to start digging into the expenses. Even though I hadn't looked at them yet, I was suspicious. Not only was the property old, but when the owner forwarded me the financials, they included the following notation: "We have removed non-property operating expenses" (whatever that meant).

Initially, the numbers looked good, but as I zoomed in, I kept finding discrepancies. Fortunately, the financials were provided to me in Excel, so I was able to dig into their formulas and pinpoint some "errors" easily, even before entering them into my own model. For example, the file that the seller provided included a formula to reduce all general and administrative expenses by 50 percent, which I assumed represented the "non-property operating expenses" mentioned above. There were smaller percentage reductions on other line items as well, but the most egregious discrepancy I found was that utility costs were omitted, even though they were paid by the landlord. This was a significant error, since water/sewer bills in particular were a lot higher than normal. When I asked about utility costs, the seller acknowledged that this was a mistake and they needed to be added back in.

Other issues we identified included a historical property tax expense that was lower than what was indicated on the real property tax report I had downloaded from the county's online database. It turned out that the actuals reflected the fact that the seller had underpaid their taxes, which made the prior years' numbers look better than they should have. We also noticed that the T-12 expenses for maintenance and labor were unsustainably low for a property of this age and condition, which we confirmed by comparing the reported expenses to nearby, similar properties.

In the end, we relied less on the expense information provided by the seller and more on our own estimates, as we usually do anyway. Seller information is helpful only for the story it tells and insofar as you can dig into anything that jumps out. You're always better served by getting actual quotes or otherwise coming up with estimates you deem to be as accurate as possible.

With the income and expenses underwritten, I was looking forward to the property tour. When the property manager and I met on Monday, I was really excited to finally be getting inside to look at things more closely, though I tried to keep my expectations in check. This was a 200-year-old property that had fallen into decline, and I knew we would find the good, the bad, and the ugly. So I braced myself and hoped for the best, knowing full well this wasn't likely to be pretty.

To be continued...

Chapter Fourteen
FINANCIAL ANALYSES

*Now the general who wins a battle makes many
calculations in his temple before the battle is
fought. The general who loses a battle makes
but few calculations beforehand. Thus do many
calculations lead to victory, and few calculations
to defeat: how much more no calculations at all! It
is by attention to this point that I can foresee who
is likely to win or lose.*

—SUN TZU, *THE ART OF WAR*

Having completed our analysis of income and expenses for Park Place
Apartments, we were able to finalize the pro forma, and it looked promising. Through a combination of lower expenses and income growth, we
were looking at an impressive increase in NOI, which was projected to
rise from about $432,000 to $765,000 over our five-year hold period. Now

it was time to complete our financial analysis and determine what price we could pay for the property while still hitting our target returns. The value-add potential wouldn't matter if we couldn't offer a competitive price.

Debt Projections

The first step after completing the income and expense pro formas is to input your debt terms. At this stage of the underwriting process, you should get verbal guidance on terms from a mortgage broker or directly from a preferred lender. Later in the process, when you get an actual term sheet, you can go back and refine things as necessary. But until you have a better handle on your own underwriting and pricing, it would be premature to hand over a loan package and start pushing for term sheets. You'll at least want to make sure you're submitting a competitive offer before imposing on a mortgage broker to devote a significant amount of effort on your behalf.

The key lending terms that will affect your underwriting include the LTV, interest rate, term, amortization period, and whether you will have an interest-only period and for how long. You should also start considering whether you will be able to fund any planned improvements with debt, which will affect the amount of equity required as well as the debt products you can secure. Some lending products will cover the cost of renovation while others won't.

If you plan to make significant improvements, your property valuation may end up being driven by post-construction cash flows and your offering price could far exceed what the in-place income would support. The problem with this scenario is that the T-12 and your pro forma may show an NOI that won't meet a lender's minimum thresholds for debt service coverage, and this can pose challenges with your financing.

Most lenders will look at the T-12 (and in some cases T-3 or T-1) as the floor for income and expect the property to satisfy their underwriting criteria for the new debt with that level of income. Note that the lender may adjust the T-12 income or expenses if there is something unreasonable or inconsistent with the property's current situation, and over time you'll learn how to look at things from their perspective.

As you begin to make your debt assumptions, you'll want to incorporate a check into your analysis that determines the loan size based on your anticipated lender constraints. You'll calculate the loan size based on the minimum debt service coverage ratio (DSCR), the maximum loan to value (LTV), and the minimum debt yield, all of which you can estimate at this stage or base on preliminary guidance from the lender or mortgage broker. If you calculate the loan amount based on each of these three constraints, the lowest loan amount will be the largest loan you can anticipate securing, depending on the lender's guidelines. Some lenders are more flexible than others.

Start with the DSCR. Look at your T-12, plug in your loan terms, and determine whether the DSCR is lower than 1.2x based on the T-12 gross effective income. Note that 1.2x to 1.25x is typical, but this requirement may vary between 1.15x and 1.3x, depending on your lender and the risk profile of the property. If you don't have adequate coverage and want to use a traditional loan product, you'll need to lower your loan amount until you reach the minimum DSCR. After this, you will check both the LTV and the debt yield, which is simply the NOI divided by the loan amount.

For Park Place Apartments we tested all three constraints against a purchase price of $8 million, the valuation we arrived at based on our initial screening. This price was lower than the seller's asking price of $9 million, but a good starting point for our financial analysis. Our project's debt constraints are shown in the table below.

DEBT CONSTRAINT TEST			
Purchase Price	$8,000,000		
T-12 NOI	$432,396		
Interest Rate Assumption	4.00%		
Term Assumption	30 yr Amort/10 yr Term		
	DSCR TEST	LTV TEST	YIELD TEST
DSCR—Min 1.200	1.200	1.258	1.222
Loan to Value (LTV)—Max 75.00%	78.62%	75.00%	77.21%
Yield—Min 7.00%	6.87%	7.21%	7.00%
Max Loan Amount	$6,289,748	**$6,000,000**	$6,177,086

Table 14-1 Park Place Apartments Debt Constraint Test

As a result of lending constraints, heavy value-add projects often require the use of shorter-term loan products with less rigid DSCR constraints, such as bridge loans. Bridge loans will increase the cost of borrowing but can reduce the amount of capital you need to close, avoid prepayment penalties, and boost your returns. After your upgrades are complete you can refinance into a permanent loan with better terms. The downside of this approach is that it introduces another risk into your project, since none of us know what interest rates or the lending environment will be, even in the near future. Due to this added risk, some investors avoid projects that can't be executed without securing longer-term debt from the outset. Others will fund 100 percent of the renovations with equity. Just keep in mind that the more cash you put in, the lower your returns will be, so funding major upgrades with cash will lower the price you can pay for the property compared to funding renovations with debt.

Equity Projections

The next step is to estimate how much cash you'll require. As we've discussed, depending on the terms of the financing secured, the equity may include part or all of the planned capital expenditures identified when underwriting income and expenses.

In addition to the cost of upgrades, you'll have to plan for a variety of cash requirements, including the following:

- **Down Payment:** The down payment for a property depends on the project's LTV and whether the loan is going to cover the cost of renovations in addition to the purchase price. If the financing is only for the acquisition, the down payment is simply the purchase price minus the loan amount.

$$\text{Down Payment (Acquisition Only)} = \text{Purchase Price} - \text{Debt}$$

If the renovations are included, you would subtract the loan amount from the total project cost, with the total project cost being the cost of acquisition plus construction.

$$\text{Down Payment} \left(\begin{array}{c} \text{Acquisition } + \\ \text{Construction} \end{array} \right) = \text{Total Project Cost} - \text{Debt}$$

- **Financing Fees:** The financing fees, including lender commitment fees and mortgage broker commissions or fees, are defined by the lender and broker. They are usually between 1 and 2 percent of the loan amount.

- **Closing and Transaction Costs:** Closing and transaction costs include things like loan documentation and legal fees (for lender and buyer); survey, title, and escrow charges; and third-party reports, such as the appraisal, environmental report, property condition assessment, and survey. On average, closing costs tend to be 1 percent of the purchase price for large multifamily acquisitions, but you should be able to get a more accurate estimate of closing costs from your lender.

- **Front-Loaded Expenses and Deposits:** You may need to pay your insurance premium at closing, as well as prorated property taxes, depending on the terms of the purchase and sale agreement (PSA). Some utility companies will require deposits for account transfers. If you incurred expenses for underwriting and due diligence activities, they would typically be reimbursed at closing.

- **Operating Funds:** You'll need to seed your operating account with enough working capital to comfortably pay your bills and operate the property until you can collect rent. You should also have an adequate cushion, or rainy-day fund, to tide you over in case things don't go according to plan. There's not much you can know for certain when underwriting, but you *can* be sure that something will go wrong at some point. Depending on the level of risk associated with the project, you should set aside an amount equivalent to at least two to three months of effective gross income (EGI).

- **Reserve and Escrow Seed Money:** Sometimes a lender will hold back part of the loan proceeds to cover high-priority property repairs identified during third party inspections, or to fund a replacement reserve account or escrow accounts such as property tax and insurance. Even if you are creating your own reserve and escrow accounts, you may need to set aside cash for this purpose.

- **Syndication Fees:** As explained in Chapter Three, if you are planning to raise equity through a syndication, you'll need to budget for any up-front fees. The most common are an acquisition fee and a loan guarantee fee.

- **Broker Commission:** The seller typically pays the broker commission. However, there are situations in which the buyer agrees to pay part or all of the commission. For example, if a broker brings you an off-market large multifamily property, you might pay them a commission of 2 to 3 percent.
- **Referral Fee:** If someone, such as a wholesaler, refers you to the seller, you will often pay a referral fee in exchange for the lead. This could be a flat fee or a percentage of the purchase price. These fees vary widely, but for larger properties, 1 percent of the purchase price is average.

At this stage, you will not know the purchase price, so for now, you can calculate the equity required by assuming you will pay either the rough-estimate price you arrived at during the screening process or full asking price. However, unlike smaller multifamily offerings, many large multifamily listings will not have an asking price. Instead, the OM will state something like "market pricing" or "market bid." In most circumstances, if you speak with the broker and establish some rapport, they will share what is commonly known as the whisper price, which is the broker's estimate of what the property is likely to sell for. The practice of not setting an asking price is designed to leave things wide open and encourage buyers to bring their best offer. Since the whisper price is often based on conversations with the seller, it amounts to an asking price.

Again, remember that underwriting is an iterative process, so your price assumption at this stage is not critical. As you get closer to nailing down a value, you will adjust your equity requirements accordingly. Experienced underwriters create the appropriate formulas in their spreadsheet to make these adjustments automatically based on changes to the purchase price.

Valuation

Now that you've completed your debt and equity projections, it's time to calculate your returns and determine a property's value. Before we delve into the formulas and calculations, note that there are different schools of thought regarding valuation. As a result, you should give some consideration to valuation at a high level before moving forward.

First, we challenge you to ask yourself, "What is my goal when valuing a property?" The most common answer is "To determine what it's worth." Then ask yourself, "What is it worth to whom? To me? Or to somebody else?" The answers to those questions may be very different.

Perhaps the most widely used valuation methodology for multifamily is the direct capitalization approach (or income capitalization approach), which we covered in greater depth in Volume I. The capitalization approach takes a property's NOI and applies a capitalization rate to it. The cap rate is the factor you use to translate NOI into market value and is expressed as a percentage. Brokers, appraisers, property managers, other investors, and market research are all great sources for determining the current cap rate.

$$\text{Cap Rate} = \text{NOI} \div \text{Purchase Price}$$

or

$$\text{Purchase Price} = \text{NOI} \div \text{Cap Rate}$$

The cap rate basically reflects what investors in that market are currently willing to pay for the NOI a property is generating. What does this mean? It means that the "value" you are calculating is an estimate of what *other people* are likely to pay for the property based on other transactions.

You are less likely to find a similar comp for your target property than for a single-family or even a small multifamily property, because most large multifamilies are unique. You can't simply say, "First Street Apartments sold for $7 million last month, so that's probably what my property will sell for." There are too many variables to consider. Since we can't compare apples to apples when it comes to property type, the capitalization approach compares the profitability of one investment to the profitability of another. Sales comps remain useful, but more for determining the cap rate and getting a rough idea of what price per unit similar properties are trading at.

Another dilemma is whether to base a purchase price on actual financials or on projected future returns. One school of thought is that you shouldn't pay for value that hasn't yet been unlocked. For example, if the rent *could* be 20 percent higher, you should not use that higher rate in your calculations because it has not yet occurred.

This approach is about making an investor feel they are paying a "fair" price, meaning they don't want to pay more than what other people would pay. In fact, most investors have a strong drive to pay *less* than others. Thinking they overpaid or were somehow taken advantage of can eat people up. Everyone wants to feel like they got a great deal!

What's wrong with this? Nothing, if paying a price that people would consider fair or getting a great deal is your highest priority. But with large multifamily, many buyers look at properties from a completely different viewpoint. Most of them are deploying funds entrusted to them by others, who are seeking certain rates of return. While these buyers need to invest their funds responsibly, they're not concerned with what other people consider fair or whether they might overpay. If they can deploy their capital and achieve their target returns, who cares? Everyone is happy.

Instead, they are looking for properties that will help them achieve their target returns with an acceptable level of risk. Achieving this goal requires them to underwrite a property as thoroughly and accurately as possible in order to project the cash it will generate and determine what price will allow them to achieve their target returns.

These investors are most interested in the performance of the property over the long run, which means making assumptions for the future. Because they are basing their purchase price on projected returns, they are likely to pay more for a property than someone who's looking only at actual numbers.

Obviously, property valuation is not done in a vacuum, and if a large multifamily investor can find (or create) an opportunity to avoid competition and scoop up a property at a price that will yield even better returns, they will jump on it and be totally psyched about it. However, the approach of larger, more experienced investors is generally more disciplined, less emotional, and less influenced by the goals and actions of other investors. Cap rates are a concern only insofar as they might affect the outcome of an appraisal.

As a result, your North Star in underwriting should be your target returns, which usually depend on the source of equity. For the most part, target returns reflect the demands of whoever puts in the cash. If you're financing a project yourself, you get to decide what you're comfortable with—but if you're raising capital, you'll need to gauge what returns you'll need to offer in order to entice investors. This will drive your target returns, which will in turn drive your valuation.

Value at Disposition

In order to calculate the project's returns, you first need to make some predictions about the value of the property at disposition (when you sell), also known as reversion value. In most underwriting, it's the sale of a property that generates the greatest returns, so the assumptions that go into the exit value are critical and have an outsize impact on projections.

While cap rates may not be the driving factor in the initial acquisition of large multifamily properties, they are relied on heavily for estimating a property's exit value. Since cap rates are driven by what the market is willing to pay for NOI, it is perfectly logical to use a so-called terminal cap rate, or exit cap rate, to predict what price a property would command for the NOI you project it will be generating on exit. Perhaps less logical is the idea that you can predict with confidence what the cap rate will be five to ten years in the future. Despite this uncertainty, cap rates are generally considered the best tool at our disposal.

In theory, cap rates are unpredictable and are as likely to move down as up. However, a solid argument could be made that the average of all these potential outcomes would be right where they are at the time you complete your underwriting. Nonetheless, standard practice is to incorporate a modicum of conservatism into this assumption and estimate that the exit cap rate will be higher than current levels. In other words, the market will be paying slightly less in the future than they are today for the same NOI.

The first step, then, in estimating an exit cap rate is to determine what you should use for the current cap rate. You can use either the "going-in" cap rate (ratio of T-12 NOI to the purchase price) or the market cap rate. If you can get good market data, the market cap rate is preferable, as there may be property-specific factors at play that could skew the going-in cap rate. (For example, current rents may be far below market, which would artificially reduce your going-in cap rate.) If you find yourself in a situation where there is no basis for determining a market cap rate, such as for a highly remote or unique property, the going-in cap rate may be the most reasonable option.

How much higher should you assume cap rates will be at the time of exit? Some investors will add a fixed amount, say fifty to a hundred basis points, or .5 to 1 percent, for a disposition five to ten years in the future. Another common practice is to assume a certain increase per year, usually ten to twenty basis points for each year of the projected holding period, which is a way of taking into consideration the progressively greater uncertainty associated with predicting cap rates further in the future.

Keep in mind that the project returns are highly sensitive to the exit cap, so try to stay objective. If your projection is too conservative, you'll have trouble finding deals that satisfy your target criteria. If you're overly aggressive and assume your cap rate won't rise at all, you'll heighten your risk of not meeting projected returns.

Therefore, the steps for calculating a property's value at disposition are:

- Calculate the property's NOI in the final year of ownership.
- Determine the current market cap rate by contacting brokers, appraisers, property managers, or other investors, or conduct other market research. If you can't get good data on the market cap rate, use the going-in cap rate.
- Estimate the exit cap rate by adding fifty to a hundred basis points (or ten to twenty basis points per year) to the market or going-in cap rate. For example, with a hold period of five years, you would assume an exit cap between .5 and 1.0 percent above current levels.
- Divide the NOI by the exit cap rate to calculate a sale price, or reversion value.
- Reduce the sale price by the estimated transaction costs and debt balance payoff to determine the sales proceeds. Closing costs will typically run in the neighborhood of 1 percent, plus broker fees. If you are syndicating the project, there may also be disposition fees.

For Park Place Apartments, you can see in the table below how the cap rate increases each year over the five-year hold period. We also found that the market cap rate of 5.75 percent is slightly greater than the going-in cap rate of 5.4 percent. The difference is primarily due to lower-than-market rents. We elected to use the market cap rate, which is the more conservative assumption. We then assumed a fifteen-basis-point increase in the first two years and a ten-basis-point increase per year for years three through five. What was the rationale for these projections? It was a judgment call we made based on the circumstances. We elected to use a higher increase in the early years because cap rates in this particular market were at historically high levels at the time we did the analysis. With little visibility beyond that, we then elected to drop the annual increase down to ten basis points starting in year three.

	T-12	YEAR 1	YEAR 2	YEAR 3	YEAR 4	YEAR 5
Price/Value	$8,000,000	$8,809,426	$10,706,805	$11,657,988	$11,848,260	$12,044,468
Effective Gross Income (EGI)	$1,104,304	$1,111,409	$1,254,794	$1,339,780	$1,379,525	$1,420,450
Total Operating Expenses	$672,272	$591,653	$607,033	$622,814	$639,008	$655,626
Net Operating Income (NOI)	$432,032	$519,756	$647,762	$716,966	$740,516	$764,824
Market Cap Rate	5.75%	5.90%	6.05%	6.15%	6.25%	6.35%
Going-In Cap Rate	5.40%					

Table 14-2 Park Place Apartments Cap Rate Projections

After you've determined the value at the end of the hold period, you can estimate the cash that would be generated from the sale of the property. Below is the cash that would be generated from the sale of Park Place Apartments, assuming a transaction cost at exit of 5 percent, primarily for commissions and legal fees.

Value at Resale		**$12,044,468**
Net Operating Income (NOI)		$764,824
Cap Rate @ Resale		6.35%
Transaction Costs	5.00%	($602,223)
Sale Proceeds Before Debt Payoff		**$11,442,245**
Payoff Loan Balance		($5,742,777)
Prepayment Penalty		$0
Gross Proceeds from Sale		**$5,699,468**

Now that you have estimated the cash that will be generated by the sale of the property, you can calculate the target returns, the most common of which are the cash-on-cash return, average annual return, total return, internal rate of return, and equity multiple.

Cash-on-Cash Returns

One of the most widely used target returns is the cash-on-cash (CoC) return, also known as the cash return on investment, which is the percentage return earned on the cash that goes into the project. Investors like this metric because it's simple to grasp and makes it easy to weigh returns against those of other asset classes. The use of leverage reduces the amount of cash needed to acquire a property, which drives up a project's CoC return and is part of what makes real estate an appealing option for so many investors, especially when compared to stocks and bonds, which enjoy no such advantage.

Calculating a project's CoC return is fairly straightforward. Traditionally, you would calculate the CoC return by taking a property's cash flow and dividing it by the total projected equity that you will invest in the project.

$$\text{CoC Return} = \text{Annual Cash Flow} \div \text{Total Invested Equity}$$

The annual cash flow used to calculate the CoC return is arrived at by deducting your debt service from your NOI and subtracting any other cash demands that the property might incur that weren't captured in your income and expense projections. Examples include planned CapEx and lender-mandated escrows or reserves that don't already show up as a line item in your expenses.

$$\text{Cash Flow} = \text{NOI} - \text{Debt Service} - \text{Non-Expense Cash Demands}$$

While calculating the CoC return is intuitive and helpful, the metric also has its limitations. CoC returns do not factor in any changes in a property's value, annual principal paydown, or tax benefits because these factors aren't directly realized in the form of annual cash distributions. CoC returns also do not account for the time value of money, meaning that future cash flows are not discounted, so the CoC return is not affected by the timing of the distributions. This failure to account for the timing of the cash flows is a weakness, since it's clearly more beneficial to get your cash back sooner rather than later.

The target CoC return for multifamily investors can vary widely but is typically in the range of 6 to 12 percent, depending on the risk profile. Investors naturally expect higher returns for riskier projects. The projected CoC returns can also vary widely over the life of a project, so it's important to calculate the CoC return for each year of the holding period. In some types of investments, such as development or major turnarounds, investors are willing to sacrifice CoC returns in the early years for larger paydays down the road.

For Park Place Apartments, we are assuming an exit after a five-year hold, as shown in the table below.

CASH-ON-CASH RETURNS	T-12	YEAR 1	YEAR 2	YEAR 3	YEAR 4	YEAR 5
Effective Gross Income (EGI)	$1,104,304	$1,111,409	$1,254,794	$1,339,780	$1,379,525	$1,420,450
Total Operating Expenses	$672,272	$591,653	$607,033	$622,814	$639,008	$655,626
Net Operating Income (NOI)	$432,032	$519,756	$647,762	$716,966	$740,516	$764,824
Less: CapEx Reserves		$36,000	$36,000	$36,000	$36,000	$36,000
Less: Debt Service Payment		$240,000	$240,000	$240,000	$363,750	$363,750
Cash Flow		$243,756	$371,762	$440,966	$340,766	$365,074
Invested Equity		$3,412,095	$3,412,095	$3,412,095	$3,412,095	$3,412,095
Cash-on-Cash Return		7.14%	10.90%	12.92%	9.99%	10.70%
Avg Cash-on-Cash Return		7.14%	9.02%	10.32%	10.24%	10.33%

Table 14-3 Park Place Apartments Cash-on-Cash Returns

If you're planning to syndicate and offer your investors a preferred return, you should aim for a CoC return that will allow you to meet this level. Note that for syndications you will need to calculate all your returns at both the project level and then separately for your limited partners. That's because in a syndication the rights to distributions are not 100 percent aligned with the sources of equity. As a result, LP returns are likely to be lower than the full-project-level returns, as you can see below.

CASH-ON-CASH RETURNS	T-12	YEAR 1	YEAR 2	YEAR 3	YEAR 4	YEAR 5
Effective Gross Income (EGI)	$1,104,304	$1,111,409	$1,254,794	$1,339,780	$1,379,525	$1,420,450
Total Operating Expenses	$672,272	$591,653	$607,033	$622,814	$639,008	$655,626
Net Operating Income (NOI)	$432,032	$519,756	$647,762	$716,966	$740,516	$764,824
Less: CapEx Reserves		$36,000	$36,000	$36,000	$36,000	$36,000
Less: Debt Service Payment		$240,000	$240,000	$240,000	$363,750	$363,750
Cash Flow		**$243,756**	**$371,762**	**$440,966**	**$340,766**	**$365,074**
Invested Equity		$3,412,095	$3,412,095	$3,412,095	$3,412,095	$3,412,095
Cash-on-Cash Return		7.14%	10.90%	12.92%	9.99%	10.70%
Avg Cash-on-Cash Return		7.14%	9.02%	10.32%	10.24%	10.33%
Limited Partners CoC Returns (@ 7% Preferred + 70% Equity Share)						
Cash-on-Cash Return		6.66%	9.44%	10.73%	8.67%	9.15%
Avg Cash-on-Cash Return		6.66%	8.05%	8.94%	8.87%	8.93%

Table 14-4 Park Place Apartments LP Cash-on-Cash Returns

Finally, note that the calculation of CoC returns is based on the total equity invested *as of the end of that period*. That means you need to base the annual return on *how much equity remains committed* at the end of each year. This distinction comes into play when you have a capital event that returns equity, such as a cash-out refinance. In other words, let's say you raise equity to fund your project through a syndication. Then, after two years, you've added a lot of value and decide to do a refinance and return half of the investors' cash. From this point forward, your CoC return would be calculated based on that remaining half that is left invested in the project, since the other half of the capital has already been returned to investors and is no longer at risk.

Average Annual Return

Many investors favor the average annual return (AAR) because unlike the CoC return, the AAR factors in all the cash distributions over the full life of the project, including both operating profits and return of investor capital from refinancing or sale of the property.

The AAR is a measure of the average return over the entire holding period and is expressed as a percentage. To calculate the AAR, you add up all the individual annual return rates of your investment and divide by the number of years you anticipate holding the property.

$$\text{AAR} = \frac{\text{S Annual CoC Returns}}{\text{Incl. Return of Invested Equity}} \div \text{Hold Period}$$

For Park Place Apartments, the AAR would be calculated as follows:

AVERAGE ANNUAL RETURN	YEAR 1	YEAR 2	YEAR 3	YEAR 4	YEAR 5
Gross Proceeds from Sale					$5,699,468
Less: Invested Equity					$3,412,095
Net Proceeds from Sale					$2,287,373
Cash Flow	$243,756	$371,762	$440,966	$340,766	$365,074
Annual Cash Flows	$243,756	$371,762	$440,966	$340,766	$2,652,447
Project Total Net Cash Flows					**$4,049,697**
Invested Equity					$3,412,095
Average Annual Return					**23.7%**

AAR = Projected Total Net Cash Flows / Invested Equity / # of Years Invested in Project

LP Average Annual Return (@ 7% Preferred + 70% Equity Share)					
LP Share @ 70% of Net Proceeds from Sale					$1,601,161
Cash Flow	$227,085	$322,240	$366,263	$295,705	$312,291
Annual Cash Flows	$227,085	$322,240	$366,263	$295,705	$1,913,452
LP Total Net Cash Flows					$3,124,746
Invested Equity					$3,412,095
Average Annual Return					**18.3%**

Table 14-5 Park Place Apartments Average Annual Return

Total Return

The total return for the project is calculated by adding up all the cash distributions over the life of the project (excluding return of capital) and dividing it by the total equity invested. This metric is also expressed as a percentage.

$$\text{Total Return} = \frac{\text{Cash Distributions}}{\text{Excl. Return of Capital}} \div \text{Total Equity Invested} \times 100\%$$

PROJECT TOTAL RETURN	
Project Total Net Cash Flows	$4,049,697
Invested Equity	$3,412,095
Total Return	**118.7%**
Limited Partners	
LP Total Net Cash Flows	$3,124,746
Invested Equity	$3,412,095
LP Total Return	**91.6%**

Equity Multiple

Another widely used metric is the equity multiple (EM), or equity multiplier, which is simply the factor by which the equity investment has increased. To calculate the EM, you divide the total cash distributions (including the return of your original invested equity) by the total equity invested.

$$\text{EM} = \text{Total Cash Distributions} \div \text{Total Equity Invested}$$

For example, if you invested $1 million and ended up getting $2 million back, your EM would be 2. Investors are typically seeking an EM between 1.5 and 3 for a holding period of five to ten years. The longer it takes to achieve your target EM, the more problematic, because like CoC and the other types of returns covered so far, this metric does not factor in the time value of money.

For Park Place Apartments, you can see in the table below the EM for the full project and for the LPs.

PROJECT EQUITY MULTIPLE	
Gross Proceeds from Sale	$5,699,468
Cash Flows	$1,762,324
Gross Total Proceeds	$7,461,792
Invested Equity	$3,412,095
Equity Multiple	**2.19**
LIMITED PARTNERS	
Return Invested Equity From Sale	$3,412,095
Gain from Sale	$1,601,161
Gross Proceeds from Sale	$5,013,256
Cash Flows	$1,523,584
Gross Total Proceeds	$6,536,841
Invested Equity	$3,412,095
Equity Multiple	**1.92**

Internal Rate of Return

The internal rate of return (IRR) is one of the most important performance metrics because it measures the annualized rate of earnings on an investment taking into consideration the time value of money. Unfortunately, IRR is also the most complex of the commonly used returns.

To understand IRR, you first need to appreciate the underlying concept of net present value (NPV), which is the value of future cash flows discounted to the present. The purpose of NPV is to factor in the timing of returns. Simply put, $1 is worth more today than it will be in the future, primarily because if you received that dollar now, you could invest it and earn interest. Not only that, but the interest you earned would compound.

The same principle applies to annual returns from your multifamily investments—getting those returns sooner rather than later is always preferable, and worth more. This is where discounting comes in. When you calculate the NPV of a future cash flow, you discount it by applying an adjustment to reflect the time value of money. It's like a reverse compounding effect that accounts for the earning potential of the money.

The formula for calculating the NPV of future cash flows is:

$$\text{NPV} = \sum_{t=0}^{n} \frac{R_t}{(1+i)^t}$$

Where:
Rt = Net Cash Flow in Year t
i = Discount Rate
t = Number of Years

For example, if you had a cash flow of \$50,000 in year five and your discount rate was 7 percent, your NPV for that year's cash flow would be calculated as follows:

$$\$50{,}000 \div (1+.07)^5 = \$50{,}000 \div 1.4 = \$35{,}714$$

In other words, if you have an alternative investment that could earn you 7 percent, then receiving \$50,000 in cash in five years would be equivalent to \$35,714 cash today. For your multifamily project, you would similarly discount each year's cash flow and add them together to find your NPV.

How does this relate to IRR? The IRR is the discount rate that would make the NPV of all cash flow equal to your initial cash investment. It's similar to an average AAR on your project's cash flows once you factor in the time value of money.

Here is another way to think about it. You already know the value today of the initial equity investment. It doesn't need to be discounted because it's going in at the start of the project before any time has passed. That initial cash invested is your NPV. That initial equity is going to grow, and the returns are in the form of annual cash flows, which you've projected. The IRR reflects those returns and is the rate you would have to discount those cash flows by to convert them back to the initial equity investment. IRR is a sort of reverse calculation in which you're backing into the rate of return.

To calculate your IRR, you will plug your initial equity investment for NPV into the formula below and then solve for IRR.

$$NPV = \sum_{t=1}^{T} \frac{C_t}{(1 + IRR)^t} - C_0$$

Where:
C_t = Net cash inflow during the period t
C_0 = Total initial investment costs
IRR = The internal rate of return
t = The number of time periods

Calculating IRR can be confusing, in part because we're far more accustomed to using an initial investment amount and then applying a rate of return in order to calculate how much money we will make. In the case of IRR, we're using the initial investment and the later cash flows in order to calculate the rate. Not only that, but in calculating the rate of return we are also factoring in the time value of money.

What is a good target IRR? That depends entirely on your goals and what kinds of projects you're taking on. If you're raising capital, it will depend on what your investors demand. Target IRRs will typically range from 10 to 20 percent or more, with the majority in the range of 13 to 17 percent. In our experience, the most common target IRR is 15 percent. In reality, the target IRR should factor in the quality of the asset and the needs of the investor. Lower IRRs should be acceptable for investments that are lower risk, while higher IRRs should be demanded for higher-risk projects.

Before wrapping up our discussion of IRR, we want to acknowledge that the equation for calculating IRR is highly complex and, frankly, beyond what most of us could reasonably expect to solve. Brandon and I are certainly not going to be calculating any IRRs with a pencil and paper—that's for sure. If we did manage to come up with a number, we'd probably have no idea whether we'd made a mistake. Fortunately, there are manageable solutions to this dilemma thanks to the miracle of modern technology.

The most widely used spreadsheets, including Microsoft Excel and Google Sheets, have functions that can calculate IRR for you, as do many financial calculators and apps, if that's your jam. As discussed in Chapter Twelve, there are commercially available software programs specifically designed to assist you with all your multifamily underwriting calculations—an excellent choice for most situations. If you'd like to further educate yourself on IRR and other return metrics, there are plenty of tutorials just a Google search away.

For Park Place Apartments we calculated the IRR using an Excel spreadsheet and the results are summarized in the table below.

PROJECT IRR				
	Invested Equity	Cash Flows	Proceeds from Sale	Total
Year 0	($3,412,095)	$0	$0	($3,412,095)
Year 1		$243,756	$0	$243,756
Year 2		$371,762	$0	$371,762
Year 3		$440,966	$0	$440,966
Year 4		$340,766	$0	$340,766
Year 5		$365,074	$5,699,468	$6,064,542
IRR				19.23%

LP IRR				
	Invested Equity	Cash Flows	Proceeds from Sale	Total
Year 0	($3,412,095)	$0	$0	($3,412,095)
Year 1		$227,085	$0	$227,085
Year 2		$322,240	$0	$322,240
Year 3		$366,263	$0	$366,263
Year 4		$295,705	$0	$295,705
Year 5		$312,291	$5,013,256	$5,325,547
IRR				15.66%

Table 14-6 Park Place Apartments IRR. This calculation was done in a spreadsheet using the IRR function.

How to Price the Property

Once you've established your target returns and completed your calculations, it's time to arrive at a purchase price. *Simply put, your maximum purchase price will be whatever valuation will achieve your minimum allowable returns.* Therefore, if any of your target returns are lower than what's acceptable to you, you'll have to reduce your price to a level such that those returns rise to meet your threshold.

For Park Place Apartments we planned to syndicate, and our target LP returns were as follows:

$$\text{Average CoC Return} \geq 8.5\%$$
$$\text{AAR} \geq 17.0\%$$
$$\text{IRR} \geq 14.0\%$$

We ran our preliminary calculations based on a tentative value of $8 million, which was $1 million below the seller's asking price, and when we calculated our returns, they came in above our minimums. In order to arrive at our maximum purchase price, we went through several iterations of adjusting the price and rerunning our calculations until we determined that $8.25 million was the maximum price we could pay for this asset and still hit our targets.

Stress-Testing Your Underwriting

The final step of your financial analysis is to do a stress test or sensitivity analysis for the project. This involves checking how the project will perform if some of the key assumptions you made during underwriting were incorrect. In other words, what would it take for the project to fail?

The number of ways to stress-test a deal is practically unlimited. You could pick any of the hundreds of variables or assumptions you made and evaluate the impact of changes to them. There are time constraints, however, and most investors will settle on a few specific scenarios to evaluate. Examples of common stress and sensitivity tests include:

- **Occupancy and Rent:** Take a look at how your project performance varies as you adjust occupancy and rent projections. How low could occupancy drop before you can no longer pay your expenses and meet your lending obligations? This is called your break-even occupancy level and is something many underwriters will scrutinize.

You should also check how fluctuations in your rent projections and rent growth will affect projected returns.

- **Change in Interest Rates:** It can take two to three months or longer to close, and the interest rate can change. Therefore, you'll want to examine how different interest rates can affect your projected returns and confirm that the project will still work if rates rise more than expected.

- **Drop in NOI:** A project's actual performance is rarely as smooth as your underwriting projections. Projects can go through cycles and suffer setbacks, resulting in peaks and valleys in the NOI. Take a look through the property's history and find those valleys. Would the property be able to service the debt and perform to your satisfaction if these levels were revisited?

- **Capital Expenditures:** For projects with substantial planned improvements, you should examine what would happen if there are cost overruns or delays. Both scenarios are common and can affect returns.

- **Exit Cap Rates and Reversion Values:** Projecting cap rates five to ten years in the future is inherently somewhat speculative, so you should consider the potential impact on returns should the exit cap fall above or below your projections.

In addition to the above, you should also test project-specific concerns. For example, maybe after careful review you remain uncertain about your staffing projections. In that case, you should check how the property would perform if you end up needing to hire another person. Let's say you are projecting pet income, but you still aren't sure that's going to work in this market. If so, you should run the numbers without it to ensure you'll be okay regardless.

Based on the results of these analyses, you will weigh the risks and determine whether you'd like to take any follow-up actions. You might want to dig further into an important assumption to get more comfortable with your forecast. Or you could decide to adjust the target returns to better reflect the level of risk involved, which would result in offering a lower price. Or you may very well determine that you're comfortable moving forward as is. We're back to that recurring theme of sound judgment. Use the results of your stress test to make the best decision you can.

Underwriting Advice

We have now covered everything you need to know to underwrite a large multifamily property—at least from a quantitative standpoint. But there's more to underwriting than just the numbers. Qualitative considerations often come into play as well. An investor's personality or emotions can influence underwriting to a far greater extent than most people realize.

Remain Objective

If another investor with the same target returns as you looks at the same property and goes through the same underwriting process as you, they will almost certainly arrive at a different valuation. Why? It has a lot to do with the assumptions behind the data you're plugging in. While the formulas for valuing a property are pretty clear-cut, you'll still be making plenty of judgment calls. The key variables that will drive your valuation include income and expense projections, capitalization rates, debt terms, and value-add strategies.

The key to good underwriting is to remain completely objective. However, plenty of investors fall into one of two camps:

1. **Overly Aggressive:** When you're interested in acquiring a property, it's easy to get caught up in the excitement and be overly aggressive with your assumptions. Maybe you're just sick of not winning deals. If you're inherently optimistic, competitive, or impatient, you'll need to make a concerted effort to rein yourself in when underwriting an investment property.

2. **Overly Conservative:** Many investors fall prey to their fear of making a wrong decision. When they underwrite a property, that insecurity will manifest itself in overly conservative assumptions. Lots of investors pride themselves on their conservative underwriting, but they can easily go too far.

Dozens of assumptions go into underwriting. If each of these assumptions is even slightly tinged by your optimism or skittishness, it can have a compounding effect and you won't get a true picture of a property. The end result? You'll either pay too much and set yourself up for failure or offer too little and miss out on what could have been a great opportunity.

Are we saying not to be aggressive or conservative? Not at all. That is entirely your choice. In fact, we would encourage people to be conservative—especially when lacking experience. Just apply that conservatism *after* the underwriting is complete. You can run some stress tests to get a better feel for the risks involved, and then go back and adjust a couple of your variables—but stay true throughout the underwriting as much as possible. Keep asking yourself, *What is most likely?*

Remain Flexible

The reality of multifamily investing is that there won't always be time to do all the underwriting outlined in this book. If you're new to underwriting, it can take as long as twenty hours to perform correctly. If you're building your own spreadsheet for the first time, it can take even longer. As you gain experience, you may be able to cut that down to eight hours or so. But sometimes you'll need to move quickly or risk missing a great opportunity. While thorough underwriting is important, how much depth to go into at this stage in the process and how much to leave until you're under contract is yet another judgment call.

You need to be flexible, but you need to be smart. Weigh the circumstances and think carefully about the consequences of missing something, which can be drastically different for every deal. If a seller or broker says there is a tight timeline and encourages you to just get an offer in, you can streamline your underwriting process and make it clear that you'll be completing a more thorough analysis as part of your due diligence. Tell them it's not ideal, but you can accommodate the timeline as long as they understand that if you find problems later, you're going to have to work things out. However, if you have adequate time, you should always try to do as much analysis as you're able to up front in order to avoid any confrontations later—particularly if you're going to incorporate a hard deposit into your purchase offer (which we'll cover in the next chapter).

Get Help

Finally, if the underwriting metrics and methodologies covered here are new to you, it's natural to feel overwhelmed. There is a lot to digest, but don't panic. Remember: There are plenty of tools out there that can help. As discussed in Chapter Twelve and in our coverage of IRR, we encourage you to use one of the many professionally developed tools available for the financial underwriting of large multifamily properties. While it's important to grasp the basics, there is too much at stake to risk errors, and very few of us have the skills to fully develop an accurate and efficient model on our own.

Also keep in mind that you don't have to go it alone. Few people venture into large multifamily investing without support or partners. Don't be afraid to ask for help from a more experienced investor, coach, or mentor.

Park Place Apartments

Although Park Place Apartments was an attractive and exciting project for us, the maximum purchase price we arrived at through our underwriting was too low to be competitive. It turned out the seller was working with other prospective buyers, and just as we were finishing up our underwriting, we were notified that the seller had already received and accepted a full-price offer.

The outcome was disappointing, but that's the norm. We underwrite a lot of deals, and the vast majority aren't wins. Nobody said this was easy. From experience, we *can* say that when you eventually land a deal, the extraordinary effort involved will feel worthwhile. We set aside Park Place and made a note to follow up with the owner in a couple of weeks in case their deal were to fall through. Then we rolled up our sleeves and moved on to the next prospect.

KEY TAKEAWAYS

- In order to complete your financial analysis, you first need to check the debt constraints and then estimate your financing terms and equity requirements.
- When valuing a multifamily property, your purchase price will be driven by your target returns, which usually reflect the demands of the equity source. Exit capitalization rates drive reversion values and have outsize impacts on returns.
- The most widely used return metrics include the CoC return, AAR, total return, EM, and IRR. The IRR, while more complex, is the only metric that takes the time value of money into consideration.
- Your maximum purchase price is arrived at by determining what valuation will achieve your minimum allowable returns. Once you arrive at a price, you should always do a stress test.

Madison Barracks: Part V

The walk-through of the Apartments at Madison Barracks proved interesting. With regard to the condition of the property, the issues were pretty much as expected, though the problems were unfortunately more extensive than I had hoped. There were more down units than we'd realized, and despite the high level of vacancy, there were very few rent-ready units. Some units had extensive water damage. One unit had fire damage. A couple of others had obvious structural issues. Most of the others hadn't been touched since the last resident had moved out; many had furniture and trash strewn around. Overall, the place was very run-down, with loads of deferred maintenance. Many of the porches and windows were starting to rot, while a number of the roofs were leaking badly and in desperate need of repair or replacement.

On a positive note, a surprising number of the units retained original architectural features such as beautiful hardwood floors, exposed brick and stone walls, and ornate custom woodwork. We also discovered a historical marker outside one apartment indicating that it had once been occupied by President Ulysses S. Grant, who served two tours of duty at Madison Barracks as a junior army officer. These unique features and history gave the property tons of character and supported my long-term vision for it.

Another unexpected discovery was that a significant number of the apartments had been merged at some point. For example, there were a couple of four-bedroom apartments that had once been leased out as four studios, and some of the two-bedroom units had been created from a one bedroom and a studio. In fact, while we counted 126 units based on the current configuration, it appeared there was the potential to add at least a dozen or more units without too many alterations.

Encouraged, I began to pull together some capital improvement plans. The income potential was there, but wow, was there a lot of work to be done. The plan of attack would be to invest in some much-needed repairs, bring most of the down units back online, make some capital improvements, lower the rents, and lease the place up.

After working the initial plans for value-add and nailing down the expense projections as best we could, we were able to create our pro forma and complete our financial analysis. Based on our underwriting, we felt we could go up to a maximum price of $5.5 million. This was far lower than the $7.5 million the seller had been asking a few years ago, but there was just no way we could pay anywhere near that much. If I squinted my eyes and tilted my head, I could maybe see it work out for us at $5.6 million—but this property was beginning to make me uncomfortable, and I don't like to squint. I like to keep my eyes wide open.

There were many variables and assumptions underlying this valuation, which left plenty of room for error. This is true for most projects, but even more so when there are significant improvement projects involved and you're dealing with an older, neglected property that is almost guaranteed to have some skeletons in the closet. You have to expect the unexpected and include some contingency funds in your underwriting.

Thank God we included contingency funds for the Apartments at Madison Barracks, because things would not go as planned. It would have been impossible to see what was coming. We would need every last penny.

To be continued...

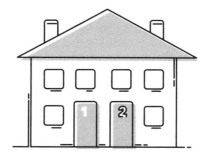

Chapter Fifteen

MAKING OFFERS AND NEGOTIATING DEALS

[The] basic rule of negotiation is to know what you want, what you need to walk away with in order to be whole.

—PHIL KNIGHT

With the underwriting complete, you're ready for the exciting next step—making an offer! But before you forge ahead, there are many factors to consider. One of the first is whether the seller is adhering to a specific timeline and process for offers or if they are willing to consider offers as they come in. Frequently when a large multifamily property is brought to market by a broker, they will work with the seller to come up with a timeline and process in advance—particularly if they anticipate a high level of interest.

Call for Offers

Brokers will often set aside a specific period of time to allow all interested parties to learn about the opportunity and complete their underwriting. This will typically be between one and three weeks but can sometimes be longer.

Usually, the listing broker will issue a "call for offers" and notify all interested parties when the offers are due. If they anticipate a lot of competition, they may require prospective buyers to complete a questionnaire in order to get a better picture of the buyers' strength as well as the depth of their underwriting efforts and their plans for the property. This questionnaire may be introduced during the call for offers or later, in the "best and final" round.

The goal is to determine how likely the prospective buyer is to follow through on their letter of intent (LOI) and close the deal without issues. Because in the end, it doesn't really matter how great an offer is if the buyer won't or can't follow through.

Best and Final

Once the deadline for offers passes, the broker will typically sit down with the seller and review all the offers. They will generally weigh the strength of the offers and buyers, select the strongest, and then go back to this select list of prospective buyers and request that they submit their "best and final" offer within a shorter period of time—usually no more than several days. If there is one particularly strong offer that stands out above the rest, they may negotiate exclusively with that one buyer.

Whether a seller adheres to a specific schedule can be good or bad, depending on what position you're in. If there's no defined schedule, that often means the buyers with earliest access to the deal will have an opportunity to wrap it up before it is more broadly marketed. If you're on good terms with the listing broker, you may be able to get a deal nailed down without having to go through competitive bidding. Otherwise, you may get left out in the cold and never even see the deal before it's been locked up by someone else.

What to Offer

In the prior chapter we covered the process for arriving at a maximum purchase price for a property, but that doesn't mean this is the price you should offer. Bear in mind that there will usually be some negotiation, and if you leave yourself no room to move, it can be harder to reach an agreement. That said, if you're trying to get through to a best-and-final round, you have to balance the desire for negotiating room with the possibility of coming in too low to make the cutoff.

It can be tempting throughout this process to seek input from the broker, and you should do so, but proceed with caution. Establishing a good rapport with the listing broker can be helpful as you figure out what approach to take, but remember that their primary responsibility is to the seller. They may also have deeper allegiances to other buyers than they do to you—especially if you haven't closed a deal with them before. Imagine they've closed a dozen deals with another buyer over the past five years, netting millions of dollars in commissions. How do you think they'll advise the seller if it comes down to you and that other buyer? Unless you have established a high level of trust with a broker, don't share anything with them that you wouldn't want repeated, and take everything they say with a grain of salt.

Another trap some investors fall into is thinking too much about what other investors are going to offer or what the seller is willing to accept. These considerations should not affect how you value a property. Such thoughts are usually rooted in a fear of overpaying and will cause you to second-guess yourself. You know what your top price is, so focus on that and work backward from there to formulate your negotiating strategy. Based on our experience negotiating on hundreds of multifamily properties, the greedier you get trying to land a property at a substantial discount, the less likely you are to get the deal. Maybe you're okay with that, because every once in a great while, swinging for the fences can actually work. It's fine to push hard for a bargain as long as you remain professional, don't burn bridges, and are comfortable missing out on a deal. Just bear in mind that finding deals that meet your investment criteria and target returns can be a real challenge, so be sure you can live with the consequences if you take that approach.

Timing

In terms of timing, you need to figure out the lay of the land. Even if the broker issues a call for offers, it's worth asking whether the seller is open to considering the right offer on a rolling basis. Some brokers maintain a strict policy of following through on their timelines, while others will short-circuit the entire process if they can get their target price from a solid buyer and wrap things up quickly.

When there is no call for offers, speed is of the essence. Occasionally properties are offered for sale, through a broker or otherwise, at a below-market asking price. That may be due to the seller's personal goals or based on a broker's misguided underwriting. In either case, if you can wrap up your underwriting and get a strong letter of intent in before the competition (more about that in a minute), you might be able to get an asset under contract at an attractive price and achieve superior returns.

Negotiation

Sometimes you may find yourself with more room to negotiate or extend the timeline, for example, when you have some level of confidence that the seller is not engaged in conversation with other prospective buyers and is unlikely to do so. This can happen when a deal is truly off-market or a property has some characteristic that makes it undesirable to other parties. In these situations, you have the opportunity to employ more negotiating tactics. Here are a few tips we have found helpful:

- **Don't bid against yourself.** Always try to get the other party to state their price first and make them counter before changing your offer.
- **Make an offer that includes two or more options.** When there are choices, the other party will tend to weigh them rather than just decline an offer or counter with a price of their own. Keep your options straightforward, and don't offer so many that they become overwhelming.
- **Use specific numbers.** Big, round numbers tend to look like they are more negotiable than something more uneven, which is more likely to be interpreted as a number you arrived at after careful calculation. Five-million dollars looks a lot less serious than $5,039,500.

Finally, recognize that the strength of an offer rarely lies exclusively in the price. Make a concerted effort to learn everything you can about the seller and gain insight into their motivations. If there is a broker involved, probe them for details, and do your own research on the seller as well. Figure out what's important to the seller, and you may be able to craft an offer that will set you apart and grab their attention.

Sometimes introducing non-monetary items can help with negotiations. For example, you could agree to retain the current staff or not to change the property's name. One time we learned that a seller hadn't taken a vacation in ten years, so we included an all-expenses-paid vacation in the offer. Understanding a seller's priorities and constraints may also allow you to be creative with your deal structure and consider some alternative financing options.

Maintain Objectivity

As with any negotiation, you'll get the best deals on your multifamily investments if you can remain as objective and detached as possible. Making offers and negotiating deals is the same as underwriting in this sense. You have to keep your emotions in check and not get attached to a property; otherwise you'll find yourself second-guessing your underwriting and seeking any possible way to rationalize a higher price point. You'll make decisions that will come back to haunt you later.

Maintaining objectivity is even more important when you're raising capital or have partners in the deal. You have a fiduciary responsibility to investors that can't be overlooked. On the other hand, if you're funding a deal entirely on your own, you are free to accept a lower return, agree to onerous terms with the seller, or do whatever else you want. That doesn't mean you'd be making a wise investment choice, just that you'd be within your rights.

You'll always make better decisions if you can stay detached and remain comfortable walking away from deals that won't meet your investment criteria. This can be hard to remember when you're in the midst of negotiating on a property you really like, but one thing experienced investors know for sure is that there will *always* be more deals. A strategy I have used to stay levelheaded while negotiating on a property I really want is to redouble my efforts to find other possible acquisitions. This keeps me from getting too emotionally invested in the deal that's on the table.

The Letter of Intent

Offers for large multifamily properties are typically delivered in the form of a letter of intent (LOI), which is a letter of understanding from the buyer to the seller that outlines the general terms of a prospective sale. The use of LOIs helps both parties avoid legal expenses prior to knowing whether they'll be moving forward. If both parties agree to the terms in the LOI, they execute the document, after which the attorneys will draft a purchase and sale agreement (PSA). An LOI generally includes disclaimers clarifying that it is not a legally binding document, but it is taken very seriously and usually honored. Once an LOI is fully executed, for either party to walk away without good cause is considered a serious breach of etiquette (although it does happen occasionally).

If you don't already have an LOI template, it's best to get one from an experienced real estate attorney. The high-level terms outlined in the LOI will end up in a legal contract, so properly crafting your LOI is critical. While there is no one standard format, an LOI will typically include the following:

- Identification of property
- Proposed purchase price
- Earnest-money deposit
- Timelines (and extensions if applicable) for PSA, due diligence, and closing
- Due diligence and financing contingencies
- A list of required seller documents

In addition, LOIs sometimes include language regarding assignment, title policy, property access, seller documentation, closing costs, 1031 exchange, and confidentiality. However, most of these items can wait to be addressed in the PSA. The exception would be any nonstandard provisions you are seeking that are likely to be objected to later on. If they are to be handled according to convention, however, you can leave them out. Remember that everything you include in the LOI is going to be scrutinized and is a potential point of contention or negotiation, so be selective and don't wade too far into the weeds.

If you want to get a jump on due diligence, it can be helpful to include a list of any documentation you would like to receive from the seller. That way they can begin to gather it while the PSA is being finalized, which can take several days to several weeks, depending on how complex it is and how much needs to be worked through. Some documents to ask for may include:

- All professional reports the seller has in their possession, including, but not limited to, environmental, survey and title insurance, termite, engineering, radon, and appraisal; in addition, any reports from the seller's insurance company, the current mortgagee, and any other documents requested or required per the agreement to be executed.

- Three years of financial reports, including income statements, capital replacements, history of rent levels and collections, updated and certified rent roll, and copies of all current lease agreements and rental applications.
- Copies of all service agreements and vendor contracts.
- Any other documents the buyer may reasonably request, such as management reports, bank statements, insurance loss run reports, property tax bills, and utility bills.

If you already have some of these in your possession, you don't need to relist them in the LOI as long as they're up-to-date. For something like a rent roll, you'll want to make sure it's current, complete, and certified (signed and dated). A rent roll should include (as a minimum) the unit numbers, tenant names, rates, security deposit amounts, current rent payment status, move-in dates, and lease-expiration dates. If outstanding balances don't show up on the rent roll, you should get a delinquency report.

When putting together an LOI, you might want to attach a sheet that includes an overview of the buyer qualifications to help strengthen your offer—especially if there is no buyer questionnaire. You don't have to go overboard, but a couple of paragraphs providing an introduction and a high-level overview of qualifications and background can be helpful. Incorporating a brief bio of yourself and any partners can make the LOI feel more personalized.

In a highly competitive bid situation, you should do every little thing you can to make a difference. At Open Door Capital, we have even included a hyperlink that the seller can click on to access a personalized video message. Remember that a sale can be emotional for the seller. A property may have been in the family for generations, or the seller may feel a strong personal connection to it.

For example, the owners of one property we underwrote recently made it clear that they would not sell to anyone who planned to dramatically raise the rents. The property had been family owned and operated for a long time, and they had developed personal relationships with many of the tenants. In this kind of situation, feeling good about who they're selling to and the buyer's intentions can be just as important to the seller as the price. Remember: People like to sell to people they like. Make it easy for them to like you, and you'll increase the chances of your offer being accepted.

Ten Ways to Strengthen Your Offer

Buyers and brokers will weigh the strength of a prospective buyer heavily as they consider offers. They want to know that you have the ability to close and to do it expeditiously. Your offer can influence their perception of you and demonstrate strength in ways besides just the purchase price. Here is a list of ten ways you can strengthen your offer.

1. **Large Deposit:** The larger your deposit, the more financial strength it will demonstrate to the seller, which is a positive indication of ability to close. Your deposit should be at least 1 to 2 percent of the purchase price, so putting down something closer to 5 to 10 percent should get the seller's attention. However, beware that if the deal falls apart and you've got a difficult seller, it can sometimes take some wrangling to get your deposit back, even if you're entitled to it under the terms of the PSA.

2. **Hard Deposit:** A hard deposit is nonrefundable, usually with very limited exceptions, such as seller default, title issues, or environmental contamination. Brokers and sellers, of course, love a hard deposit as it indicates a high level of confidence from the buyer that they intend to close. A hard deposit also helps mitigate a seller's losses if the deal falls through. For the buyer, however, this is a high-risk move—so do not put down a hard deposit unless you are prepared to lose it. You should also make sure that you've completed a thorough underwriting and have a high level of confidence in your ability to close. It's not uncommon for us at Open Door Capital to include hard deposits of $200,000 or more. Yes, it increases our risk, but we tend to follow the simple adage, "No risk it, no biscuit!"

3. **Short Timelines:** Sellers tend to hate long, dragged-out contingency periods because an extended timeline is viewed as more opportunity for things to go wrong. Tightening up the timelines may make your offer more compelling. Just don't do anything that will prevent you from completing your due diligence.

4. **All-Cash Offer:** If you have the financial wherewithal to pull off an all-cash closing, that can be the foundation of a very strong offer.

Large hard deposits and all-cash offers are both strong enough plays to sometimes get your LOI selected over competing offers with significantly higher purchase prices.

5. **Limited Contingencies:** Being willing to accept a property "as is" or waive any of the standard contingencies will strengthen your offer. Again, you should only entertain this option if you've completed an extremely thorough underwriting.

6. **Proof of Funds:** Providing copies of bank statements or otherwise proving that you have adequate funds at your disposal can improve the seller's perception of your ability to close.

7. **Reference Letters:** A reference letter from your lender or mortgage broker attesting to your experience and qualifications as a borrower can be helpful. If you've closed multiple properties with another broker, a letter from them attesting to your follow-through and noting that you don't retrade could also be helpful—as could reference letters from other sellers you've closed deals with.

8. **Term Sheets:** If you have already secured a term sheet by the time you're submitting your LOI, you can include a copy to demonstrate that you already have an early indication of financing for the project.

9. **Demonstrated Interest:** Brokers and sellers will be less comfortable with LOIs that seem to come out of the blue with little prior communication or expressions of interest. Demonstrate that you're serious by asking intelligent questions, touring the property, and engaging with the broker as much as possible without being annoying.

10. **Raise Your Price:** This may seem fairly obvious, but our intention in this list is to provide ideas for ways to strengthen your offer *without* diminishing your returns. The question becomes: Are there things you can ask for from the seller that will allow you to raise your price but still hit your target returns—or even improve them? One of the most common ways to do this is by incorporating some kind of seller financing arrangement into your offer. If you are uncertain how this will be received, you might include two options in your LOI—one with the lower price and no seller financing, and one with a higher price that includes seller financing. In some instances, we have put a veritable smorgasbord of options in front of sellers so that they could see different prices and how they would relate to financing alternatives.

Just to clarify, all the above methods will make your offer stronger, but that doesn't mean you should use any of them. It's great to make a strong offer, but only if the situation is right. You need to objectively gauge the situation, the risk involved, and your comfort level before deciding to incorporate any of these into your LOI. How well do you know the property, market, and seller? The more you offer at this stage, the stronger your underwriting needs to be and the higher your level of confidence in both the price and your ability to close. Will you be okay if things go sideways, as they often do? Just remember that deals fall apart all the time, deposits are lost, and the risk is real.

Purchase and Sale Agreement

If the seller signs your LOI, the next step is to have your attorney draft a PSA. The attorney will incorporate the terms of the LOI into the PSA and include a laundry list of provisions to make sure your interests are protected. All the legal performance requirements are defined for both parties. For large multifamily deals, it is highly recommended that you leave the PSA to a well-qualified real estate attorney. Each transaction is unique, the contracts can be complicated, and there is just too much at stake to handle this part of the transaction yourself. One small mistake in the PSA could cost you far more than you would ever spend on legal bills.

Some more seasoned investors have a PSA template they are comfortable with and will use that as a starting point. If the seller's attorney doesn't make too many exceptions, a buyer may be able to wrap up the contract without legal counsel. For large deals, however, doing contracts yourself is not advisable in the vast majority of circumstances, and it's never wise for an investor without a lot of experience under their belt.

If you don't already have an established relationship with a real estate attorney, try to get a referral from a broker, a lender, or another investor who is active in your target market. You'll want an attorney who brings extensive experience with large multifamily transactions as well as knowledge of local customs.

Follow Up

If you submit your LOI and don't get the deal, don't be discouraged. You're going to lose out on far more deals than you're going to win, or else you're doing something wrong. While you should accept the loss gracefully, don't give up entirely until the other buyer actually closes. By this stage in the process you will have invested too much time and effort to just walk away without looking back. As we've already said, deals fall apart all the time, and then they can go back on the market. Sometimes when a deal falls out of contract, it's marketed broadly, and sometimes it's quietly offered directly to another buyer rather than going through the whole dog-and-pony show all over again. If the deal is discreetly offered to a backup buyer, you want to make sure that buyer is you.

Throughout the course of underwriting, you will have also laid the groundwork for a relationship with the broker, and potentially the seller. You shouldn't let your efforts go to waste, so regardless of the outcome, it's worth building on that foundation. You never know how it will pay off down the road.

And if your offer is accepted and you put it under contract? Take a moment to celebrate, but don't pat yourself on the back for too long. Now it's time to roll up your sleeves and get to work on due diligence.

KEY TAKEAWAYS

- When a property comes to market, it's important to understand the timelines and process the seller will follow for receiving, evaluating, and responding to offers. When there is no call for offers or when offers will be evaluated on a rolling basis, speed is of the essence. If you can respond rapidly, you might get an asset under contract at an attractive price and achieve superior returns.
- When you have an opportunity to negotiate, you should avoid bidding against yourself, make offers with more than one option, and use odd numbers.
- There are a variety of tools at your disposal to strengthen your offer besides raising your price, including large or hard deposits, quick closings, limited contingencies, all-cash offers, proof of funds, reference letters, term sheets, demonstrated interest, or other terms favorable to the seller.

Madison Barracks: Part VI

As we worked through our underwriting and financial analysis for the Apartments at Madison Barracks, we began to recognize that we were going to be somewhat limited in our financing options. Despite its upside potential, the property was not cash flowing well and would need a significant capital infusion for us to complete the necessary renovations.

As part of our underwriting, we had researched the property's debt and decided to try to assume the seller's mortgage of $4.7 million. We didn't like the terms, but this would allow us to secure a higher leverage than new financing and let us use our cash for the necessary upgrades. Multiple roofs had to be replaced right away, and it would take a significant amount of work to get the units rent-ready. Some of the down units had extensive damage, and estimating the full cost for rehab would be difficult.

In order to mitigate our risk and reduce the amount of cash required, we planned to leave the worst of the units down and focus on those that weren't as bad. We would execute on our value-add and then refinance within thirty-six months—hopefully into better, long-term debt. At that time, we would pull some cash out and reinvest it in additional upgrades, bringing the rest of the down units back online. Fully restoring this property was not economically viable right now because the rents wouldn't support it. While certainly doable, returning the property to its full former glory would have to be budgeted for and accomplished piecemeal over the long term.

Although I felt confident in the plan, it was risky. The underwriting supported the valuation, but in the end, the decision of whether to extend an offer was a judgment call. In addition to the financial analysis, I weighed other factors that were meaningful to me. This was a property where I had once been a tenant. It was located in a community I cared about. It was a property with history—and it was now a property in severe distress. If I could reverse its downward trajectory, that would be as rewarding as any financial returns.

As my plan came together, I began to realize with dismay that my investment decision might be getting clouded with emotion. I have always tried my best to remain objective, but that's easier said than done. I was breaking my own rules! Even though I feared it could end up being my downfall, I shrugged these concerns aside and made an offer anyway.

To be continued...

Chapter Sixteen
DUE DILIGENCE

It's the little details that are vital. Little things make big things happen.

—JOHN WOODEN

Once you have a large multifamily property under contract, it's time to drill down even more and make sure you know what you're buying. This means taking a microscope to the financials, the market, the legal documentation, and the property itself. It's a deep dive into the details, but an essential step in the process to protect both your interests and, if you're raising capital, those of your investors.

We're not sure why, but when you're an active large multifamily investor, the deals never seem to reach fruition at a smooth and steady pace. You might go six months or even a year with no luck, and then you'll somehow manage to get three properties under contract in a week.

Brandon and I recently found ourselves in a similar situation at Open Door Capital. After a long dry spell, multiple deals came together at the same time. This development was super exciting, but it also meant we had to plow through a ton of overlapping due diligence in a short time. Fortunately, one of our partners, Ryan Murdock, stepped up and really took the bull by the horns.

Over a span of nineteen days, Ryan flew more than 16,000 miles and drove another 3,100 to visit not only the three properties we had under contract but another thirty that were comps or that we were underwriting. He took seventeen flights (three of which were red-eyes), rented five cars, and ate too many bags of cheesy crackers to count.

While we do not in any way advocate the consumption of excessive amounts of snack foods, we were otherwise impressed with and grateful for our partner's dedication to ensuring that thorough due diligence was completed for each deal.

Toward the end of his trip, I was fortunate enough to meet up with Ryan during one of his many layovers and grab a late dinner with him. He was starving and visibly exhausted. He had been hopping back and forth between time zones and obviously wasn't getting much sleep, but it wasn't affecting the quality of his work—the on-site videos and reports he was providing were excellent, as always.

"What a crazy trip! I can't imagine how tired you must be," I said. "Thanks for doing this—it's much appreciated."

He looked at me, smiled, and said, "I love this stuff."

And that's Ryan for you. He's fueled by an excitement and passion for our business, and always willing to go the extra mile.

Given the circumstances, it would have been easy to rationalize cutting corners, but Ryan knew that wasn't the right thing to do. Due diligence is critical, and he made sure the job got done, and done well. It's this kind of penchant for stepping up and doing whatever it takes that can make a real estate investor successful at the highest levels, and it's what made Ryan such a highly respected and indispensable member of our team when we first started Open Door Capital.

Digging In

What is the goal of due diligence? At a high level, it is intended to provide you with the clearest possible picture of the asset so that you go in with eyes wide open and can accurately assess the risk involved. Different investors look at due diligence in different ways, particularly with regard to underwriting. The question is, where should underwriting leave off and due diligence begin? There is no single right answer, but there are some pretty good incentives to do a large portion of your research up front in the underwriting phase. If you save too much for due diligence, you're far more likely to end up retrading or exercising your option to cancel a contract during the due diligence period. You'll also risk being known as an investor who doesn't follow through and honor their agreements, which can undermine future opportunities. If instead you do a thorough job of vetting a project beforehand, you are much more likely to close.

As we said earlier, sometimes thorough underwriting simply isn't feasible. Time constraints may not allow it, or the broker may even encourage you to put in an offer with the understanding that you'll evaluate the property more thoroughly once under contract. In some situations, sellers will even refuse to release any information until the property is under contract.

Regardless of the circumstances that may have led to less-than-thorough underwriting, the first step in the due diligence phase is to complete any of the remaining underwriting tasks we've already reviewed in the previous chapters. Completing these items requires little additional capital. Remember, if you find a major problem with any area of due diligence it could kill the deal, so starting with tasks that don't require you to invest more cash makes a lot of sense.

You'll also need to decide what parts of due diligence you're going to do yourself and what you're going to outsource. When you're digging this deep for a large multifamily acquisition, some activities can be very time-consuming and require a level of expertise you might not have. Other aspects of due diligence will be dictated by your lender and mandatorily outsourced to third parties. For these reasons, among others, the largest investors will frequently outsource most major due diligence items.

Financial Audit

During underwriting you should have reviewed the property's income and expense statements, including their T-12 and the last three calendar years. You'll want to get an updated T-12 during due diligence to make sure nothing has changed significantly. In order to further vet the financials, many investors will hire a real estate consulting firm to conduct a full financial audit of the documents provided by the seller. An audit involves cross-checking the income and expense records with the tenant leases, bank statements, and rent rolls. Getting journal entries from the seller can also be useful.

The audit report will provide you with an overview of the findings. It can help you identify any discrepancies and provide a thorough accounting of income, expenses, and other cash-flow requirements that serve as the basis of your pro formas. Armed with the information in the report, you can then refine your financial projections as necessary and hopefully move forward with a higher level of confidence in your income and expense assumptions.

Lease Audit and Rent Roll Analysis

A lease audit and rent roll analysis can be outsourced or completed in-house, since it is fairly straightforward. If you are working with a property management firm, they may be willing to complete this task on your behalf.

To perform a lease audit, you'll need copies of all the leases. You must make sure you have a lease for every unit shown as occupied on the rent roll. Once you have all the leases, review them to confirm that they match the information on the rent roll. You will be checking things like lease dates, rent amounts, security deposits, fees, and other ancillary charges. You'll keep track of all discrepancies and then work with the seller to resolve any discrepancies.

The other thing to watch out for is any concessions. Sellers will sometimes offer excessive concessions in the months or years leading up to a sale in order to artificially inflate the rent roll and secure higher rents. Uncovering such a tactic can be challenging without going through every single lease.

Property Inspection

Early in the due diligence period you should schedule a personal walk-through inspection, preferably with the help of your property manager and contractor. At this inspection you will thoroughly walk the grounds, examining all the common areas, structures, amenities, and utilities, the parking lot, and the units themselves. You'll be looking at the condition of everything and making note of any issues you find. You should examine everything closely, inventory any equipment you observe, count the number of parking spaces, and so on. It's a good idea to take lots of videos and photos you can refer back to later. Be sure you take pictures of the management office, supplies, and inventory to include on a personal property list for closing. Items will sometimes disappear before closing—particularly if you're going to be making a change in property management.

Some investors will inspect a random sampling of units, which can be tempting when you're inspecting a very large property, but we recommend checking inside every single unit. You'll want to prepare in advance, make careful notes about the condition of each unit, and identify any potential maintenance problems. Take note of the appliances, fixtures, and finishes. Your property manager and contractor should closely examine mechanical system components and look for any structural problems. They should also closely examine any balconies and stairs for signs of corrosion or deterioration. If they are experienced, they ought to know what to look for. Many property management firms have developed checklists to help keep track of items as you work your way through the property.

While inspecting the units, you should also cross-check them against the rent roll to confirm its accuracy. Make sure that the unit types and occupancy status are correct. It is rare not to find mistakes. On more than one occasion we have even discovered additional units that weren't on the rent roll!

If you encounter any units that are in such disrepair that they are not suitable for occupancy (known as "down" units), you may be entitled to a price adjustment. Some investors will even include a clause in the PSA defining a purchase price adjustment for any down units discovered during due diligence.

If the property charges pet rent (or you plan to start doing so after closing), you should also make note of which units appear to have pets and cross-check that against the rent roll or individual leases. You're likely to discover at least a handful of occupants with unreported pets that you can track down and start charging for after closing.

Finally, the unit inspection can also be a good opportunity to identify problem tenants or situations that may need to be dealt with after closing.

Market Survey

A market survey, also called a market report or market study, will evaluate the subject property's rental market. The need for a market study will vary, depending on how comfortable you are with the level of research completed during underwriting. If you have a high level of confidence in the comps you've identified and current market dynamics, you may not need a full market survey—especially if your initial survey work was done with the assistance of a property manager with a strong knowledge of the submarket.

With a full market survey your goal is to delve deeper into supply-and-demand issues, identifying market trends and rents that take into consideration class, amenities, unit type, and so on. You could do this research yourself or have your property management firm do it. Another option is to contract with a real estate consulting firm, which would likely provide you with the most in-depth overview of current market conditions that may affect the property going forward. Some lenders may ask for a market survey; others may even mandate one.

Lender-Driven Due Diligence

As we discussed in Chapter Seven, a number of important due diligence steps are typically driven by the lender and must be completed by lender-approved vendors. These include the property condition assessment (PCA), Phase I environmental site assessment (ESA), appraisal, survey, and title report.

Not all lenders require these items. For example, a portfolio lender may not require a PCA or Phase I ESA. The same is true of some private lenders and deals that are seller financed. In cases where these items are not lender mandated, you may need or want to complete them for other purposes—primarily for the same reasons that lenders usually require them, which is to uncover any potential risks you might not otherwise be aware of. A survey and title report should be completed regardless.

For some due diligence items required by the lender, you may want to complete your own version in-house too. One example is the PCA.

Property Condition Assessment

Most multifamily lenders will require that a PCA be completed, which involves a thorough physical inspection of the property and all its component systems. The report will identify any near- or long-term repair issues and estimate the cost of the work involved.

The lender may require that items identified as "critical" or "high priority" either be addressed prior to closing, or more likely, that proceeds from closing be held back in an escrow account until the work is completed. The lender will also use this report as the basis for calculating the replacement reserve requirement. This is important because the reserve requirement affects the property's cash flow. Also, going forward, only work done on the items specifically identified in lender documents will qualify for reimbursement from the replacement reserve.

While the PCA is valuable, unfortunately the results are often not available to the buyer until after the due diligence period has expired. For this reason, some investors will hire a licensed commercial contractor to do their own internal PCA and obtain a more thorough assessment of the physical condition of the property.

Additional Due Diligence

In addition to these key, standard items, there are a variety of other tasks you will want to complete. Some should always be done, while others may be property-specific. Think back through everything you've done thus far and try to determine whether there are any areas worth digging into further.

The following are examples of additional due diligence items you might want to complete:

- Get a copy of the most recent survey and seller's title insurance policy and conduct a preliminary review with your attorney to get a head start addressing any potential title issues and avoid last-minute surprises.
- Review all third-party contracts that are in place and make sure you understand the terms. Note that contracts with telecom or laundry vendors may include a one-time lump sum payment to the seller in exchange for ongoing obligations that you will inherit, in which case you should be entitled to a prorated credit at closing.
- For properties located in known seismic zones, complete a seismic risk assessment and structural analysis, and confirm compliance with building stability standards.
- Check that there is a valid certificate of occupancy, and confirm that

there are no outstanding code violations. If there are any required fire, code, or other mandated property inspections, get copies of the most recent reports.

- Confirm that parcels are zoned correctly. You should also get a copy of any required local licenses or permits.
- Review tenant applications to see what type of screening was done.
- Search the online sex offender database to see whether any convicted offenders are residing at the property.
- Contact the police department to further research criminal activity. If possible, secure copies of police reports for the past couple of years and get some qualitative insights from local law enforcement.
- Contact the local planning office and development authorities for information on any pending development or housing projects that could affect supply or demand.

Keep in mind that even if you've completed your underwriting, time passes, and things can change. For example, we once learned of a shooting that occurred at a property less than a week after we had put it under contract. The seller never told us about the incident, and we never would have known about it if we hadn't done a new online search during due diligence. We dug deeper into the criminal activity and grew increasingly concerned over the community's safety. This incident caused problems with our lender, who notified us that it would affect our financing terms. As a result of the shooting, we ended up terminating the contract and walking away from the deal.

Retrading and Contract Termination

As discussed earlier in the chapter, you should make every effort to avoid retrading or terminating a PSA by doing your homework up front. Nonetheless, sometimes you'll discover issues that are significant enough to prevent you from moving forward. You would then have to decide whether to retrade (renegotiate the contract purchase price or terms) or exercise your right to cancel the contract. Either retrading or terminating would generally be considered acceptable if you were to discover one of the following:

- Information provided to you by the broker or seller during underwriting was false or misleading.

- There is an underlying and significantly problematic situation at the property that you couldn't reasonably have been expected to find during underwriting.
- A significant change in the condition or situation at the property has occurred since you put it under contract.

In order for any of the above issues to merit a change in price or walking away, they should be substantive. Experienced investors know and accept that no property is perfect, and it's reasonable to find a host of issues that are unfavorable. Unless the issues impact the property enough to materially diminish its value or your projected returns, they should either be accepted or addressed by requesting that the seller rectify them if possible.

What if you need to walk away or renegotiate for some less significant reason? In the end, you should never proceed with the acquisition of a property that isn't going to work for you. If you need to walk away, just do it. Maybe you made a mistake, or lost a key investor, or have been saddled with a major personal issue. Whatever the reason, once you realize the deal is not right for you, buck up and pull the plug. It won't be pleasant, but if you wait and allow the seller to continue to spend time and money, it's going to be worse. Terminate the contract. Will it affect your reputation? Perhaps. But buying a multifamily property isn't like buying a kitchen gadget that you can just stow away in a hard-to-reach cabinet. Moving forward with a bad multifamily deal is a huge mistake that you're going to have to live with and could adversely affect a lot of people for a long time.

KEY TAKEAWAYS

- Due diligence entails taking a microscope to the financials, the market, legal documentation, and the property itself. It's a deep dive, but an essential step to protect both your interests and, if you're raising capital, those of your investors.
- When it comes to due diligence, it's best to err on the side of thoroughness. At a minimum, you should perform a financial audit, a lease audit, a rent roll analysis, a property inspection, and a market survey. Refer back to the list in this chapter for additional recommended due diligence tasks.
- You should make every effort to avoid retrading, but if you discover unexpected issues during due diligence, you will have to decide whether to proceed with a deal. You should never acquire a property that isn't going to work for you. If you need to walk away, just do it.

Madison Barracks—Part VII

Based on our financial analysis, we determined that the Apartments at Madison Barracks was worth approximately $5.5 million, which was a full $2 million lower than the asking price just a few years ago. The property had deteriorated since then, though, and I felt confident that we would be negotiating from a position of strength. The NOI was weak, there was a ton of deferred maintenance, and as far as I knew, there were no other prospective buyers.

I asked the owner what price they would be willing to accept. They adamantly refused to provide an asking price but said they were open to offers. I don't like to be the first to put a number out there, but I agreed to do so in this case because I did not want the negotiations to stall before they even got started. I decided on a number I thought was low but not entirely indefensible. I prepared a purchase offer in the amount of $5 million and delivered it to the seller, with an email supporting my valuation and outlining my position.

I let the seller know that the purchase price represented a cap rate of less than 5 percent, which was significantly lower than properties were trading at in that market. I pointed out that this cap rate was based on their T-12 expenses, even though some of them were too low. I also gave the seller some background on challenges faced by the local housing market, which had struggled to absorb new construction and as a result had experienced some rent compression.

Despite the challenges, I stated that we were prepared to make the investments necessary to turn the property around, but for this to be viable, we had to acquire the property for no more than $5 million. We were also willing to assume their mortgage of $4.7 million and thereby help them avoid a prepayment penalty, even though the current income would not cover the debt service.

Finally, I let them know that should they accept our purchase offer, we were prepared to move forward quickly and expedite due diligence. We would accept the property in "as-is" condition, with the exception of some roof work the seller claimed was already scheduled for completion before the proposed closing date.

Five days later, after my offer had expired, I got a one-line email from the CEO: "Brian, we accept this offer and will execute first thing next week."

Wow. Not at all what I had expected. I changed the dates on the offer and sent it back for signature, although the fact that I didn't get a counteroffer made me very uneasy. At this stage in my investing career I had been involved in hundreds of deals, and I couldn't recall a negotiation for a large property where my first offer had been accepted without any counter. It seemed like a great opportunity, but I couldn't help but wonder if I had missed something.

Within days, a purchase agreement was fully executed, and we had a 126-unit multifamily property under contract for $5 million. We would be assuming the mortgage, which meant that we'd only have to come up with a $300,000 down payment plus closing costs and the funds necessary for planned improvements. While the lack of negotiation made me apprehensive, my excitement outweighed my concern.

I forwarded the seller a list of due diligence documents we were looking for and scheduled an inspection. While the initial tour was more cursory, at this stage I wanted to get some contractors in there and make sure we saw every single unit. Maybe due diligence would help put my mind at ease. The deal seemed almost too good to be true. Unfortunately, we all know what that means.

To be continued...

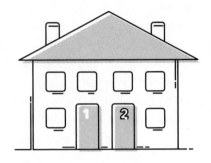

Chapter Seventeen
CLOSING

All great changes are preceded by chaos.

—DEEPAK CHOPRA

When your due diligence as the buyer begins to wind down, your attorney will work in cooperation with the seller's attorney, the lender's attorney, and (depending on where the closing occurs) an escrow or title agent to prepare closing documents and line everything up. The lender's attorney usually produces a closing checklist enumerating every matter that must be addressed in order to close, together with notations on which party is responsible for each item. You will then work with your attorney to satisfy the requirements as outlined on the checklist. As these items are addressed, any number of issues can come up that will have to be resolved. Some might be legal matters, which the attorneys can handle but you should still stay apprised of. Others will require input from third parties.

In order to be responsive and make informed decisions, it's a good idea to have a basic understanding of the core legal issues associated with the closing, starting with title, the deed, and title insurance.

Transfer of Title

As the buyer, it's important to confirm that the seller has the legal right to convey the property and that after closing you will have legal ownership. In other words, you want to make sure that you will receive "clean title." In real estate, there is no single document that constitutes title. Instead, title consists of a combination of documents, records, and acts that together indicate a property's ownership. In some cases, the documents and records are consistent and point to a clear and unencumbered ownership, but sometimes ambiguities, inconsistencies, records, or situations emerge that make things a little messier and constitute "clouds" on the title. Examples include old ownership claims, open mortgages, liens, easements, encroachments or other lot line issues, legal disputes, ancient mortgages (generally, mortgages over thirty years old), or property access issues. These types of problems are not uncommon and can usually be uncovered through a title search and survey.

The Deed

The seller's deed is the main written document that transfers title from one party to another. To be valid, a deed must be signed and notarized, and meet a host of other legal requirements that can vary by state. In many states, a properly formatted deed must be recorded in the public record by the appropriate government official or risk being subject to legal challenges.

There are various types of deeds, including quit-claim deeds, bargain and sale deeds, grant deeds, general warranty deeds, and special warranty deeds (or limited warranty deeds). General warranty and special warranty deeds (or grant deeds in California) provide the buyer with some level of protection because the seller warrants against certain claims arising from title issues. The only difference between a general warranty and a special warranty deed is that the special warranty deed is limited to title defects arising during the seller's period of ownership. A bargain and sale deed, on the other hand, comes without any warranties.

A quit-claim deed transfers whatever interest the seller actually has in the property, if any. A quit-claim deed is often used when a seller transfers a property to the seller's own family or related entity (LLC).

Title Insurance and Survey

Seller warranties that are conveyed with the deed have limitations. For one thing, a seller warranty is only as strong as the seller. There are also limits to how much you can rely on the results of a title search. Generally, title searches are performed by human-beings and as such, human error remains a risk. What you're really going to be depending on for protection of your interest in the property is an owner's title insurance policy and an up-to-date survey that has been reviewed by your attorney and is referenced and insured in the title policy.

Title insurance is basically an insurance policy that affords you protection from any future claims related to title issues, including legal fees related to proving your valid ownership. Your lender is almost always going to require title insurance and an updated survey because they want to protect their own interests. Along those same lines, you should be purchasing an owner's title insurance policy for those same reasons.

Depending on what state the property is in, your title insurance agent will initiate a record search to identify any potential title risks. Once the agent has reviewed and analyzed all the information collected, they will usually issue a title commitment. However, if the title agent finds something problematic, they could refuse to issue a policy or, more often, take exceptions in the title insurance commitment. The title agent will provide a list of such exceptions for review and response. Depending on the type of exceptions, some may need to be addressed by you, your attorney, and the seller's attorney prior to closing. The attorneys may also be able to work with the title agent to have exceptions deleted or modified, which in some jurisdictions can result in a higher premium. The lender's attorney will also have to be satisfied with any resolutions.

Title issues are not uncommon, and they will often come to light right before closing. Fortunately, many title issues can be resolved without too much drama. For example, sometimes an old mortgage lien is still recorded even though the debt was paid off long ago. This may simply require some additional research as you track down the prior lender so that the appropriate paperwork can be recreated and then subsequently filed with the county clerk. Or there may be a mechanic's lien on the property because the seller failed to pay for work that was done. These liens can usually be discharged by paying the amount owed, negotiating a settlement, or finding a procedural defect in the lien.

In the worst-case scenario, an exception cannot be resolved to the satisfaction of the lender or buyer and poses a significant enough risk that it derails the transaction. Other exceptions that are not deleted may be deemed acceptable by the lender and buyer and will be considered permitted exceptions. A common example would be a utility easement that serves another property, which would not generally be cause for concern. Your attorney will advise you regarding title issues and any associated risks.

Not all lenders require title insurance, and it is not mandatory. Nonetheless, owner's title insurance is always highly recommended to protect a buyer's interests in the real property, whether that's the down payment at closing or the equity in the property at a future date when a claim against the property is made. The title insurance premium is limited to a one-time fee that is paid at closing, but the protection it affords will continue even after you sell the property. While the premium is an added expense at closing, it won't affect your property's long-term cash flow or NOI because it is a one-time fee.

Uniform Commercial Code Searches

In addition to the search completed by the title insurance agent, another way that buyers and lenders help ensure a clean title to the property is to complete a Uniform Commercial Code (UCC) search through the Secretary of State. A third party conducts the search on both the seller and the property to make sure that any portion of the asset hasn't been pledged as collateral for any loans or other financial agreements. Generally, a UCC would be filed to protect a lender's interest in personal property (appliances, trade fixtures, etc.), although at times a UCC will be filed to protect the lender's interest in the event that membership interests or shares are pledged as collateral for a loan.

Bill of Sale

When a buyer acquires a large multifamily property, they are usually purchasing more than just the land and the physical structures: They are generally acquiring a variety of equipment and other personal property as well. This may include vehicles, lawn care and snow removal equipment, maintenance and repair inventory, office equipment, tools, and ladders. While the value of this personal property is typically minor relative to the total purchase price, it is part of the purchase and should be conveyed to the buyer unless otherwise agreed to.

The catch is that personal property is a lot more mobile than a building and will sometimes disappear between the time a property goes under contract and closing. An unscrupulous seller or property manager may move personal property to another of their communities, swap it out for lesser quality equipment, or sell it off, and employees who learn they aren't going to be retained may start to take things home. We have experienced this on multiple occasions. (Remember the River Apartments?)

The lesson learned is that you should always request a list of personal property, including approximate age, brand, and model number, from the seller, and whenever possible this list should be included as an exhibit in the purchase and sale agreement (PSA). Then a bill of sale will be prepared for closing that conveys the personal property to the buyer. A bill of sale is essentially a deed for the personal property. Absent a personal property list, your attorney should still draft a bill of sale using general language, such as "all personal property located at the premises not owned by the tenants and used in the operation and maintenance of the real property."

Vehicles, mobile homes, trailers, and other items on the personal property list that have a certificate of title will need to be conveyed separately, and a property tax liability may be incurred at the time of transfer. You should confirm with your attorney whether or not you would like these conveyed to the same legal entity as the rest of the property.

Corporate Documents

As part of preparation for closing, the buyer's attorney will create a legal entity for the transaction. In most cases this will be what is known as a single-purpose entity (SPE), which is usually a limited liability company that is created exclusively to finance and acquire a specific asset. When investing in large multifamily properties, the size of the investment will generally make it a bad idea to put multiple properties in a single entity due to the level of risk involved. Be aware, however, that a lender may undermine this separation of risk to some extent through a cross-default clause. In other words, if you have multiple loans with the same bank, they may include a provision that an event of default on one borrower's loan will constitute an event of default under all other loans the lender made to you, regardless of the actual borrowing entity.

For syndications or other sophisticated investment structures, you may need to form multiple entities for a single property. The entity type and corporate structure may also be driven by lender and investor requirements.

In preparation for closing, your attorney will generally prepare and distribute copies of the following, which will be reviewed and accepted by your lender's attorney and the seller's attorney:

- Articles of organization and all amendments
- Operating agreement and all amendments
- Member consent or resolutions for the loan, purchase, and signer(s), if necessary
- Current certificate of good standing from the state where the entity was formed
- Federal tax ID number

Settlement Statements

The document summarizing the disbursements, charges, and credits associated with closing are listed on a settlement statement, also known as a closing statement. The settlement statement will start with the property purchase price and then itemize all credits and deductions. Based on this breakdown, it will show the cash that the buyer must contribute at closing and the proceeds that will be disbursed to the seller.

Generally, each party is responsible for their own legal costs, and you will be responsible for all of your lender's expenses related to the closing. But who pays for what in a transaction is negotiable, and convention can differ depending on where the property is located. Regardless, the responsibilities reflected in the settlement or closing statement should reflect the terms of the PSA, which takes precedence.

The fees and expenses that typically show up on the closing statement include all financing and third-party report fees, prepaid interest, lender-mandated charges (such as escrow and reserve funds), various title/escrow charges and recording fees, legal fees, commissions, and adjustments.

It's a good idea to obtain a draft closing statement in advance of closing, review all the numbers thoroughly, and make sure the closing cost responsibilities align with your understanding of the PSA. You'll also want to confirm that fees are consistent with any quotes you may have received along the way. As a buyer, you should pay particularly close attention to the adjustments, which usually include prorated rents, property taxes, and security deposits. Other prorations, such as for utilities, may also appear, although they are less common. There can also be secondary financing.

When it comes to property taxes, rents, and security deposits, the prorations on the settlement statement will have been calculated by an attorney or paralegal. This person is probably not very familiar with the property, so errors and omissions are not uncommon. As the party who spearheaded the due diligence, you as the buyer are likely better qualified than your attorney to catch potential mistakes. We highly recommend that you check these numbers closely.

Prepaid Property Taxes

There are generally four steps to take in order to calculate the prorated property taxes. The first step is to determine what the taxing jurisdictions are, the fiscal year, when taxes were due, and what taxes were owed on the property you're buying. The second step is to check the tax receipts and confirm that taxes were actually paid in full and for what time period. The third step is to prorate the taxes paid to determine what portion of the payment covers the period prior to the closing date, and what portion will cover the period after closing. The portion of the payment that covers days post-closing are considered "prepaid" and can sometimes result in a credit to the seller. Note that if the due date for taxes falls after the commencement of the tax calendar year and taxes are not yet paid, there could be a debit resulting from unpaid taxes. You should proceed with caution, because in some jurisdictions property taxes are prepaid, while in others they are paid incrementally or at the end of the fiscal year.

Local custom regarding the treatment of prepaid taxes varies. In some locales, the seller is expected to have fully paid all taxes due prior to closing, but there are no prorations, so the seller is not reimbursed for the portion of property taxes that was prepaid. Meanwhile, in many other areas its customary for the property taxes to be prorated and for the buyer to reimburse the seller at closing for prepaid taxes. Regardless, the settlement statement and adjustments should reflect the terms defined in the PSA regarding the treatment of adjustments at closing. Only if something is not specifically addressed in the PSA would the process default to what is customary or presumed by statute.

Rent Proration

Most PSAs will include a provision for the proration of rent. The easiest way to prorate rent is to first convert the monthly rent into a daily rent. You can then multiply the daily rent by the number of days remaining in the month at closing to calculate the rent due to the buyer. You should review the most recent certified copy of the rent roll to determine what rents and other fees are scheduled for collection during the month of closing. It's a good idea to reconcile this newer rent roll with your lease audit, because any prior rent roll mistakes you picked up on the audit are likely to have carried over into the most current rent roll.

Proration of rents becomes tricky when the PSA states that the rents are to be prorated but doesn't specify whether the rents to be prorated are limited to those actually collected or include rents that are scheduled but have not yet been paid. A well-crafted PSA will clarify this calculation, address who is entitled to rent on the day of closing, and expand the proration to include other fees or revenue that might be due from the tenant. For example, if a property has utility bill-backs, these charges may reflect a prior time period. If their prorated amount is not addressed in the PSA, it may be hard to reach an agreement on how they should be handled.

Prorations that are left unclear can create significant confusion at the time of closing and thereafter. Responsibility for who is collecting rent also becomes confusing. If you as the new owner are expected to collect the remaining rent, you may find that some payments have already been mailed to the seller but are not reflected on the proration, while other tenants may claim to have paid the rent to the seller but be unable to produce evidence. On the other hand, if the seller is expected to collect the remaining rent, they may find they no longer have the leverage to enforce collection. If there is any back-due rent, sellers will also want to first apply any rent collected toward prior months instead of the month of closing. In the end, buyers and sellers will end up passing checks back and forth, returning them to tenants, trying to track down missing payments, arguing over who gets what—in short, a real mess and one worth avoiding.

You can work with your attorney to draft an appropriate clause for the PSA to help make things go smoothly at closing. Ideally the PSA should require the seller to collect past-due rent and prorate rent as if current. Here's an example of rent proration language you might find in a PSA:

In the event the Closing Date is not the first day of a month, all rents, fees, and other charges shall be prorated based on the scheduled income in an amount equal to one-thirtieth of one month's rent for each day from and including the Closing Date to but excluding the first day of the next month.

For large multifamily properties, the proration of rents can amount to a significant credit to the buyer at closing. All things being equal, favorable rent proration terms would motivate you as the buyer to close as early in the month as possible. Closing earlier in the month also allows you more time to ensure that all tenants have been notified of the change in ownership and understand how to pay rent to the new owner moving forward.

Security Deposits

Security deposits held by the seller should always be transferred in full as a credit or by separate check to the buyer at closing. As the buyer, you should compare the list of security deposits on the certified rent roll to the results of your lease audit, and then confirm the credit on the draft settlement statement. Be careful—unethical sellers may draw down security deposits before closing and apply them to past-due rent. It is not uncommon for tenants to later demand the return of security deposits not handed over or noted on the certified rent roll. Be prepared to have these tough conversations and to refer the unhappy tenant back to the seller.

Everything Else

While many closing responsibilities are related to legal matters, you'll still need to address a number of other matters in preparation for closing. At the top of the list will be shepherding financing through the final stages of the lending process. You should expect a steady flood of requests, questions, and clarifications right up until closing, and you'll have to stay on top of everything to avoid delays. Fortunately, much of the necessary information will have already been gathered as part of your underwriting and due diligence efforts. As soon as the draft loan documents are ready, you and your attorney should review them. You'll want to ensure the terms are consistent with the commitment letter. If you find any discrepancies, you should try to have them addressed. A savvy attorney will know which items in the loan documents require further negotiation, rather than signing the lender's standard documents. This is what truly separates an adequate attorney from a stellar attorney. You may not see value in this now, but when a potential default exists or when you are paying off the loan, a good attorney can save you time, money, and aggravation.

In addition, if you're raising capital for a syndication, that process should be at or nearing completion. You'll be wrapping up the activities outlined in Chapters Three and Four while coordinating with your securities attorney to finalize the necessary documentation and ensure compliance with securities laws.

Finally, by the time due diligence is completed you should have concluded your property management arrangements and be working closely with your property manager to make sure that everything is lined up and ready to go for a smooth transition after closing. Your property management agreement should be executed and, if required, a copy provided to your lender.

Prior to closing, you will probably have to perform the following in cooperation with your property management team:

- Prepare and review a final operating budget for the project.
- Make and approve staffing arrangements.
- Hire contractors for any work you plan to commence after closing.
- Establish an operating account (the bank will need your corporate documents).
- Gather utility account numbers from the seller and provide them to the property management firm so that utility providers can be notified, readings can be scheduled, and accounts transferred on closing day.
- Once you have a closing date nailed down, get an insurance binder that satisfies your lender's requirements and provide a copy to your lawyer, who will forward it to the lender's counsel for review and approval.
- Assemble a list of people and organizations that will need to be contacted after closing. This would include local emergency services and third-party service providers.

- If there are motor vehicles or other assets with certificate of title involved in the transaction, secure insurance and coordinate with your attorney to confirm registration and title transfer requirements in preparation for closing.
- Draft tenant letters announcing the change in ownership, which should include any new contact information and instructions to tenants on how to pay rent moving forward. Also request tenant letters from the seller.
- Conduct a final walk-through inspection immediately prior to closing to ensure that there have been no substantive changes to the real or personal property under contract.

Between legal work, lender requests, capital raising, and property management, the days and weeks leading up to closing can be chaotic, to say the least. The nearer you get to closing day, the more frenzied it gets. Trying to get a large deal closed can feel a bit like trying to steer a vehicle as it slides down an icy hill. You're trying to avoid obstacles and navigate your way by frantically turning in one direction and then the other, occasionally spinning in a circle or two. Getting safely through requires your full attention, and maybe even a little luck, to avoid collisions and stay on the road.

The good news is that things are usually a lot more controlled than they seem, particularly if you have a good team in place. Not only are you not alone, but you're likely working with people who are accustomed to managing the whirlwind that surrounds the closing of a large multifamily deal. With a competent real estate attorney, mortgage broker, property manager, and other professionals working on your behalf, closing will be very manageable. In the words of minister and Yale professor Halford Luccock, "No one can whistle a symphony. It takes a whole orchestra to play it."

When it's all finally ready for signature, take a moment to admire how prodigious the legal teams have been in their output—and then bite the bullet and go through everything one last time. While your attorney will certainly review the documents on your behalf, it's still a good idea to go through them yourself. Don't be afraid to ask questions or request clarification—you're entitled. Pay particularly close attention to the final closing statement and loan documents. You should have had the opportunity to review drafts in advance. What you'll want to focus on at this point are any changes that have been made since your prior review.

If everything appears to be in order, it's time to get out your lucky pen and sign your life away. After you've drained your pen of ink, the funds will be transmitted and the sale recorded. An absurdly large number of keys will usually be handed over, half of which will never be matched to any lock. Congratulations! You're now the owner of a large multifamily property. Let the adventures begin.

KEY TAKEAWAYS

- There are many procedures, documents, and considerations associated with closing, so it's imperative to have good counsel and a strong team to look out for your interests and help you navigate the process.
- Always closely review closing documentation. As the buyer, you're in the best position to find mistakes because you're more familiar with the property and have the broadest knowledge of all aspects of the deal.
- The time leading up to closing can be chaotic, but an experienced team will help you pull everything together and get across the finish line.

Madison Barracks: Part VIII

Getting a signed purchase agreement for the Apartments at Madison Barracks was a big, exciting step, but it was only the beginning of a long journey. Due diligence can get complicated for a large property, especially one in distress, but our underwriting process had been fairly thorough. In the end, we didn't find any major surprises—just lots of reminders that we were taking on a real challenge.

It was the mortgage assumption that proved far more difficult than we had anticipated. The target closing date came and went, with the assumption process having dragged on for more than four months. Painful by any measure, the process involved repeated and lengthy negotiations with all the mortgage stakeholders.

Our primary point of contact was the loan servicer—the company that administers the loan on behalf of the lender and manages all aspects of dealing with a borrower. Once we contacted them and requested that they begin the assumption process, they informed us that they would first need to complete an initial analysis. They provided a list of documentation they would require, as well as a host of nonrefundable fees we would have to pay. After we submitted the full documentation and wired the initial fee deposit of $28,500, they would conduct the initial analysis. If the results of this analysis met their satisfaction, the lender would proceed with their full underwriting of the request.

While no part of the process was particularly user-friendly or expedient, the most cumbersome was the lender's full underwriting. After the loan servicer completed their own review, they handed off the underwriting to a third-party firm whose demands often seemed senseless and never ending.

Ultimately, the biggest obstacle we faced was convincing all the parties involved that they should allow us to assume the mortgage, with a principal balance of $4.7 million. Since we were paying only $5 million, this resulted in a 94 percent LTV, a ratio that was well above their lending guidelines. It wasn't just the third-party underwriter that needed to be satisfied: They had to get approval from the loan servicer, who in turn had to get approval from the lender. They also had to get approval from another bank that was the "master servicer." Each party seemed to have their own concerns, which they wanted to be addressed differently. Getting all parties on board seemed impossible at times.

From our standpoint, this should have been a no-brainer. We had an extensive track record of successfully turning around distressed properties (including several with the same lender) and were prepared to invest a substantial amount in capital improvements. We were willing to jump in with both feet and turn this property around, which would benefit all parties and reduce the lender's credit risk.

Of course, the lender would have preferred that we make a large principal paydown at closing to reduce the LTV, but that just wasn't going to work for us. We strongly believed that the funds we had available for this project would be better invested in property improvements as opposed to paying down debt.

The most frustrating part of the lengthy assumption process and lender negotiations was that in the meantime, the current owners were running Madison Barracks into the ground. Now that the property was under contract, they had pretty much stopped doing anything at all.

They had stopped turning units, until there were literally no rent-ready units left, which in turn brought leasing to a standstill. Routine maintenance wasn't being completed and occupancy was dropping by the week. Meanwhile we were neck-deep in endless requests for documents, frustrated by a process that moved at glacial speed, and trying to negotiate agreements with a litany of people who either didn't understand the situation or didn't care.

After protracted negotiations, we agreed to establish a debt service escrow, a large new replacement reserve, higher monthly replacement reserve payments, and a variety of other items totaling approximately $700,000. The improvements we agreed to make were clearly defined, and the funds would be held in escrow until the work was completed and we provided proof of payment. The loan servicer ran this past all parties and thought it would satisfy everyone's needs.

Finally, a glimmer of light at the end of the tunnel. I thought we were finally nearing the finish line. Due diligence was done. The mortgage assumption was about to be approved. Maybe we could finally get this thing closed. Or maybe not.

To be continued...

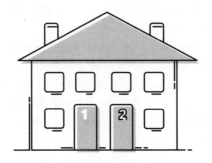

Chapter Eighteen
ASSET MANAGEMENT

We have two ears and one mouth so that we can listen twice as much as we speak.

—EPICTETUS

In Chapter Eight, we explained why it makes sense for most large multifamily investors to outsource property management, but electing this option doesn't mean you won't stay involved and provide oversight. There is far too much at stake to simply outsource property management and then walk away. Large multifamily investors assume a higher-level function associated with property management called asset management. As we discussed in Chapter Three, asset management basically means managing the property management company. In other words, you'll be keeping an eye on what the property management company is doing and making sure they are performing at a satisfactory level.

How to Be a Good Asset Manager

The biggest challenge you'll face as an asset manager is understanding all the nuances of property management. While property management is not particularly complicated, it does involve a lot of moving parts. There are countless responsibilities and considerations, as well as numerous situations that can arise, and the knowledge required to handle them successfully is picked up primarily on the job. Not surprisingly, one of the best qualifications for being a good asset manager is property management experience. Otherwise, it's hard to know what to look for in a property manager and what questions to ask.

Getting some property management experience under your belt early on with smaller properties can be valuable and pay dividends later as the size and number of your investments grow and your responsibilities evolve. What if you don't have this type of experience? You can either partner with someone who has the necessary background to be an effective asset manager, or do everything within your power to educate yourself about property management through books, videos, articles, podcasts, social media groups, seminars, meetups, and industry events.

Be a Good Listener

Regardless of how much property or asset management experience you may have, trying to come across as an expert in an attempt to impress or intimidate your property manager would be a mistake. No matter how much you think you know, there is more to learn—and every situation is different.

The first key to being a good asset manager is to focus on listening. Most of us could stand to listen more, but for an asset manager, it's crucial. The art of listening will come in particularly handy for those asset managers with limited experience. In the words of Mark Twain, "It is better to keep your mouth closed and let people think you are a fool than to open it and remove all doubt."

Ask questions that will facilitate an open dialogue and allow you to learn about any challenges the property manager is facing. As an asset manager, you aren't expected to know all the day-to-day details, but you should try to stay abreast of big-picture issues and make sure the property is on the right path and progress is being made. Good property managers take pride in their work. If you're an effective listener and can build trust with them, you will find that most are willing to share plenty of information—and the more you listen, the more you'll learn.

You can gain more practical knowledge from routine phone calls, video calls, or face-to-face meetings with a property manager than by taking a class. Jump in, ask questions, listen, and soak up all the info you can.

Most experienced property managers already know what they need to do. They just need to get it done. What will help? Knowing that somebody cares, is on their side, and recognizes when they make positive contributions and is grateful for their efforts.

Weekly Asset Management Meetings

A good asset manager will have standing weekly meetings with the property manager. If a property is fully stabilized, meetings can be reduced to biweekly or even monthly, but in the early stages it's important to stay on top of what's happening and build a solid relationship. Although face-to-face meetings are ideal, they often aren't practical. A video call is the best alternative, followed by a phone call. Written communication is the least effective format for weekly "meetings."

Celebrate Wins

A great way to start things off is by encouraging the property manager to share some wins to set a positive tone and put them at ease. Ask them to share accomplishments both large and small. It might be something major, like successfully completing a difficult project or reaching an occupancy milestone. It could be something minor but meaningful, such as a note of thanks from a tenant, a particularly speedy after-hours response to an urgent tenant need, or an act of kindness by one of the staff members.

Working in property management is a lot like working in an IT department: It's mostly about routine maintenance and problem solving. People don't stop by the IT department just to thank them because their email has been working great. If anyone is stopping by, they probably have a complaint. Likewise, people in an apartment community don't normally pop in at the management office just to say things are running smoothly; they usually have a problem. As a result, property management teams can feel unappreciated and start to find their work unrewarding. A good asset manager recognizes this, keeps it in mind, expresses gratitude, and creates opportunities to celebrate the positives.

Review Challenges

After you recognize your property manager's accomplishments, you should dig into some of their challenges and areas that need improvement. There could be quite a few, particularly if you've recently taken over a property that is distressed or has been poorly managed in the past, or that you're repositioning. These are the situations where good property managers will really earn their fees. Again, you can start with broad, open-ended questions, or dig in further with more probing questions if you have enough familiarity with an issue to do so. Mostly, though, you should listen attentively, because the property manager usually already knows what the solutions are to their own challenges.

Encouraging property managers to expand on issues they raise during your meetings is another key to learning about what's going on and building a solid working relationship. In his excellent book *Never Split the Difference*, author Chris Voss introduces a concept called mirroring, which is designed to keep people talking: You simply repeat back the last three words a person says to you. This may be uncomfortable at first, but it's a highly effective way to put people at ease and get them to open up. Voss explains that when you repeat back what a person says, "your counterpart will inevitably elaborate on what was just said and sustain the process of connecting."

Assess Key Performance Indicators

In addition to wins and challenges, you can also use your weekly meetings as an opportunity to get updates on key performance indicators (KPIs), which are select metrics for tracking performance. Most of a property manager's reporting will be done on a monthly cycle, but some items can be tracked weekly. There are no industry-wide standard weekly KPIs, so decide which items are your highest priorities, and whenever possible, find an appropriate metric to track them. Not everything important can be measured, but when you can find a good KPI, it can be motivational.

Common KPIs you might consider tracking on a weekly basis are expanded on below. Note that some of these may be more appropriate for monthly measurement and review, depending on your priorities and the situation at your property.

- **Project Milestones:** If you are undertaking projects such as major repairs and replacements, unit upgrades, or other value-add improvements, your property manager should prepare a construction schedule. At each meeting you should discuss progress versus established milestones and any associated issues.

- **Occupancy Rate:** Occupancy is one of the most important KPIs to track and should be included in weekly updates. Review the number of move-ins, move-outs, and renewals, and try to understand what is behind any increases or drops in occupancy levels and whether any changes should be made moving forward. The inverse of the occupancy rate is the vacancy rate, which would essentially be the same KPI.

- **Retention or Renewal Rates:** You should monitor your retention rate (the percentage of tenants who renew) and get regular updates on how many leases came up for renewal and how many were renewed. Property managers should always speak to residents who provide notification of non-renewal to find out why they want to leave and determine whether there is anything that can be done to retain the tenant. Note that the inverse of this metric would be the turnover rate (or churn rate), which is the percentage of tenants who do *not* renew and is basically the same KPI.

- **Collections and Delinquency:** You may want to get routine updates on how much rent is past due, and what steps are being taken to minimize collection losses. You can readily see resident delinquency by reviewing an accounts receivable aging report. A good metric to track is the percentage of scheduled rent that is collected by the end of each month.

- **Leasing Leads:** Finding out how many new leasing leads came in over the prior week and discussing the source of those leads can be helpful. Other valuable metrics may include the average response time to leasing inquiries and average number of follow-ups on the leads that come in, both of which have a strong impact on conversion rates. You can also gain insights from the percentage of leads converted to showings/tours, and the percentage of showings/tours converted to signed leases. Periodically correlating these conversion rates back to the source of leads can be a valuable way to gauge the relative effectiveness of various lead sources. By dividing the advertising cost of each lead source by the number of resulting signed leases, you can calculate your new resident acquisition cost for each source, which can help you evaluate whether to reallocate your marketing budget.

- **Average Days to Lease:** This often-overlooked metric tracks the average amount of time a unit remains vacant between the departure of one tenant and the move-in of the next. As a component of this metric, the property manager may also want to track the average number of days to turn a unit and make it rent-ready. Any progress in reducing the average days to lease can help raise annual rental income.
- **Service Requests:** To ensure good customer service, you can track how many service requests (or work orders) are opened, how many were closed, and the average time to close. To avoid this metric's resulting in sloppy, rushed work, the management staff should also conduct follow-up calls to measure resident satisfaction with service request resolution.
- **Rent-Ready Costs:** Monitoring the cost to turn units can be useful for managing repair and maintenance costs.

Many of these KPIs can be captured and reported using commercial leasing and property management software programs, but some may be more cumbersome to deal with. Data is valuable, but not if the benefits are outweighed by the effort it takes to collect, analyze, and report it. If you go overboard in requesting KPIs, you may find that on-site staff are spending too much time collecting and analyzing data to the detriment of other responsibilities. You should consult with your property manager when deciding which KPIs are going to be most helpful without overburdening staff or upending processes. The relative importance of certain KPIs may evolve as a property stabilizes or otherwise changes over time.

Monthly Management Reports

The bulk of the property management reporting will be captured in a larger monthly deliverable that is sometimes called an owner's report, or just a property management report. You'll want to schedule a monthly meeting to go through these management reports. In order to be well prepared and get the most out these meetings, it's a good idea to obtain reports in advance of the meeting and review them thoroughly. If your weekly meetings are with the property manager, you'll probably also want to include the regional manager in the monthly meetings, which is who most property managers report to.

There are a lot of different potential components and information that you might find in a property management report. Most property management firms' reports have a standard format and content, though they are usually willing to tailor them (within reason) to suit your needs. As with weekly meetings, there is a balance to be struck between providing enough information and overdoing it, so don't go overboard with your requests for customization or it could detract from the time your property manager should be spending on actually running the property.

What follows is a real-life example of the eight sections of an actual property management report for a large multifamily property that was prepared by a reputable property management firm that manages more than 10,000 units. We have also included some comments on how an asset manager might find each section of the report useful.

Not all property management reports are this comprehensive or include the same components. This is a great example, but it is not a one-size-fits-all solution. There are countless other reports and variations that can be equally beneficial. As an asset manager, you should be open to working with your property management firm to come up with a set of reports that will work best for both of you, the property, and your particular circumstances.

1. Narrative
The first two pages of the monthly management report are a narrative, which serves as an executive summary. The narrative is broken down into the following nine sections, each of which includes a one-paragraph summary:

- **Financial Summary:** States the total monthly operating income, operating expenses, and net operating income for the property, together with the percentage favorable or unfavorable to budget for each of them. The narrative also briefly summarizes the principal reasons for any excess or shortfall relative to budget.
- **Occupancy:** States the average physical and economic occupancy for the month and an explanation for any differences between the two. Also includes the number of move-ins and move-outs, the number of leases renewed, and the number of month-to-month leases. States the occupancy at month end, net units leased, and number of notices to vacate.
- **Advertising and Marketing:** Gives an overview of advertising and

leasing considerations, including leasing programs, specials, and concessions offered during the month. Lists each of the places the property is being advertised.

- **Traffic:** Outlines the results of monthly marketing and outreach efforts, including the number of inbound phone calls, email/text leads, and resulting number of applications. Of the applications received, states how many were approved and how many were pending at month's end.
- **Comparable Property Overview:** References high-level data from the market survey in the body of the report, including market occupancy estimates and how it compares to prior months. Also states how the subject property rents compare to average comparable rents. Notes plans for rent bumps and lists any properties under construction that could affect supply.
- **Resident Relations:** States the number of service requests completed during the month and notes any trends or general comments related to completion of the requests and customer service levels.
- **Delinquency:** States the total amount of delinquency at the end of the month and notes any reasons and actions being taken. Discusses plans to address past-due rent going forward.
- **Capital Projects:** Provides an update of ongoing improvement projects, including estimated percent completion and costs relative to budget.
- **Property Team:** Gives an overview of any staffing changes, promotions, compensation issues, and human resource issues.

A narrative like this one, either within the report or as an accompanying email, is important because you can quickly read the highlights and get some context for the numbers. It tells the story behind the data. Having read the narrative, you'll be in a better position to digest the rest of the report and go into your monthly meeting with a more complete picture of what's happening at the property. If your property management firm is not able to complete a full narrative, you can use the list of sections above as a structure for your discussion and review them orally.

2. Market Survey

The market survey consists of a table that summarizes leasing information for a half-dozen nearby comparable properties. The table includes estimates of current and prior occupancy levels, as well as current rents for each unit type, security deposit requirements, application fees, administration fees, and current specials and concessions being offered to new renters.

The market survey also includes the average for each of these metrics, providing you with an easy basis for comparison. The subject property is listed so that you can view it relative to the competition, though it is not included in the averages. Any reports similar to this one can provide a valuable snapshot of the market and where your property fits into the bigger picture, which can be useful for making decisions about changes in rent and concessions. It can also raise red flags. For example, if your property has lower rents than the competition and also has lower occupancy levels, you'll want to invest some time and effort in understanding why and figuring out how to address the problem.

3. Leasing Data

The leasing section of the report shows the occupancy, number of move-ins, move-outs, applications, renewals, and positive reviews for each of the trailing twelve months, which is a great way to track trends. Viewed in conjunction with the market survey, it can give you a good picture of a property's position and health from the perspective of leasing. This property management firm also includes the total operating income for each month alongside the leasing data. The operating income is presented in three columns: total charges, total collected, and a rolling three-month average to smooth out aberrations and allow you to easily see high-level income trends. Including the operating income allows you to readily see the impact of the leasing activity.

4. Budget Variance Report(s)

These valuable reports show the actual, budget, and variance for all major categories of income and expenses. They show the variance for the month and the year to date. Perhaps most importantly, one of the reports includes a "variance explanation" for every category and a few sentences providing insight into why the actuals are above or below expectations.

Note that these kinds of variance reports may roll budget line items up into major categories to make the information easier to digest. You can then reference more detailed reports to drill down into any areas of potential concern.

5. Cash Flow Report(s)

The cash flow reports are great because they not only show all your income and expenses, but also other non-operating items that affect cash. Examples would be capital expenditures, principal payments, and investor distributions. These reports were provided with monthly breakdowns for each month in the calendar year, as well as a second version with both the prior month and year to date. They are helpful for understanding how much cash the property is producing and consuming. Among other things, you can use a cash flow report to make decisions about investor distributions or capital improvements.

6. Balance Sheet

An updated balance sheet lists all the assets and liabilities for the property as of the end of the prior month. This can be helpful for tracking things like unpaid bills, debt principal, and how much you've paid in distributions so far in the current year.

7. Check Register

A property's check register is one of the most valuable reports you can request. Assuming your property is not paying for things in cash (which it shouldn't be), this document lists every payment that a property made during the prior month. It will include the name of the vendor, check or ACH number, date, whether the check has cleared, payment amount, the general ledger account name and number, and a brief description.

If you really want to understand where all the money is going at a property, this report can be a gold mine. An experienced asset manager will probably spend as much or more time digging into this report than any other.

8. Rent Roll

The final section of the report is a detailed rent roll as of the end of the month. This will include the unit number, unit type, tenant name, status, square footage, market rent, actual rent, security deposit, lease dates, and move-in date.

A rent roll can help you identify rents that are outliers or specific units that are responsible for loss to lease. It's also a handy source for detailed information when you're discussing issues that arise with a specific resident or unit in the community.

Purpose

Finally, try to remember that reports and data are great, but there is so much more to getting the most out of your property management team. Despite what you might think, your property management team is probably not leaping out of bed in the morning telling themselves they can't wait to get to work in order to make you more money. Far more likely is that they begin to take pride in the community they're managing and pride in performing their job at a high level. Good property managers also feel a sense of ownership and become a sort of "mother hen" to the residents, many of whom they are likely to grow attached to and feel some level of responsibility for. You'll notice that they use possessive terms, referring to the community as "*my* property" and the residents as "*my* tenants." This shows that they feel a sense of ownership, which is a very good sign and something I look for and encourage.

These are the kinds of attitudes that will help a property manager find their work rewarding and help you as the asset manager draw out the highest level of work performance from them and financial performance from the property. The financial rewards are a *by-product* of a job well done by people with other motivations. That's not to say you shouldn't have metrics associated with income and expenses, but you should remember to tie these things back as much as possible to aspects of property management that the people on the front lines can take pride in.

Other Asset Management Responsibilities

While providing oversight of property management is traditionally the asset manager's primary responsibility, the scope of duties can vary widely depending on the circumstances. For example, if you are doing syndications and have partners who are dividing up responsibilities, one of the GPs will typically have primary responsibility for capital raising and investor management. However, the asset manager may sometimes perform some of these duties, or both roles can be filled by a single person.

Some asset managers will also blur the lines of responsibility with their property management firm and assume a more active role than is the norm. This is particularly true when there is an extensive renovation or development involved. Given the critical importance of such projects, it's not unusual for an asset manager with construction experience to assume extra responsibilities in an effort to make sure things go well.

KEY TAKEAWAYS

- Some of the keys to good asset management include property management knowledge, being a good listener, and having regularly scheduled meetings in which you celebrate wins, review challenges, and assess KPIs.
- Your property manager should provide a set of comprehensive, monthly management reports that are designed to work best for you, the property, and your particular circumstances.
- Financial rewards are a by-product of a job well done by people with other motivations. You should remember to tie financial metrics back to aspects of property management that the people on the front lines can take pride in.

Madison Barracks: Part IX

The loan servicer for Madison Barracks informed us that an agreement had been reached, which I assumed meant we were ready to proceed. When a week passed with still no official word, I asked for a status update. Per their response: "The underwriting is almost complete, and we should be able to submit the request this week to management. Once approved, the request will be sent to the Master Servicer for their concurrence. We estimate the approval process to take 30 days once we have a final complete package." Unbelievable.

The assumption had dragged on for several months, and word began to get out that the property was going to be sold. We'd tried to keep it under wraps, but you can only do that for so long. Between the seller's staff, contractors, attorneys, insurance agents, and a host of third parties there were now dozens of people aware of the pending deal. What we didn't realize at the time is that public knowledge of the deal would come back to haunt us.

When we actually got the all-clear to proceed with closing, I was incredibly relieved. The occupancy kept dropping and the holidays—a notoriously slow time for leasing—were approaching. We needed to start righting this ship before it took on too much more water or it would sink us after closing. I met with the property management team to make sure everything was ready for the transition. With the property in rapid decline, we needed to hit the ground running. I also took the time to talk about the importance of this property to the community, its place in history, and how we could make a real difference in the lives of the residents. This was a project that would test us, but one that we could all take a lot of pride in.

Unfortunately, with only days to go before closing, I got a phone call from our property manager, who was out at the complex checking on things in preparation for the pending change in ownership. Apparently, a problem had come up that could prevent us from closing. Ugh! This was the last thing I needed. I desperately hoped it was something that could be resolved, because my patience was running out. If we didn't get this closed soon, we wouldn't have any tenants left.

To be continued...

Chapter Nineteen

ADDING VALUE

Companies that solely focus on competition will ultimately die. Those that focus on value creation will thrive.

—EDWARD DE BONO

About a year after I'd bought my first investment property, I was lucky enough to meet my future wife. While I think we both took an immediate interest in each other, I'm not sure it was exactly love at first sight. In fact, she later shared that initially, she wasn't overly impressed with everything she saw—at least not on the surface. My wardrobe was a liability in her eyes and needed to be "brought up to date." I also kept my BlackBerry in a leather case clipped to my belt at all times, which I thought made me look cool but was actually just nerdy.

Fortunately, my wife looked deeper and saw potential. In fact, I think it would be fair to say she took me on as a bit of a value-add project. She saw possibilities: someone who could become a better person with her love and support. Did it work? Well, I guess it depends on whom you ask. I've come a long way, but I'm still a work in progress. Then again, aren't we all?

Adding value to multifamily properties isn't really that different. You're looking for a property with good underlying fundamentals that has the potential to shine—potential that hasn't been reached due to factors you can correct. Ideally, you can find upside that isn't already factored into the price. Every real estate investor is looking for a return on their investment. While some investors are content with the returns they can achieve with the status quo, most are looking for more: trying to figure out how to boost income, lower expenses, or both. If an investor can do this, the property will generate more cash. It will then be worth more and drive up your investment returns, sometimes to fantastic levels.

Fortunately, properties are more concrete than human relationships, and there are formulas to help you estimate the value that can be added through improvements before you implement them—or before you even decide to purchase a property to begin with.

The Fundamentals

The potential you're seeking for value-add in a multifamily property amounts to any changes you can implement that will either increase the revenue a property is producing or decrease the expenses it is incurring. As we covered in more depth in earlier chapters, the difference between revenue and expenses is the NOI, and the goal of value-add is to find cost-effective ways to increase this number.

The real beauty of value-add for multifamily properties is that, unlike for single-family homes, their market value is a direct multiple of their NOI, and the multiple used to convert NOI into market value is the cap rate. In Chapters Eleven through Fourteen, we covered how to incorporate value-add into a property's valuation, but you can use the same formulas to directly calculate the incremental value added by a specific change using the following formula:

$$\text{Value-Add} = \text{Change in NOI} \div \text{Cap Rate}$$

For example, if you're able to increase a property's NOI by $100,000 and the cap rate is 5 percent, you can add $2 million in value. But is this

$2 million real or just theoretical? That depends in large part on your intentions. If you plan to hold the property forever and not refinance it, you're not going to realize the benefit immediately, but you'll still reap the ongoing rewards of the higher cash flow associated with the jump in NOI. If you plan to refinance or sell the property, on the other hand, you can reap the rewards on an accelerated timeline. The market value will be higher, so the property will command a higher price when you sell. If you don't want to sell, you can realize the value through a cash-out refinance, in which the value-add will be reflected in a higher appraised value.

Regardless of whether you plan to hold or sell, there is real opportunity in value-add. The challenge is to identify the changes that will create the highest amounts of value relative to the cost of implementation. Fortunately, most properties offer plenty of options to generate healthy returns.

Boosting Income and Lowering Expenses

The vast majority of opportunities to add value to multifamily properties lie in the multitude of simple and creative ways you can increase a property's income and reduce expenses, driving up your NOI. On most properties, the only limit is your imagination.

How do you find value-add ideas? Generally, investors rely on a combination of personal experience, anecdotal information, and their own inventiveness. To help address the lack of information out there, we have included three comprehensive, bonus supplements that share proven and practical ways to add value on both the income and the expense side.

Bonus Supplement I provides an overview of how to boost rental income, while Bonus Supplement II covers ancillary income, which includes the revenue sources that a multifamily can generate in addition to rent. Bonus Supplement III then delves into the numerous ways you can reduce a property's expenses. These value-add supplements can be accessed at www. biggerpockets.com/mmbonus.

Between the material presented in this chapter and the bonus supplements, you'll find dozens of tips, tricks, and strategies. While you may already be familiar with many of them, we're confident you'll discover some new ways to add value to your multifamily assets.

Beyond the ideas in the bonus supplements, perhaps the single most widely used value-add strategy for large multifamily properties is to reposition them and upgrade the units. This approach can be more complicated and entail more risk than some of the simpler, practical methods we've included, but it can also offer outsize rewards. If you plan to undertake a repositioning project, the risks can be mitigated by executing the plan in cooperation with an experienced property manager.

Repositioning Properties and Upgrading Units

As mentioned, one of the most common strategies for adding value to large multifamily communities is to reposition a property in order to charge higher rents. Repositioning a property involves making improvements that tenants are willing to pay for. In some instances, it will involve a change in class, perhaps elevating a Class C property to a Class C+ or B. Or a Class B property could be elevated to a Class B+ or A, for example.

How exactly do you accomplish this? Identifying and implementing the improvements that will yield the highest return is as much an art as a science. The first step is to understand the market dynamics in the area where the property is located. As part of your due diligence, carefully study the submarket and competition to see how much renters are willing to pay for different combinations of location, features, and amenities for each unit type. You'll want to look at a range of properties to get a feel for how rents vary along a spectrum. This means looking at comparable properties that are similar to your property's current state, as well as properties that have already been improved. Only then can you determine fair market rents for the current project, and which improvements will yield the optimal return (see Chapter Twelve for more details).

Getting good comps is particularly important because one of the most common mistakes value-add operators make is to over-improve, especially on unit upgrades. This normally happens because they assume a rent premium for certain unit upgrades without documenting local comps that are successfully getting the same premiums with similar upgrades. You should avoid planning to blaze a new path for rent premiums. Let someone else be the guinea pig—the risk is too high.

As discussed in our section on underwriting, there are many sources of information on market rents. You can learn a lot from community websites, advertising, and reviews, but you can also call the competition and "mystery shop." Once you engage someone on the phone, take the opportunity to dig in and understand the full range of offerings and rents a property has available, as well as trends and even information on competitive properties. Ask them what sets their property apart from specific competitors in the area, or why someone should live there over other alternatives (including the property you're hoping to acquire). Prompting leasing agents or property managers to share information on their competition can yield some pretty interesting insights. Property tours can be even more enlightening, and they will give you a better feel for a property's appeal, convenience, and surrounding neighborhoods.

Every market and submarket will have varying supply and demand for different sizes of units and features. Since there is often more than one way to fulfill a tenant's wants and needs, a fair amount of creativity and vision are involved when evaluating upgrades—but there are also tried-and-true approaches. The goal of this chapter is to review some of the more common improvements that consistently yield attractive results. These improvements may be to the exterior or the interior of the property or community wide.

Improving a Property's Exterior

To determine what improvements to make on a property's exterior, you'll want to complete a thorough inspection of the grounds and structures to decide what repairs and upgrades might be necessary both immediately and over the next few years. A good property management firm should be able to help with an initial assessment, and this can be followed up during underwriting with a full property condition assessment (PCA). Special attention should be given to all major components, such as roofs, windows, doors, sewer lines, roads, and parking areas. While not necessarily value-add, priority repairs should be included in your up-front budget, in addition to work that is more cosmetic in nature. You can consider longer-term replacements when determining replacement reserves.

When identifying ways to reposition a property, consider the entire customer experience from the moment they first pull into the location. In addition to the architecture and physical structures themselves, a property's signage, landscaping, cleanliness, and overall appearance are what create that critical first impression. Based on the property's "curb appeal," potential residents will make an immediate judgment regarding its overall desirability. You want to ensure that first impression is consistent with the class of property you're striving to achieve. The good news about curb appeal is that some of the most impactful improvements are straightforward and not that expensive.

Landscaping, Painting, and Cleaning

We consider landscaping, painting, and cleaning the "big three" in terms of achieving value-add on a property's common areas. These three types of improvements often turn out to be low-hanging fruit, meaning the necessary investments are usually very modest relative to the resulting change in image of a property and eventual return on investment through higher rents and occupancy. Landscaping, painting, and cleaning can often be handled by low-cost labor or even do-it-yourselfers or anybody who has the inclination and capacity to roll up their sleeves and get to work.

The big three have an outsize impact on a potential resident's critical first impression of a property. Every significant turnaround project we've ever undertaken has involved some level of cleanup and landscaping improvements, with the exception of urban properties with no green space. That's because landscaping, painting, and cleaning are some of the first things to be neglected by inattentive management—but they're also fairly easy to correct. A cleanup, a fresh coat of paint, and some mulch, tidied greenery, and beautiful flowers in the most visible locations can not only set a positive tone but really make a property pop. Our favorite places to enhance are the area immediately surrounding the property sign and the outside of the rental office, which is often prominently situated and will see more traffic.

Be careful not to get carried away while upgrading a property's image as part of repositioning. Some landscaping improvements can be expensive to implement and maintain, so make your design choices with an eye toward minimizing longer-term costs. It's wise to utilize sustainable and low-maintenance landscape features wherever possible. Planting perennial flowers instead of annuals, for example, can significantly reduce future expenses. The costs can be a little higher up front, but the property also won't need to buy new plants and flowers every year or incur the labor costs associated with purchasing, transporting, and planting them. In areas subject to drought, it behooves landlords to choose drought-resistant landscaping, which can both reduce the amount of water necessary for maintenance and help ensure plant survival. Instead of live landscaping features, property investors should consider materials like stones and rocks, which don't require watering or trimming.

Finally, better landscaping doesn't always have to mean a large investment in new plantings. Some of the most dramatic changes can result from the pruning or even elimination of overgrown trees, shrubbery, and plants. At more than one investment property, we've made significant improvements by completely clearing out unruly landscaping and replacing it with grass or gravel. This can make the property look tidier and more professional while reducing maintenance costs.

Parking and Sidewalks

When repositioning a property, consider the state of the parking, roads, and sidewalks. You'll want to ensure they're in a condition commensurate with the class of property you're striving for. Quality parking, roads, and sidewalks should be invisible to most non-investors. If new visitors to your apartment community are complimenting the quality of the concrete and asphalt, you've probably gone overboard. But if a visit involves encounters with potholes, haphazard parking due to lack of striping, and crumbling sidewalks, you're off to a really bad start.

Does this mean you need to tear it all out and start from scratch? Maybe. But in most instances, some patching, sealing, and striping can make a world of difference. While perhaps not as notable to new visitors, these types of improvements can make an outsize impression on current residents and help with retention when rents rise. As a side benefit, the repairs will mitigate the risk of liability associated with falls and accidents.

Front Doors

When a prospective tenant approaches a building, the entry door is front and center. It sets the tone as someone enters a property, and its importance can't be overemphasized.

Imagine this: You walk a prospective tenant up to the front door. As you stop to fumble through your keys, the tenant takes note of the beat-up old door, which is slightly askew. The paint is missing in some spots, as is a piece of the trim. At one turnaround property I purchased, the glass above the door was riddled with bullet holes. If you had to guess what waited on the other side of that door, what would you say? The prospect could be ready to tell you they'd changed their mind before ever setting foot inside!

Now imagine we replace that old beat-up door with a brand-new, gleaming glass one with a bronzed aluminum frame. The large glass window lets in light and gives the prospective tenant a glimpse of the well-lit, inviting lobby on the other side. They glance up and notice a small camera angled toward the front of the door, which gives them a feeling of safety and security. You pull out your compact electronic key fob and wave it in front of a sensor off to the side. You both hear a solid click as the door unlocks and the small red light turns to green. You then pull the door open and step aside to let your prospect enter. What a difference! They'll smile and think "I'm home" before they even enter a unit.

Security

Every tenant wants to feel safe in their new home, and nothing creates a better first impression of security than having cameras at the entrance to the property and camera monitors strategically positioned in the leasing office. You can enhance that positive impression with an electronic entry system such as a security card or fob system. The security card is the size of a credit card, and the key fob is an electronic device small enough to fit on a keychain. Either will unlock the door when you press it against a pad mounted next to the doorway. These are particularly impressive if such systems are uncommon in your marketplace or among your competition.

The great thing about cameras and electronic entry systems is that they not only create the impression of security and high standards but are actually effective deterrents to mischief, vandalism, and criminal activity. People are less likely to enter a property with the intention of committing a crime if they know their image is being captured. A security camera might also help identify people who damage the front of your property. At one of our properties the manager was able to figure out who cracked a picture window this way. After reviewing the footage, they discovered that a tenant had returned home drunk late at night and literally fallen over into the glass. Using this evidence, we were able to hold the tenant responsible for the cost of repairs.

Electronic entry systems offer even more brilliant advantages: You can maintain a record of who owns each card or fob, so you have a log of who is entering a property and when. Better yet, they can be deactivated when lost or stolen. Same thing with bad tenants who are evicted or leave on their own but decide to keep the card or fob: Simply deactivate it (which can be done remotely) and they'll never gain entry without authorization again. This sets cards and fobs apart from traditional key systems. Over time, keys are lost or stolen but remain in circulation. The only way to "deactivate" a traditional key is to change the locks to the property and swap out all the tenants' keys. That might be reasonable for a fourplex but is a much more involved and expensive task for a high-rise apartment building.

Some properties may also benefit from good old-fashioned security personnel, who can be hired on a permanent or temporary basis to physically drive and even walk the property throughout the day or only at night. Many operators have successfully used security service companies to help eliminate resident misbehavior and crime at takeover or during periods of heightened criminal activity. You can choose an appropriate level of service to fit your needs and budget.

Refurbish Lobbies

Imagine your leasing agent escorting a prospective tenant into the lobby or foyer as they continue to tell them about the property. While they stand there looking around, what do they see? Stains and an overflowing wastebasket, or a clean lobby with nice finishes? What do they feel? Is the temperature comfortable, or is it too hot or too cold? Perhaps just as important, how does the lobby smell?

Multifamily investor JC Castillo, who owns Velo Residential and specializes in repositioning large multifamily properties, gets it right when he likens the lobby of an apartment building to the lobby of a car dealership: "It's where you showcase the lifestyle the customer can have if they buy the car! By the time the prospective tenant leaves the lobby, they are already leaning significantly in one direction or the other."

Upgrading Units

As important as the common areas are, what they're doing is setting the stage. They're creating a first impression that the units either need to overcome or live up to, depending on the circumstances. Arguably the most critical upgrades you can make on a property are within the units themselves, because this is where tenants will spend the vast majority of their time, and this is where they'll be looking for the features that tend to be highest on their list. The units are usually where final renting decisions are made, and where prospects determine whether there is enough value to justify the rent you're charging.

One of the greatest ways to add value is to invest in new finishes. By this I primarily mean paint, flooring, and fixtures. These elements play a very large role in determining how a space is perceived—and they tend to have a significant impact relative to cost.

I've found that a fresh coat of paint provides the best return on investment. Flooring and fixtures aren't far behind. Giving a grungy old apartment a fresh coat of paint and changing out dated light fixtures (along with a few plumbing fixtures if necessary) will do wonders for how it shows. It should certainly lease more quickly and/or command enough additional rent to give you a quick payback period and a healthy return. Improving lighting and adding USB ports can be a nice touch, as can adding blinds for the windows. Blinds also offer the benefit of uniformity of appearance from a property's exterior. When you leave window treatments to the discretion of tenants, you never know what may end up draped over the windows.

Higher-end flooring can also enhance a space. We usually use hardwood or a hardwood-appearance product such as luxury vinyl plank (LVP). We also like luxury vinyl tile (LVT). These types of flooring tend to be durable and will reduce maintenance costs over the long term. It is a good idea to install hard-surface flooring in high-traffic and wet areas to reduce wear and tear. All improvements should be chosen with a similar eye toward cost-efficiency. This means choosing products that are more durable while also stressing uniformity in order to simplify inventory and repairs.

When leasing apartments, prospective tenants tend to scrutinize appliances very closely. New, higher-end, and energy-efficient appliances can make a very favorable impression and tilt a prospect toward signing a lease, particularly if the appliances are better than expected for the class of apartment you are offering.

If an apartment has an underutilized space that could accommodate a washer-dryer unit, adding washer-dryer hookups is another great upgrade option. This amenity can be a strong competitive differentiator and help you command a higher rent. There is a significant population of renters who feel washer-dryer hookups are a nonnegotiable requirement—and in many markets the supply for this amenity falls far short of demand, particularly in older housing stock.

Structural elements should be approached with caution as they tend to have a lower return. For example, all-new cabinets or counters might be nice (and perhaps necessary for higher-end properties), but they are among the costlier items to replace. Sometimes they can be painted or stained instead. In many cases the cabinet faces and doors can be replaced instead of tearing everything out and starting over. Adding a new backsplash is another cost-effective improvement that can do wonders for the overall appeal of a refurbished kitchen.

Multifamily properties with ground-floor units and enough green space can effectively expand the footprint of those units by adding patios, decks, and/or privacy fences. Expanding a unit with outdoor living space makes it much more desirable and can help command higher rent.

Larger improvements, such as new HVAC equipment, replacing or adding balconies, or changing floor plans, are sometimes necessary but can dramatically escalate your renovation costs and should be approached with care. You just want to be sure the payback is there. Knowing what *not* to upgrade is almost more important than knowing what *to* upgrade.

In assessing unit upgrades, you also need to consider any possible logistical complications. Many of the upgrades discussed here would be extremely challenging if not impossible to accomplish while a unit is occupied. Because of the disruptive nature of rehabbing a unit, you'll need to consider whether to relocate tenants or to do upgrades only as units become available. Most management firms will have experience navigating such circumstances and can be a great resource when you're determining the best course of action.

Finally, creating a unit upgrade template, not only per property but also per unit type, can help achieve uniformity of the finished product each time you stamp out an upgraded unit. Taking the time to create an Excel template for each unit type with upgrade items, vendors, unit pricing, color and finish specs, and designating which elements are to be completed in-house versus contracted out will ensure that every new resident gets the same end product at move-in with as little variance as possible. This level of detail also makes the cost for unit upgrades more predictable on the front end and helps avoid budget overages, frustration from the onsite staff if no blueprint exists for how to upgrade units, and bad online reviews from disgruntled and misled tenants.

Model Units

A well-planned model unit is also a critical part of any unit upgrade plan. The model unit is where you sell the dream. For example, the model unit should have all the upgrade finishes that are contained in your upgrade template, meticulously ensuring that not a single thing differs from what the resident would get at move-in. For example, if the resident sees granite counter tops in the model unit but gets sprayed laminate countertops in their unit at move-in, that will be a source of frustration not only for the resident but also for the onsite staff, who will instantly lose credibility with their resident base.

The model unit should also be fully furnished and well designed. Consider consulting with a professional interior designer on things like space planning and furniture, which can help residents immediately envision their dream unit.

Amenities

Multifamily amenities are common features and services that a community offers to its residents above and beyond their living space. When it comes to amenities, the possibilities are practically limitless. Anything you can think of that would be appealing to renters is worthy of consideration. Some examples are :

Playground/Play Area	Game Room
Library	Dog Park
Pet-Washing Station	Pool
Gym/Fitness Area	Sports Courts/Fields
Walking/Running Path	Video Intercom
Community Room or Clubhouse	Community Wi-Fi
Outdoor Kitchen or Grilling Area	Business Center/Workspace
Garages	Private or Covered Parking
Security Fence and Gated Access	Doorman or Security Guard
Bike Racks/Storage	Online Portal for Payments & Work Orders
Mail Room with Package Lockers	Electric Car Charging Stations
Recycling Center	Valet Trash Service

When repositioning a property, determining what baseline amenities are necessary to meet tenant expectations is not always straightforward. Determining how much a given amenity will allow you to raise rents is equally challenging, if not more so.

There is a clear correlation between amenities and rent levels, and it increasingly comes into play as you move up the quality scale to better-class apartments. Higher rents come with higher expectations. But the relation of cost to benefit varies. Expectations vary as well, depending on what can be found at other properties. The key is to provide tenants with superior value. As such, when repositioning a property, the first step in determining what amenities to add is to do a survey of the competition. This will give you a better feel for the baseline in the area and where you need to be in order to be competitive.

The second step is to consider the merits of each potential amenity and how much perceived value it would add for your tenants. We say "perceived value" because this can differ significantly from actual value. For example, in some areas, a pool may be considered necessary for higher-end properties, even though it may not be used frequently. In the end, its presence may create a lot more value from a marketing standpoint than from its actual usage.

You should also consider the demographics of your target residents and what they value. Are you hoping to appeal to older or younger residents? Technology executives or blue-collar workers? Families or singles? These factors and others can make some amenities more appropriate than others.

Societal trends weigh in favor of amenities targeted at pet owners. Pet stations, walking paths, washing stations, and pet parks are all highly desirable for residents with pets. The up-front and maintenance costs of such features are also fairly modest relative to those of other amenities, making them a good value-add investment for many multifamily projects. For properties with ample green space, dog parks are one of our favorite amenities to add.

Create a Community

In addition to physical improvements, creating a stronger feeling of community among the residents can elevate a property. Improving communication by using social media, newsletters, and memos is one of many ways to do this. Increasing activities is another. Some landlords encourage tenants to stop by their rental office by offering coffee, light snacks, or candy. Some communities host classes, barbecues, yard sales, and other events that encourage socializing. If tenants get to know their neighbors and feel they're part of a closer-knit community, they'll be more reluctant to relocate.

Rebranding

There are two aspects to repositioning a property: One is improving it physically; the other is improving its reputation. The latter can be challenging. A certain amount will happen organically over time by word of mouth; unfortunately, this can take years. Here are a few ways to accelerate the process:

- If the property has a bad history or reputation, consider renaming it. This can be particularly important if it has a lot of bad reviews online.
- Put up promotional signs and advertise the property as "under new ownership" and "newly renovated."
- Offer referral bonuses to tenants to encourage them to talk about all the improvements.
- Chronicle the property's transformation on social media with plenty of videos and before-and-after photos.
- Issue a press release and pitch a turnaround story to local news media.
- Host a series of open houses. You can also invite community leaders and press for a private tour.
- Actively encourage residents to post positive online reviews if they are happy with the improvements to the community and the new management. The best times to get reviews are at move-in and after a successfully completed work order.

Sample Repositioning Project

For an example of what a repositioning project might look like, let's review an actual plan to improve a large multifamily property. Based on a survey of neighboring properties, it was determined that if the apartment units were upgraded and a few more amenities were added, rents could be raised from an average of $1,100 per month to an average of $1,300 per month.

Proposed unit renovations included new stainless-steel appliance packages, new wood-style flooring, granite countertops, new cabinet doors with updated hardware, a modern lighting package, undermount sinks, two-inch faux-wood blinds, new tile backsplashes, and private fenced-in yards for ground-floor units.

The community had an existing tennis court in a state of disrepair that received minimal usage. The plan was to remove the concrete and repurpose the court area to house a new playground and a dog park.

The cost for all the work combined was estimated at approximately $10,000 per unit. In order to determine whether this project would provide an attractive return, you would need to determine the value it would create through the incremental increase in rents. Since similar properties in this market were trading at a 6 percent cap rate, the value added to each unit by increasing the rents by $200 per month could be estimated as follows: ($200 per month × 12 months per year) ÷ .06 = $40,000 per unit

Spending $10,000 per unit in order to create $40,000 per unit in value-add is an excellent plan that will dramatically drive up the project returns. This is a great example of how to increase the value of a property. A savvy multifamily investor will know the market and be on the lookout for value-add projects that can generate these kinds of gaudy returns.

KEY TAKEAWAYS

- Value-add is driven by changes in NOI. You can easily estimate value-add by dividing the increase in NOI by the cap rate. Once a value-add idea is implemented, the value you create can then be extracted through an exit or a refinance.
- The most widely used value-add strategies include straightforward ways to boost income or reduce expenses. *A multitude of ideas can be found in the bonus supplements.*
- If properly planned and executed, repositioning a property and upgrading its units can be an effective way to add significant value. Due to the risks involved, this type of value-add project should be planned and undertaken in cooperation with an experienced property manager.

Madison Barracks: Part X

With the closing finally in sight, my property manager visited the Apartments at Madison Barracks to check on things and called to report what he had discovered.

"Bad news," he said. "Apparently, a couple of the contractors who have done work out here were never paid. They heard about the sale and are going to be filing liens. One of them even gave me a copy." He hesitated for a bit before adding, "It sounds like there might be more coming too."

Oh man. I didn't think we'd be able to close if there were liens on the property—and I knew the seller didn't have the funds to pay these debts. I wondered what it would take to clear this up, and how long the legal process would drag on. Our attorney assured me that something could be worked out. He didn't seem as concerned as I was.

However, right before closing word came in that the seller's property manager (the one who slept in the property management office) was also going to place a lien on the property. Apparently, he had not only paid some contractors out of pocket but was even supplementing the pay of onsite staff! As bizarre and unlikely as this seemed, he had documentation to back it up.

In the end, the attorneys agreed that a portion of the proceeds from the sale would be set aside until the liens were released, thus placing the full responsibility for paying the liens on the seller. The closing itself was anticlimactic, at least from my perspective. It came to light that my attorney had performed a variety of legal acrobatics to get us across the finish line. I had trusted him to get it done, and my trust was well-placed.

Getting past the closing was such a huge relief. Now we could assess just how far things had deteriorated at the property while it was under contract and start down the long road of making the improvements we'd so carefully planned. We were finally in control and could begin to turn things around. Time to start upgrading units and repositioning the property.

Unfortunately, that feeling of being in control would prove all too fleeting. Even though working with the servicer on the loan assumption had been such a long and painful process, I really hoped our relationship would get better once we took over the property. I could have never imagined how much worse it would actually get—bad enough to make the project fail.

To be continued...

Chapter Twenty

LEGAL AND ACCOUNTING CONSIDERATIONS

> *To me, a lawyer is basically the person that knows the rules of the country. We're all throwing the dice, playing the game, moving our pieces around the board, but if there is a problem the lawyer is the only person who has read the inside of the top of the box.*
>
> —JERRY SEINFELD

As a multifamily investor, you will encounter a wide range of legal and accounting issues that will play a significant role in your journey. Some will affect your income, while others can determine whether you end up incarcerated. If you've already developed a good general understanding of the rules of the game through prior investing experience, you already know the value of getting support from legal and financial experts.

As discussed in Chapter Eight, having a solid real estate attorney and accountant in your corner is essential. Sometimes things are straightforward, but other times they're complicated. It's not always easy to distinguish between the two because we don't know what we don't know. With large multifamily properties, relatively small issues can have outsize implications, especially when compared with dealing with a duplex.

What follows is an overview of the legal and accounting issues you may encounter as a large multifamily investor. This is just an introduction—and not in any way meant to be a substitute for getting sound, professional advice!

Forms of Ownership

Whenever you acquire a multifamily property, you'll need to create an ownership entity. While you could technically hold a large multifamily property in your personal name, which is known as a sole proprietorship, this practice is rare for two important reasons. First, having a property in your name creates personal liability. If you are sued for anything at all, everything you own could be at risk. Insurance may offer some protection but has limitations and exclusions. Ultimately, insurance companies are profit-seeking ventures, so we use them only as our first line of defense. Apart from the liability issues, obtaining financing as a sole proprietorship is difficult for large assets.

The types of entities you can form in order to acquire a multifamily property are C corporations, S corporations, limited liability companies (LLCs), limited partnerships, and trusts.

C Corporations and S Corporations

A small number of investors elect to incorporate, usually due to specific tax situations. Holding property in a C Corporation (C corp) limits any potential liability to the assets held within the corporation in an entity that is likely to satisfy a lender.

However, a major drawback to C corps is that they may be subject to double taxation. The entity pays corporate income taxes on its profits; then, once it distributes its after-tax profits to shareholders, the shareholders pay income taxes on those dividends. Due to the tax implications alone, C corps are rare in the multifamily world.

Corporations can mitigate the unfavorable tax treatment by applying to the IRS for a Subchapter S Corporation (S corp) tax designation. S corps are more attractive from a tax standpoint because most states do not tax them at the entity level, so there is no double taxation. Instead, the tax liability is determined when the profits and losses are passed through to the corporation's shareholders, which are limited to no more than a hundred people. S corps do have one potential disadvantage, however. If more than 25 percent of their income is passive, the excess is taxed at the maximum corporate rate, which can pose a problem for real estate investors.

A couple of other limitations to note are that, with certain exceptions, shareholders must be individuals, not other legal entities, such as LLCs. Finally, both C corps and S corps come with a host of filing and administrative burdens.

In the end, unless there is a unique tax or legal incentive making corporations particularly appropriate for specific circumstances, they are not generally an appealing choice for real estate investors. Instead, most real estate investors opt for limited liability companies, limited partnerships, tenancy in common, or trusts.

Limited Liability Companies

LLCs are by far the most popular choice among multifamily investors because they offer the same kind of liability protection as corporations while avoiding onerous taxation issues. An LLC typically will elect to be treated as a partnership, so income and expenses flow straight through the LLC to the members' returns. The filing and administrative burdens are also less costly and cumbersome than a corporation's, making an LLC more attractive from that standpoint as well. LLCs offer greater flexibility with regard to how profits and losses are distributed, which can accommodate a wide range of deal structures and investor demands. LLCs are typically also viewed as a favorable type of entity by most lenders.

The downsides associated with LLCs are fairly limited. There are some modest filing requirements, which vary by state. In general, you can expect to go through an initial registration process and then pay an annual filing fee, which also varies by state. Some states also have annual reporting or information statement requirements. But overall, LLCs usually provide great benefits with minimal downsides.

Series LLCs

The SLLC is a type of "master LLC" with separate divisions, or "series," that each provide separate liability protection. Each series can own separate properties and have different managers and members. The aim of an SLLC is to provide the same liability protection you would receive by using separate LLCs, but within a single entity.

The benefit of an SLLC is that you can pay a single set of annual state fees and have a reduced administrative burden. Nothing beats an SLLC for long-term asset holding while minimizing administrative costs and time. Concerns expressed about SLLCs are primarily associated with unresolved tax issues and a lack of clarity regarding liability protection between the series in states that do not have established laws governing SLLCs. If you choose to use an SLLC, find a professional who uses them frequently and in multiple states and situations.

It is notoriously difficult to obtain financing as an SLLC, so all financing would need to occur through a different legal vehicle and be transferred to the SLLC after the fact for long-term holding.

Partnerships

There are two types of partnerships: limited partnerships and general partnerships. A limited partnership (LP) is often a good entity choice when raising private capital from passive investors. LPs work well for syndications and are covered in some depth in Chapter Three.

Unlike LPs, general partnerships (GPs) do not offer protection against liability to the partners. A GP is really just an agreement between two or more people to own and operate a business together. GPs are similar to sole proprietorships in that their absence of liability protection makes them less attractive for real estate transactions. In fact, GPs are actually worse than sole proprietorships because one partner can be held personally liable for the actions of another partner on behalf of the partnership.

Tenancy in Common

Tenancy in common (TIC) is an old form of ownership that is unique in that it constitutes direct ownership of a property. There is no limit to how many TICs can have an interest in a single property, but you'll have to limit the number of co-owners to thirty-five to remain eligible for a 1031 exchange (which we'll discuss later in this chapter). With other legal entity structures, such as LLCs and partnerships, the entity owns the property, and it's the ownership of the entity that gets divided up among investors. The owners of the TIC have direct ownership of their undivided interest in the property, almost as if the TIC didn't exist. In fact, the distributions and tax benefits are allocated in direct proportion to the percentage of the property each person owns.

Why and when would you use a TIC? TICs are used almost exclusively for people who want to do a 1031 exchange, which allows you to reinvest the proceeds from the sale of one property into another "like-kind" property. The IRS doesn't consider purchasing a portion of an LP or LLC a like-kind exchange because you're technically exchanging into an ownership stake of an entity, not a property. Since a TIC gives investors direct ownership in the property, the IRS considers a partial interest in a TIC as a satisfactory like-kind exchange.

Nonetheless, some unique aspects of TICs can make them cumbersome. For example, all the co-owners are required to vote on major investment decisions and to sign on any loans. As a result, most lenders are reluctant to provide financing for acquisitions that will be held by TICs. From a lender's perspective, having to underwrite and monitor up to thirty-five borrowers on a single property can also be a significant administrative burden.

Trusts

A trust (or a land trust, depending on the state) is a vehicle used to pass property on to one or more beneficiaries. A trust can be either revocable, meaning the creator may keep control of the trust and make changes, including terminating the trust, or irrevocable, meaning control is generally ceded to the beneficiary when the trust is created, and only the beneficiary can make changes—although the grantor may retain certain rights. Trusts that are created for estate planning purposes while you are still alive are called living trusts, while trusts that don't go into effect until you are deceased are called testamentary trusts.

Trusts are most commonly used for estate planning or for privacy reasons. Placing a property in a trust can help ensure that the property is not subject to probate. Probate is a legal proceeding that will render all your assets and who gets them part of the public record.

There are some significant downsides to trusts as well. First, trusts are more complex and costlier than other legal entities. By itself, a trust provides little in the way of asset protection, so it is typically used in conjunction with LLCs and other entities. The combination provides anonymity and protection, but at slightly higher legal costs. In addition, the rules associated with estate taxes are notorious for changing frequently, and any modifications to the trust will incur additional legal costs. Finally, trusts can complicate the lending process. Since the property could convey to the beneficiary at any time, you should be prepared for lenders to underwrite all parties.

Delaware Statutory Trust

A Delaware statutory trust (DST) is a unique type of trust that was created through the enactment of legislation in the state of Delaware. Multifamily investors typically use DSTs to pool investor funds, with each investor holding a fractional interest in the trust, which has title to the property.

DSTs offer investors several advantages. They are relatively easy to form and maintain compared to more traditional trusts, and they provide limited liability protections to the trustees, managers, investors, and beneficial owners similar to those of LLCs. They also provide a lot more flexibility with respect to the rights and responsibilities of the parties. Unlike in TICs, all the investors are not required to vote and there is only one borrower. Two additional features of DSTs make them particularly appealing for many real estate investors:

- When set up appropriately, DSTs can provide a high level of anonymity, which can discourage lawsuits. In order to build a case against you, an attorney would first need to identify who you are, which can be very difficult with a DST.
- Investors can do a 1031 exchange and roll the proceeds of a sale into a DST, which provides benefits similar to those of a TIC, but without many of the downsides.

As a result of the IRS ruling that allowed ownership interests in a DST to be an acceptable replacement property for a 1031 exchange, DSTs are often used as a vehicle to pool funds for similar purposes as an LP or TIC. Multifamily investors raise capital for their projects using a DST structure because it can attract capital from people who have sold properties and are seeking to defer capital gains by rolling the proceeds of their sale into a passive investment.

Although DSTs do have downsides, they are relatively modest compared to the benefits. A DST is an illiquid investment for people who roll their capital into it through a 1031 exchange, and those investors are also entirely passive, with no control or say in how the DST's assets are managed. For the deal sponsor, there are a variety of constraints that could cause concern, including the inability to accept future capital contributions or reinvest the proceeds from the sale of any assets. There are also a variety of debt, lease, and capital expenditure restrictions to contend with. Finally, all cash other than necessary reserves must be distributed to investors.

These DST restrictions are not likely to be significant when a property is performing well, but they could definitely become problematic if a property goes into distress. If the restrictions must be violated, Delaware law does allow for a provision to convert the trust to an LLC, which is known as a springing LLC. Converting a DST to an LLC would unfortunately disqualify any tax-deferral benefits, but having it as an option in case of emergency helps make lenders more comfortable with DSTs.

DSTs are complicated, so we would like to remind you again that you should consult with an experienced attorney with the appropriate expertise before making any decisions.

Managing Liability

Each type of legal entity has its own level of liability protection, but there is still risk that must be considered and managed. The level of exposure will depend on the specific circumstances and type of debt, the type of legal entity and corporate structure, and liability insurance coverage. Large multifamily investors manage their liability exposure in several ways.

Debt

Unless you are investing as a limited partner (in which case your liability exposure is limited to the funds you invest), the liability protection you are afforded through the ownership entity is not going to absolve you of debt obligations. Even if you were to lose ownership of the property, you'd still be on the hook for the remaining mortgage debt. The exception is nonrecourse debt. As explained in Chapter Seven, some debt is full recourse and other debt is nonrecourse. Loan guarantors on full recourse debt are personally liable in the case of default, while with a nonrecourse loan, liability is limited to "bad acts." When evaluating debt options, investors who want to limit risk exposure will prioritize nonrecourse loans.

Entity Structure

Beginning investors often ask, "How many properties should I put under one LLC?" and "Should I create a new legal entity for every property?" The answers depend on your tolerance for risk. Every time you add another LLC (or any other legal entity) there are additional costs and administrative tasks, but there is also an additional level of protection. Many investors will compromise and elect to place multiple properties in one LLC, but only up to a point they are comfortable with. The limits for how many properties they are willing to combine might be based on an aggregate market value for properties financed with full-recourse debt, or aggregate equity for those properties financed with nonrecourse debt.

However, the potential consequences of losing a property rise to an entirely new level when it comes to large multifamily transactions. When you're investing in assets with market values in the millions of dollars, the benefits of creating separate ownership entities for each property far outweigh any modest burdens. Yes, the likelihood of a lawsuit resulting in the loss of all properties owned by an entity is low, but there is just too much at stake not to take simple precautions. Many lenders agree and will make this a loan requirement.

There are many other ways that investors will try to shield themselves from potential liability:

- Some investors build multiple layers of protection into their corporate structure. For example, you can make the property ownership entities wholly owned subsidiaries of another entity with liability protection.
- Investors who have their own management company or are self-managing will usually create a separate entity for property management. This will separate liability associated with operations.
- Investors will also take pains to keep all finances separate between properties, management operations, and personal assets. It is best to keep boundaries clear and not blur any lines.
- Investors will use "equity stripping" tactics to remove equity from their properties so that the loss of an asset is financially bearable.

Some of these approaches may work for you; others may not. Be sure to review these and any other strategies carefully with your attorney and accountant to determine what steps are most appropriate for your specific property and situation.

Insurance Coverage

Most steps to limit liability through the use of separate entities are about confining your loss to a specific asset and not putting other properties or personal assets at risk. However, even if you successfully contain the risk to one property, if that property is big enough, the consequences can be dire.

That's where insurance comes in. Insurance coverage is your front-line protection—not only to guard your assets but also to pay for legal defense, which can be very expensive whether or not a claim has merit. If you are securing agency debt or working with other large multifamily lenders, the minimum coverages will typically be defined as a condition of the loan. These tend to be quite expansive, since lenders don't want you to lose the property any more than you do. Still, you should consult with a broker about filling any possible gaps in coverage. You'll want to seek out an insurance broker who has extensive experience with large multifamily and get their advice on appropriate coverage.

Large multifamily investors also tend to secure an umbrella policy to provide coverage above and beyond what is provided through the primary policy. Umbrella coverage is usually fairly economical and can be limited to a specific property or extended to an entire portfolio, depending on individual needs. In addition, having a broker periodically review your coverage to identify any gaps or unnecessary overlaps is always good practice.

Tax and Accounting Considerations

While the choice of legal entities, corporate structures, and insurance is driven in part by a desire to manage risk and mitigate losses, tax considerations should also be weighed in your decision-making. Income taxes don't usually have a direct impact on property valuation, but they can have an outsize effect on after-tax cash flows and after-tax internal rate of return (ATIRR), which is calculated the same way as IRR (see Chapter Fourteen) after adjusting cash flows to reflect income tax.

Tax treatment of different entities is not the only factor to consider. Other accounting issues that can have a dramatic impact are depreciation and capital gains. Two of the most widely used tools available to help investors leverage depreciation and minimize capital gains include cost segregation and like-kind exchanges.

Cost Segregation

When it comes to taxes, depreciation can be a real estate investor's best friend. As explained in Volume I, depreciation effectively offsets income and helps reduce an investor's tax burden. The more depreciation, the more income can be offset, which reduces your income tax burden.

The most common way that multifamily properties are depreciated is to allocate a portion of the purchase price to the value of the land and the rest to the improvements, which are then depreciated using the straight-line method over 27.5 years. For example, if you purchase a property for $5 million (including closing costs), your accountant may allocate $1 million to the land and $4 million to the improvements. The amount allocated to the improvements is the "basis" for depreciation. The $4 million would be depreciated over 27.5 years, at a rate of $145,454 per year. The basis would subsequently be reduced each year by the amount depreciated or increased due to the addition of capital improvements.

The problem with this method is that you've assumed all the components of the property have the same useful life as the building or structure itself, even though the IRS has published guidelines for the timelines over which a taxpayer can depreciate the various components (aka "recovery periods"). For example, any personal property you purchase for the property—such as computers, appliances, and carpeting—can be fully depreciated over a five-year recovery period, while office furniture is considered seven-year property. A fifteen-year recovery period applies to items like roads, fences, and shrubbery.

In order to unlock the accelerated depreciation schedules for different components, you may want to retain a consultant to complete a cost segregation study. This study will typically identify somewhere between 15 and 40 percent of a property's basis as falling into the five-, seven-, and fifteen-year recovery periods. All structural components, such as the roof, HVAC units, doors, and windows, will be separated as well. When these items are replaced, you can write off that portion of the basis.

A properly completed cost segregation study involves an on-site inspection and an engineering study that properly quantifies the building components and their associated values. The cost will likely be between $3,000 and $10,000, depending on the size and complexity of the property as well as the scope and quality of the work performed.

In the end, the benefits of cost segregation will typically far outweigh the expense of the study, which ironically can also be written off. Cost segregation can yield tremendous tax benefits from the accelerated depreciation deductions, not to mention the write-offs when building components are replaced down the road.

Note, however, that cost segregation does not create additional depreciation. Instead, it changes the timing of depreciation, pulling the tax advantages forward so that they can be realized sooner. You are then left with a lower basis, which is used to determine the size of the gain on which you will be taxed at the time of a sale. In other words, the more you depreciate, the lower your basis, and the larger your gain at the time of sale. That means it will eventually catch up to you—right? Maybe not. Investors have the unique opportunity to defer their gains through a 1031 exchange.

1031 Exchanges

When you sell a property, your accountant will determine the amount of gain and the amount of income tax on that gain. However, there is another option: a 1031 exchange, so called after Internal Revenue Code (IRC) Section 1031.

IRC Section 1031 contains provisions for an investor to exchange one property for another within a specified timeline and elect to defer the gain until the replacement property is sold (or exchanged for another property). While this provision is pretty fantastic, it comes with a host of requirements that must be adhered to, which can make compliance challenging. An experienced tax attorney or CPA can help you navigate the process. In the meantime, here are some highlights to be aware of:

- If any proceeds from the sale come into your possession, even for a short period of time, those proceeds will be subject to taxation. For this reason, investors who want to do a 1031 exchange should engage a third party called a qualified intermediary (QI) to receive the proceeds and then transfer the proceeds to the seller of the replacement property. The QI should be able to prepare all the necessary documentation associated with the 1031 exchange, alleviating that administrative burden.
- The replacement property must be of like-kind, though the definition of "like-kind" is fairly broad. In general, any investment real estate asset would be considered suitable.
- The replacement property must be of equal or greater value than the one sold. Otherwise, a portion of the proceeds from the sale will be subject to taxation. You also need to replace the full amount of any

debt you paid off when you sold your property with equal or higher debt on the replacement property.

- The replacement property must be identified within forty-five days of the sale of your property. You are permitted to identify up to three properties as prospective candidates regardless of value. You can identify more than three properties if the aggregate value of the properties identified doesn't exceed 200 percent of the value of the property sold. Alternatively, you can identify an unlimited number of replacement properties as long as the acquired properties are valued at 95 percent or more of the replacement cost.
- You must close on the replacement property or properties within 180 days. Otherwise, the gain will be subject to taxation.

Finding a suitable replacement property within the specified timeline is not always easy. We've both done 1031 exchanges in which we were under the gun to locate another property to buy. You could end up purchasing a property that you would not have otherwise pursued, which isn't advisable. While the potential tax savings can be considerable, you should not compromise your standards. Sometimes paying extra for a property that meets your investment criteria can make more sense. When searching for a replacement property, be sure to weigh the potential tax savings when evaluating prospective returns.

It is also possible to complete a reverse 1031 exchange, which involves acquiring the replacement property before selling the property to be exchanged. This transaction is less common and more complicated. In order to complete a reverse exchange, the property title must be transferred to an exchange accommodation titleholder (EAT) and a qualified exchange accommodation agreement (QEAA) must be signed. The timeline requirements for a reverse exchange are forty-five days to identify the property you will sell and 180 days to close.

Finally, if you want to spread your capital gains out over time or invest proceeds into something other than real estate, you can consult with a specialist regarding a tax strategy called deferred sales trusts. A deferred sales trust does not sell the property directly to the buyer. Instead, an installment contract with a third-party trust will be executed. The property transfers to the trust, and the trust in turn sells the property to the buyer. Taxes are deferred until receipt of installment payments that contain principal, and in the interim, you can reinvest the proceeds into stocks, bonds, or other investments through the trust. If you don't want to pay capital gains taxes, the installment contract could be set up for interest-only payments, which will allow deferral of the capital gains tax indefinitely.

KEY TAKEAWAYS

- Legal forms of ownership and tax designations at your disposal include C corps, S corps, LLCs, SLLCs, LPs, GPs, TICs, trusts, and DSTs. Each type of entity comes with its own legal, tax, and business advantages and disadvantages.
- Beyond the protection afforded through your choice of legal entity, you can manage your liability exposure through your choice of debt, corporate structure, and insurance coverage.
- Two of the key tax and accounting tools available to help investors leverage depreciation and minimize capital gains include cost segregation and 1031 exchanges.

Madison Barracks: Part XI

After we finally closed on the Apartments at Madison Barracks, our property manager jumped in with both feet. Top priority was to get units rent-ready and start filling the place up. During the time we had the property under contract, occupancy had fallen to 55 percent, and there wasn't a single rent-ready unit. We definitely had our work cut out for us, but the property management team knew what they were doing. Contractors were lined up and ready to go.

We also got a couple of proposals to have a cost segregation study completed and discovered that about 20 percent of the depreciable assets fell into categories that could be depreciated over five, seven, or fifteen years instead of 27.5. The potential net after-tax benefit would be about $200,000 over the first six years of ownership. In addition, completing the cost segregation study would also allow us to write off structural components that we planned to replace, which could result in even more tax savings. The benefits were just too good to pass up.

Our work progressed well over the first couple of months, and we were ahead of schedule. We were banging out the property improvements we had planned. Unfortunately, our loan servicer was about to derail us.

At first, the issues with the loan servicer were really nothing more than an annoyance. For example, less than two weeks after closing they demanded a full property inspection, even though a thorough property conditions assessment had already been completed by a third party less than a month earlier. Yes, it was a disruption for the property staff, but more importantly it was yet another intrusion for the community's residents, who for the most part had patiently put up with multiple walk-throughs not only by us, but by the lender's third parties and our insurance company. One tenant, however, got fed up. She accused us of "targeting" her because of how many times her unit had been inspected.

We also received a notice from the loan servicer warning us that the property's financial reports from two quarters ago were overdue. We explained that we didn't own the property two quarters ago, but that didn't seem to matter as more threatening notices and warnings would follow for months. This was yet another clue that they really didn't have their act together.

More significantly, although we were completing the agreed-upon improvements, we couldn't get our expenses reimbursed from the funds we had set aside for this purpose at closing. First, our repeated requests for a point of contact and instructions on how to submit reimbursement requests were ignored. By the time our new client relations manager finally contacted us and provided a copy of the necessary escrow disbursement form, we were already overextended financially and desperately needed access to our funds.

We immediately assembled and submitted our request for reimbursement for the work we had completed to date, but several weeks later it was denied. Our client relations manager informed us that we should redo the escrow disbursement form so that they could more easily match up the invoices with the repair items, even though we had followed their instructions exactly. We immediately redid the form in the format she requested, but a couple of weeks later the request was again denied, this time with a note that said: "Per the attached escrow disbursement form all the invoices submitted under current request are toward unit upgrades (interior). However, unit upgrades are not listed under exhibit C of loan agreement. Hence we will not be able to reimburse funds for this."

This was beyond frustrating. Unit upgrades were the single biggest improvement we had agreed to make as a condition of assuming the mortgage, and at closing we deposited the funds to make these improvements into the replacement reserve. The wording the lender had included in the loan exhibit was apparently not explicit enough for the person reviewing our submittal, but I had been on all the conference calls where all parties agreed that this was to be the primary use of the funds. We explained this to anyone who would listen, but to no avail. After three more weeks, we got a senior executive at the loan servicer to intervene on our behalf, and the reimbursement was finally approved. After another couple of weeks, we finally received our first reimbursement.

By the time the check arrived, we were ready to submit numerous additional requests. We were also running low on funds, not only because we'd had to extend more for repairs than expected but also because another major problem cropped up: The loan servicer was taking large sums of money from our bank account without our knowledge or authorization. We called our client relations manager seeking an explanation, but she had no idea what we were talking about and was unable to help. What the heck was going on? Was this fraud? We were at our wits' end and running out of cash.

To be continued...

Chapter Twenty-One

RECESSION RESISTANCE

*Expect the best. Prepare for the worst. Capitalize
on what comes.*

—ZIG ZIGLAR

What's the greatest fear of real estate investors? Typically, a major correction in the market. In fact, it's difficult to have a conversation about real estate without someone pointing out how overvalued properties are, how hard it is to find a deal, and how we're headed for a crash. This is true regardless of where we may be in the economic cycle.

Thanks to an abundance of fearmongering, it can be hard for real estate investors to maintain objectivity. If you listen to the pundits, we're perpetually on the edge of a veritable Armageddon—a massive sinkhole of a recession that's going to suck us all into oblivion. Tenants will stop paying, notes will be called prematurely, locusts will swarm, and life as we know it will cease to exist. However, for some investors, the prospect of a downturn is no more than a nagging worry in the back of their mind stemming from endless chatter and speculation. An annoyance. Kind of like a mosquito buzzing around that never lets you get fully comfortable.

What Does the Future Hold?

How can you determine whether we're on the edge of a downturn? The truth is that no one ever knows for certain. The more definitively people state what's going to happen, the more self-deluded they are. If anyone could accurately predict such things, they'd be swimming in their piles of gold coins like Scrooge McDuck instead of publicly prognosticating.

Will real estate values decline at some point? Most certainly. They always do, because real estate follows a cycle, and what goes up must come down. But no matter how frothy the market might seem at any given point in time, there is no way to know whether we've reached a peak. We can never know for certain when values will drop, how far they might fall, or at what rate they will decline. In the words of famed investor Howard Marks, "'Prices are too high' is far from synonymous with 'The next move will be downward.' Things can be overpriced and stay that way for a long time...or become far more so."

Likewise, when values decline, there is no way to know when we've reached the bottom. We don't know what will happen in the lending environment or the economy. We don't know when a geopolitical event, natural disaster, or global pandemic might bring the world to a screeching halt. Yes, people can make educated guesses based on history and theory. But investors must understand that guesses are all they are, even when they're rooted in a grain of truth that can make them highly seductive to people craving some clarity in a world chock-full of uncertainties.

Before you get sucked into anyone's apocalyptic predictions and decide to throw in the towel, know this: Although the threat of a downturn is real, it's always there and it's not going away. The threat will exist even when cap rates are double their historical average. Should you stop investing? Should you sell everything? That depends on your personal circumstances, goals, and tolerance for risk. Certainly if you stop investing and sell your properties and then the market tanks, you'll look very smart—but to call that anything other than outcome bias would be hubris.

Should you dive in and ramp up your investing? That's a tough one. It's easy to be paralyzed by fear. If you wait for a time when there's no apparent threat of a drop in real estate prices, you'll never buy anything. Yes, there will be a correction at some point—but it's difficult to make objective decisions if you let your mind run rampant with doomsday scenarios.

What should a real estate investor do? Regardless of where we are in the cycle and what your expectations are, we recommend that you invest selectively and take the necessary action to make sure you're ready for an eventual correction. Because even though we can't know when or how it will come, we know one will come eventually. Remember that and get your house in order, so to speak. Periodically taking stock of your real estate positions and shoring things up a bit is always good practice.

Complete a Self-Assessment

The first step to manage your risk and better position yourself to withstand any potential downturn is to periodically conduct a simple, objective assessment of your risk exposure. Your degree of exposure will be a key determinant of what actions you might take. For example, if you lived in the projected path of an approaching storm, you would consider factors such as whether you're in a floodplain and how sturdy your home is. Someone residing in a concrete building might board up the windows and choose to ride it out, while someone living in a straw hut might decide to flee. The appropriate response depends on each individual's situation.

Preparing for a correction in the real estate market is a lot like bracing for a major weather event. Whether you shore things up or head for the hills will depend on your risk profile, so take a good look in the mirror and do a self-assessment.

Cash Is King

What are you really afraid of? What constitutes a truly catastrophic situation for a real estate investor? Most would agree that it would be pretty bad if a property or portfolio stopped cash flowing. The wheels really fall off when you can't meet your debt obligations.

Not paying the bills is how you end up losing a property. Worse yet, if you default on full-recourse debt, you may be personally liable. If a property cash flows, however, you can see things through and live to fight another day, preserving the potential to see attractive returns over the long term.

Cash flow is where the rubber really meets the road. As David Greene, cohost of *The BiggerPockets Podcast*, says, "Cash flow is a defensive metric. It ensures you don't lose the property in bad times, so you can hold on until you build wealth in the good times." Too many investors assess their risk level by monitoring their ratio of debt to equity, but this is a flawed approach. Equity is too subjective and doesn't pay the bills. When cap rates start rising, equity can evaporate like a puddle on the pavement under the hot, beating sun.

Portfolio Debt Service Coverage

Since everything depends on your cash flow and ability to service your debt, to assess your vulnerability you need to analyze your portfolio in aggregate and determine how much cushion you have above your debt obligations. This cushion can be measured by calculating your debt service coverage ratio (DSCR), which is also known as your debt coverage ratio (DCR) and is covered in detail in Chapter Seven. There is a reason that lenders rely so heavily on this metric. Calculating your DSCR is the first step in assessing your risk exposure.

As you may recall, to calculate your DSCR, divide your NOI by your debt service. You can do this for an individual property or for a portfolio. To best assess your risk, we suggest doing it at both the property and the portfolio level. For example, if you own several properties that generate a total NOI of $800,000 per year and your mortgage payments total $400,000 per year, your portfolio DSCR would be 2.0x. In this scenario you have a very comfortable cushion in place that will help you weather a storm. Your portfolio is generating double the cash flow necessary to pay your mortgage, so if your rental income gets cut in half you'll still be able to meet your obligations.

A word of caution when analyzing DSCR at the portfolio level: You can't always use all the cash flow from one property to cover the debt service of another—for example, when you have different partners and ownership stakes in each asset—so certain properties could face significant risk even if the overall portfolio has a high DSCR.

What is a good DSCR for a portfolio? That depends on your tolerance for risk and the stability of the income. For context, keep in mind that lenders typically prefer this number be no lower than 1.2x or 1.3x for individual properties. As the DSCR approaches 1.0x, lenders may start to consider drastic actions, so you'll want to be familiar with the clauses in your mortgage that could be triggered by a low DSCR. At the portfolio level, we prefer to see this number stay above 1.5x.

Knowing your DSCR makes it relatively simple to stress-test your property or portfolio for various scenarios. For example, what would happen if you lost 20 percent of your tenants? How about if your rents dropped by 20 percent? In either case, you'd obviously need to have at least a 20 percent cushion to cover the decline. So if your DSCR is greater than 1.2x, you should still be able to meet your debt obligations.

You should also take into consideration any cash demands that aren't reflected in your NOI. Common examples include mandatory reserves and escrows imposed by your lender and necessary CapEx. Anything that consumes cash affects your ability to meet your debt obligations.

If you raised capital for your acquisitions through a syndication, another cash demand would be investor distributions. While paying investors should come secondary to your debt obligations, the potential inability to meet investor returns certainly merits consideration when weighing risk. If you're concerned about not being able to pay investors, you can easily modify the formula for DSCR to gauge your ability to both pay your mortgage and make investor distributions. We call this the debt service and distribution coverage ratio (DDCR).

$$DDCR = NOI \div (Debt\ Service + Investor\ Distributions)$$

It's also important to remember that the DSCR is only as reliable as the two factors that determine the DSCR, which are your cash flow and your debt. To accurately gauge your risk, go a little deeper and examine each of these to determine how stable they are. Obviously if one or both of these inputs were to change unfavorably, it could create a problem.

Quality and Diversity of Cash Flows

Now it's time to objectively assess the quality and diversity of the cash flows your properties are generating. Is the cash flow vulnerable? To answer this question, you must weigh things like the type and class of the assets, the stability of the income and expenses, and the location. For example, projects located in high-growth areas are less likely to experience a steep drop in income.

Within multifamily the most recession-resistant properties are probably workforce housing, which tends to have a blue-collar, lower-middle-class tenant base. Workforce housing can also appeal to retirees and others either receiving subsidies or on a fixed income. Class C apartments, mobile home parks, senior housing, and subsidized housing are all likely to stand up well in hard economic times. That's because people still need a place to live when times are tough, and they need housing that is affordable.

The size and diversity of your portfolio is another factor to consider. Single-asset risk should be avoided if possible. Obviously, the more properties within a portfolio, the more you're able to spread out any risk. The same applies to geographic diversity. The more spread out your properties are, the more easily you can absorb the loss of income associated with a localized downturn.

All the risks discussed here play a role in determining the future stability of your NOI—and when there is a higher degree of uncertainty in NOI, your DSCR is more suspect. Unfortunately, there is no clear and simple formula to calculate the quality of your income. I'm sure a model could be created, but the inputs would be highly subjective.

The good news is that you don't always need a number to gauge risk. While some may find comfort in running calculations, qualitatively weighing the factors at play can be just as valuable. There is no substitute for deliberate reflection, consideration, and good judgment. Thinking through the cash-flow risks outlined above will help you get a real sense of where you fall on the spectrum and decide whether that's within your comfort zone.

Strength of Debt

The next step in assessing your level of risk is to evaluate your portfolio's debt. You do this by determining what exposure you have to changes in your mortgage payments over your desired time horizon. Debt instruments that put you at the whim of future interest rates should be avoided wherever possible. Variable-rate mortgages and bridge loans are examples of debt that can pose significant risk.

If you haven't already done so, we highly recommend creating a debt schedule that lists the pertinent dates, rates, and so on for each of your properties. Having things laid out in a schedule will make it easier to identify, for example, when your fixed rates expire and when balloon payments are due. You'll then be able to see where your vulnerabilities and opportunities might lie.

Discussions with your mortgage broker or trusted lenders *before* any issues arise should help you better understand how flexible the lender is likely to be should something bad happen—and whether you need to have more or better contingencies in place.

The Big Picture

The final step of completing your self-assessment is to weigh all the above factors in aggregate and look at things from a broader perspective. By evaluating the long-term stability of your income and debt, taking into account your tolerance for risk, you can decide whether you're comfortable with your DSCR. For most investors, an acceptable portfolio-level DSCR will be somewhere between 1.3x and 1.5x. If you don't feel comfortable evaluating your portfolio on your own, consider consulting with a third party such as a trusted investor, lender, or advisor to help identify areas of risk exposure.

Note that while having a high DSCR might help you sleep better at night, it also diminishes your returns. Because more leverage will likely result in a lower DSCR, in most cases, that increased leverage will also yield higher returns. If you're in growth mode, sitting on a lot of equity will slow you down. You need to strike a balance that works for you.

In the end, the goal is to be fully aware of how much exposure you have and make an educated decision you're comfortable with. Everyone has a different tolerance for risk, and everyone's situation is unique.

This is why it's not advisable to look at your real estate investments in isolation. Taking the steps outlined in this chapter will help you assess your real estate portfolio but not the rest of your holdings and income streams. How much risk you can tolerate within your real estate holdings likely depends on how large a part of your income it represents, how stable your other income sources are, and what other obligations you have. In other words, you need to look at the big picture.

If you follow the steps outlined above and decide you'd like to increase your DSCR and reduce your risk exposure, there are a variety of ways to accomplish that, starting with your debt.

Clean Up Your Debt

The first way to reduce your risk is to clean up your debt. In the words of Robert Kiyosaki, "Good debt is a powerful tool, but bad debt can kill you." This is especially true when tough times come around. How do you clean up your portfolio's debt? Refinancing is a fairly low-cost option that should be seriously evaluated on a routine basis. Improving your debt terms with a refinance is one of the most straightforward ways to increase your DSCR and reduce your risk exposure. Author J Scott likens refinancing to giving your airplane a longer runway: "Even if the plane doesn't generally need it, it's nice to know that it's there in an emergency!"

Unfortunately, the tendency is not to think about mortgages until the end of the term is approaching, but keeping your head in the sand can be a costly mistake. Not only can ignoring your debt options result in missed opportunities to improve your cash flow, but if you wait to refinance until you're required to, you'll be at the whim of the lending environment and no longer in control of your own destiny.

It's easy to understand why so many investors avoid refinancing. Navigating the lending process can sometimes be akin to a prolonged, unpleasant dental procedure. But as much as most people hate dental work, the end result is a healthier set of teeth and less pain over the long run. The lending process can be similarly unpleasant but equally worthwhile. A couple of strategic refinances can result in a stronger, healthier portfolio and a dramatic reduction in risk. You're less likely to feel the pain over the long run, and more likely to keep your smile intact.

To see whether refinancing might make sense for you, create a schedule of your debt and review the list to identify opportunities to improve your debt position. You have one goal here: to make your future debt payments as low and predictable as you can for the longest period possible.

Here are some red flags to watch out for:
- Debt with high interest rates (relative to current rates)
- Any variable-rate debt
- Fixed rates scheduled to expire in the next three to five years
- Bridge debt (or any other short-term debt instrument)
- Balloon payments
- Full-recourse debt that could be refinanced into nonrecourse debt
- Amortization periods that are shorter than what's available through a refinance

Any debt within your portfolio that falls into one or more of these categories should be evaluated further to determine whether you could reasonably refinance or restructure it into a better product. To make this determination, you'll need to take the following steps:

1. Look at each property to determine whether it is suitable for securing replacement debt. If the property is distressed or in turnaround, you may need to stabilize it before you can refinance.
2. Examine each of your current loans to make sure you understand

the consequences of a refinance. Check whether there are prepayment penalties or other costs associated with an early payoff. If the mortgage needs to be defeased, it's easy to get a quote for that.

3. Work with a mortgage broker or preferred lenders to get some preliminary quotes and model what the new debt would look like. For the purpose of managing risk, you'll want to prioritize longer terms and longer amortization periods. You want to lock in low payments for as long as possible.

4. Compare your current debt for each property to the potential future debt, also weighing all the costs and benefits associated with the prepayment and refinancing. What is your mortgage payment right now? How long is it fixed? What will your new mortgage payment be, and how long will that be fixed? Will the new debt allow you to change a full-recourse position into a nonrecourse position?

Once you've gone through this exercise, you should have enough information to make an educated decision about whether to refinance. Sometimes the answer is obvious. Other times it's less clear, particularly when there are steep prepayment penalties or you're uncertain about how long you plan to keep a property. Going through a refinance might be too time-consuming and costly if you plan to exit soon.

In the end, the decision will be driven in large part by your personal goals and risk tolerance. Ironically, conservative investors may find this approach to managing risk particularly challenging. They tend to gravitate toward shorter amortization periods with the goal of paying down debt faster. This can be an effective strategy for some investors and works well in a stable environment. However, it locks in a higher mortgage payment, and if things don't go well, these investors could find themselves needing to lower their payments through a refinance at a time when banks might not be willing to lend. The hope is they will have paid down enough debt by then that they'll be able to work something out.

A word of warning about refinancing: Investors can get pretty excited at the prospect of refinancing with the idea of pulling out some cash. The lure of tax-free cash can be pretty enticing! But remember that if your goal is to manage risk and strengthen your position should there be a correction, adding leverage is not usually a good way to accomplish that.

Value-Add

Apart from cleaning up your debt, what else can you do to reduce your risk? You can create as much additional cash flow as possible. As already discussed, one of the better indicators of how much risk you have is your property's and/or portfolio's DSCR. You can improve this metric and strengthen your ability to survive setbacks by adding value.

Investors usually evaluate value-add projects based on how much they will improve a property's market value. However, if you want your property to be more recession-resistant, you should place a higher priority on the resulting cash flow and increase in the DSCR. The DSCR is not traditionally considered in evaluating value-add projects, but it should be. A higher DSCR represents an increase in the property's cushion to weather hard times.

As covered in Chapter Nineteen, there are practically limitless opportunities to increase a property's income and reduce expenses, driving up your cash flow and NOI. Some methods are straightforward and others more creative. You're limited only by your imagination. If you want to make your properties more recession-resistant, carefully explore all options on both the income and expense side, both in Chapter Nineteen and the Value-Add Bonus Supplements.

The best time to undertake changes that add value to a property is not when you're at the peak of distress—by then it might be too late. Stay ahead of the curve and make decisions today under the assumption that a period of distress will come at some point, because it will. Be motivated and grateful that you still have the opportunity to shore things up. Avoid regrets by making sure you've done everything you can to be ready if and when a day of reckoning comes.

Buying Properties

Just because you may be concerned about a future downturn doesn't mean you should necessarily refrain from making acquisitions. In fact, if you buy right, you can actually improve your risk profile and better position yourself for an impending downturn. Sometimes, you can find the best deals precisely when people are becoming more nervous about the future. Industrialist J. Paul Getty has been quoted as saying, "Buy when everyone else is selling and hold until everyone else is buying. That's not just a catchy slogan. It's the very essence of successful investing." Warren

Buffett echoed this advice when he famously encouraged investors "to be fearful when others are greedy and to be greedy only when others are fearful." While Getty and Buffett were referring to other types of investments, their advice certainly applies to real estate as well.

Unfortunately, following sage advice is not always simple in practice. What if the fear is well-founded? What if a recession is imminent? Should you still buy? That depends in large part on your comfort level, but even if your timing is off you can still get great returns if you are judicious about what you buy and how you finance your purchase. Again, you need to buy *right*.

Buying right means finding a property that can generate a stable income and maintain strong debt service coverage if and when the economy tanks. It means financing deals with good debt that has a ten-year term or longer. It means picking a property with lower inherent risk, whether due to a good location or a large tenant base with stable and diversified sources of income.

It's great to be a buyer in times of uncertainty and fear in the markets, because much of your competition will prefer to stay on the sidelines. While risk aversion is understandable, if you can lock in the right property with the right financing, the risk is substantially mitigated. That said, risk will *always* be there. You just need to decide whether it's acceptable to you, knowing that if you wait for everything to be perfect, you'll never get started.

Pruning Properties

Another way to reduce your risk exposure is to sell properties that are either dragging down your portfolio's DSCR or have the greatest potential to do so in the future. Of course, there are costs associated with divesting of properties and substantial benefits to buying and holding long term. Even when a property is cash-flow break-even, it's creating wealth for you through principal paydown, so you should not take the decision to sell lightly.

Of course, everyone's business plan and tolerance for risk is different. If you're looking to take some chips off the table and reduce your downside exposure, pruning a property or two could make sense. Therefore, in the next chapter, we'll dig into when and how to sell properties.

KEY TAKEAWAYS

- Nobody can predict the future, but it's still a good idea to periodically conduct a simple, objective assessment of your risk exposure.
- You should create a debt schedule, check your DSCR at the property and portfolio level, assess your debt, and take steps to clean it up.
- Additional options for managing your risk exposure include the execution of value-add projects, selective acquisitions, and pruning marginal properties from your portfolio.

Madison Barracks: Part XII

Executing on our plan for the Apartments at Madison Barracks was proving to be far more difficult than necessary, and all because of our lender. The problems reached a pinnacle when we noticed that large sums of money were being withdrawn from our operating account without any explanation.

Eventually, we figured out what had happened. At closing, we had agreed to the lender's requirement for automatic electronic payment of our mortgage, but the amounts that were being withdrawn were far more than that. After dozens of phone calls and emails, we learned that someone in the loan servicer's tax escrow department had run a new tax escrow analysis based on the previous year's tax bills, and had accidentally included all of the previous owner's unpaid water bills in their calculation. As a result, they overestimated our taxes by more than $100,000. To cover this, the loan servicer pulled an extra $93,542 from our account for their tax escrow "deficit" without notifying us. To make matters worse, our request to correct this error and refund the money was denied.

Next, the loan servicer withdrew another $50,000 from our bank account to pay an insurance bill even though we had already paid the entire insurance premium for a full year at closing. After countless additional emails and phone calls between ourselves, our insurance broker, and multiple people at the loan servicer, it was determined that the loan servicer had accidentally paid the insurance bill for another property and assigned it to our account. This triggered an escrow deficit, which resulted in the $50,000 withdrawal.

Our client relations manager apologized for this mistake and explained that the employee who paid the bill was actually located in India, as if that were a satisfactory explanation. We didn't care where the employee was located—we just wanted the money returned. However, the insurance company was refusing to return the funds to the loan servicer, and the loan servicer would not return the funds to us until they received a refund from the insurance company. The whole thing was so preposterous, it seemed it should be illegal.

The amount of time wasted and the number of phone calls that went unanswered throughout this process were mind-boggling—and the financial strain it was causing was entirely unexpected. Who budgets an extra $150,000 in case your lender mistakenly withdraws it from your bank account without telling you? You go into a project like this concerned about finding unexpected physical problems at the property, or maybe construction cost overruns, or even an economic downturn. You certainly don't expect to get blindsided by your lender, but that's what happened, and our relationship with them showed no signs of improving. The lesson learned is that unexpected things always happen, and there's no way to guess what they might be. You deal with it and forge ahead.

The other lesson learned was that there is a lot more to "good debt" than the terms of the loan. Once you commit to a lender, you're stuck with them (or whomever is servicing the loan on their behalf) for the duration. How difficult they are to deal with and the quality of the service you receive can have just as much of an effect (or more) on your operations as the interest rate, the term, or how many months or years of interest-only payments you're able to secure.

Here we were doing everything possible to pull a property out of distress, and a lender with a vested interest was actually dragging us under. What the heck? It was beyond frustrating and seemed unfair, but feeling victimized and bemoaning our misfortune wasn't going to make things better. It was time to set emotions aside and buck up. I decided to reevaluate my plans. I was determined to take some positive steps forward to change our situation.

Little did I know that a simple solution was about to unexpectedly present itself. But then again, I've never been one to take the easy way out.

To be continued...

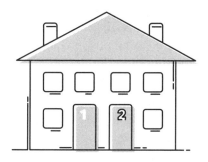

Chapter Twenty-Two

SELLING YOUR MULTIFAMILY

Much success can be attributed to inactivity.
Most investors cannot resist the temptation to
constantly buy and sell.

—WARREN BUFFETT

Before we delve into why it may be a good idea to sell a multifamily property and how to go about it, let's acknowledge that there can be tremendous benefits to *not* selling. Few strategies in real estate can match the risk-adjusted returns from combining value-add with buy and hold. Why is buy and hold often preferable to selling? Here are four reasons.

Reason Not to Sell No. 1: Lower Expenses

There are high costs associated with buying and selling properties. These include the obvious transactional expenses such as commissions and closing costs, but also the less obvious costs related to all the time that can go into transactions. This is particularly true when you're acquiring a property and have to go through onboarding and potentially stabilizing it. When you acquire a new property, the workload tends to be front-loaded. There is a learning period, relationships to be established, and processes to be put in place and refined. Over time, you realize efficiencies and income rises: You've built a well-oiled machine. When you sell a property, you're losing that machine you built. Yes, you're unlocking the equity, but you're also giving up a cash-flowing, wealth-building machine.

Reason Not to Sell No. 2: Principal Paydown and Appreciation

If you've done a good job putting together that wealth-building machine, it should continue to build equity as rents rise over time and expenses either flatten or drop as a result of operational efficiencies. With amortizing debt on the property, you're also paying down the principal every month, which can create a lot more wealth than most investors realize.

For example, let's say you finance a $10 million property using a mortgage of $8 million with a thirty-year amortization at a 3.5 percent interest rate. In this case you would increase your equity in the property by $1.8 million during the first ten years based solely on the reduction in principal from making your mortgage payments every month. That means that after a ten-year hold period you could bank $1.8 million in profit by selling the property (minus closing costs) even if the value didn't increase at all. One of the key things to note here is that principal paydown increases every year, providing you with greater annual benefits the longer you hold the property. The same benefits of long-term hold periods can be realized through appreciation. If this same property's value were to rise a modest 3 percent per year, you would create an additional $3.4 million in equity over ten years thanks to the power of compound interest. With 3 percent annual appreciation and principal paydown combined, you would create a combined $5.2 million in equity.

Reason Not to Sell No. 3: Tax Advantages

When you buy and hold, you have a means at your disposal to access the equity without selling or incurring any tax consequences—you can refinance. Pulling out cash through a refinance is a way to put cash into your pocket tax-free and with no obligation to follow the stringent timeline and other requirements of a 1031 exchange.

Reason Not to Sell No. 4: Risk Diversification

Holding your properties and adding new ones to build a portfolio divides your risk among multiple assets. The more properties you have, the less concentrated your risk. To illustrate this, imagine investor A acquires their first property, adds value, sells it, and then does a 1031 exchange to reinvest 100 percent of the proceeds into a larger property. They then do the same all over again, moving into an even larger property. Investor B takes a different route. They acquire their first property, add value, and then use the proceeds from a cash-out refinance to purchase a second property. They do the same in a few years and buy a third. Both investors A and B face a tragic circumstance at one of their properties, causing the asset to fall into distress. Which of the two investors is in a better position? Investor A is at risk of losing everything. Investor B has two other properties that are still performing well and can help them cover any shortfalls while weathering the storm.

Do these four reasons mean you should never sell a property? Absolutely not. But you should always proceed with caution and make sure you're comfortable that a disposition is the right plan given your specific circumstances.

Why You Should Sell

There are any number of reasons why you may feel the need to sell a property, some more justifiable and financially prudent than others. You could, for example, be compelled to sell by your business plan. If you raised outside capital, your investors may either need or be expecting a return of their capital through an exit. When other people entrust you with their capital, you have a fiduciary responsibility to consider any opportunity that's going to generate strong returns. This obviously includes a sale.

In other cases, a sale could be prompted by significant changes in business or life circumstances. You may be ending a partnership and need to liquidate shared assets. You could be retiring. Or you could be faced with an unforeseen change in personal circumstances, such as a medical emergency, family issue, or job loss. Life can throw us a wide variety of curveballs that result in a need for cash, prompt a shift in priorities, or just make continued ownership less feasible or desirable.

Finally, people sell properties all the time for less-than-sound reasons—say, to pay for rampant spending or settle gambling debts. While such decisions may be financially imprudent if not disastrous, they all boil down to personal choice. Part of the beauty of being a real estate entrepreneur is that you don't have to justify yourself to anyone: You can do whatever you want with your properties—within reason. If you've been investing for a long time and have a large portfolio, you may have earned the right to be a little frivolous.

Still, before moving forward, take the time to consider all your options and make sure a disposition is ultimately the right choice for your situation. You may find it helpful to think back to your reasons for investing in rental property to begin with. What were you hoping to achieve, and how have your goals evolved over time? How does a disposition fit with your current goals? An investor's needs, perspectives, and priorities will often change as their portfolio grows.

Selling to Mitigate Risk

Sometimes an investor is interested in selling assets to take some chips off the table and scale back their holdings. This may be motivated by a desire to diversify, build up cash reserves, shore up their portfolio, or otherwise mitigate risk. Perhaps you are motivated to make your portfolio more recession-resistant, as discussed in the previous chapter. The question in that case would be deciding which asset to sell.

When trying to manage risk through a property sale, a good place to start is with the self-assessment outlined in Chapter Twenty-One. This will help you identify the properties in your portfolio that present the most risk. Keep in mind, however, that while looking at individual DSCRs is a good place to start, but you can't use that as your sole criterion. There are other factors to consider. For example, which of the following two properties poses more risk?

Property A

Property A has a dubious 1.1x DSCR but the income stream is steady as a rock, and it's in a great neighborhood within walking distance of a university and a major hospital. The property is in a thriving market with steady, diversified job growth. The major systems have all been upgraded or replaced, so expenses are predictable and low. It has nonrecourse debt with a competitive interest rate that is fixed for the next ten years.

Property B

Property B has a stellar 2.0x DSCR. It's a nice property but has started to experience high turnover and is located in a neighborhood that is falling into decline. The local employment base centers on one large manufacturing facility owned by a company that has been steadily moving operations overseas. The property's infrastructure is older and periodically gets hit with unexpected expenses. It also has a balloon payment coming due in a couple of years.

Which of these two properties is more apt to make you lose sleep at night? Which one is more recession-resistant? The answer would depend on your personal comfort level with various factors, but regardless, you can see that risk and recession resistance can't be determined simply by crunching numbers. There is judgment involved, and the factors that must be weighed are property-specific.

That's not to say a property's DSCR isn't extremely important as you assess risk. In the example above, Property A seems wonderful, but that low DSCR should give you pause—and that goes double for any property that is not generating enough cash to cover its own debt. Review your debt schedule and carefully scrutinize the laggards. Sometimes selling a single property can give an entire portfolio a boost and may even generate cash that can be redeployed elsewhere with a superior return.

Other factors to consider when deciding whether to prune a property from your portfolio to reduce risk include the following:

- **Trends:** Be careful not to look at numbers in isolation. Yes, the T-12 may be a great place to start, but how does that compare to the prior year? In what direction are things moving? Properties whose occupancies and rents have been trending downward should raise concern.
- **Potential:** As value-add investors, we're always looking for ways to improve a property. If a property is operating at or near its peak,

lower returns will be realized going forward. We may be able to achieve superior returns by cashing out and redeploying the proceeds somewhere with more upside potential.

- **Operational Efficiency:** How much time and attention a property consumes relative to what it yields in returns is significant. We have both pruned properties because of the opportunity cost. They may have been good properties, but we decided our time and resources could be better leveraged with other investment opportunities.
- **Lack of Diversification:** If you are too highly concentrated in a specific market or type of asset, selling a property could free you up to expand into new areas and improve your diversification, which helps to mitigate risk associated with a localized downturn. Of course, you must weigh this against any operational efficiencies due to properties being in close proximity.

How to Sell a Property

Once you've decided to sell, how should you go about it? At a high level, there are five steps to take.

Step 1: Prepare the Property

Invest the time and effort necessary to ensure you'll get the best price. In terms of the property itself, the most effective actions will depend largely on how much time you have to work with. If you're looking at a lengthy time horizon, focus on keeping occupancy and income levels as high as possible and keep a close eye on expenses. Ideally, the months or even years leading up to a sale are when you're reaping the full financial benefits of any value-add projects. That should be reflected in additional income and lower expenses, driving up your property's NOI. The more months of data you have demonstrating that higher value, the more comfortable a buyer will be incorporating the higher numbers into their property valuation.

When you are closer to the listing date, focus on making sure the property shows well and eliminate any potential surprises when a prospective buyer tours the property and conducts inspections. This is not the time to take on big capital improvement projects. Instead, you should prioritize improving the property's curb appeal so that it creates a good first impression. At a minimum, make sure that the grounds and common areas are clean and appear well kept. Consider freshening up some paint and making other cosmetic fixes. You should also do a quick, routine maintenance inspection of every unit in the months leading up to listing a property. If a unit hasn't been inspected in a while, you never know what you might find. You don't want a prospective buyer discovering a plumbing issue, pest infestation, or something even more disagreeable.

Step 2: Assemble the Documentation

The next step is to assemble all the necessary documentation. That means all the information and documents *you* would be looking for if you were the buyer. Gather up everything you'd want for your own underwriting and due diligence, including a rent roll, T-12 and historical financials, and so on. For specific items, you can refer to the lists of high-, medium-, and low priority documents in Chapter Eleven.

Finally, you should do your own pro forma and valuation using the same process you would go through when analyzing a property you're buying. The only real difference is that you should paint as positive a picture as you can, within reason. What value-add projects remain? What could the buyer do to drive income and cut expenses? You'll want to bake those into your pro forma to show some upside potential. You're going to continue to refine this pro forma based on input from brokers or other advisors, but in the end it's likely to be the basis for an asking price and a starting point for negotiations. Your goal is to be on the top end of a potential valuation range without being unrealistic.

Step 3: Evaluate Listing Options

After you've pulled together your documentation and completed your initial valuation, the next step is to determine how best to bring the property to market. As discussed in Chapter Nine, there are pros and cons to selling a property off-market versus listing it with a broker, and a variety of ways a broker can bring a property to market. Our position is that there's too much at stake not to thoroughly consider all your options. Even if you're tempted to sell a property off-market and avoid paying a commission, we recommend you go through the process of meeting with brokers, hearing them out, and evaluating their proposals.

By the time you're ready to sell a property, you should know who the most active brokers are in your market. If not, it's worth spending some time looking at who is bringing most of the properties to market and speaking with fellow investors, mortgage brokers, your property manager, and others to develop a short list of the most appropriate brokers to list your property.

Once you've identified the best options for brokers, contact them about the possibility of their taking your property to market. At this stage, it's appropriate to share the property information you've collected but *not* your internal pro forma and valuation. A good broker will use the property's rent roll and historical financials to prepare their own investment analysis. They should be able to share a pro forma and all the assumptions that went into it. They should also be able to produce a valuation summary showing a range of potential market values based on assumptions that range from conservative to optimistic. Reviewing a broker's financial analysis is a great opportunity to validate your own projections and gain valuable insights into prevailing market cap rates.

Comparing multiple broker analyses will give you a good idea of what your property might sell for. However, beware overblown valuations that are hyped to get you to sign a listing agreement. Bad brokers love to tell you your property is worth more than it is because they think it's what you want to hear. Experienced, ethical brokers know that misleading sellers in this way is not in anyone's long-term best interest. Unfortunately, over-promising is not uncommon. You'll also want to carefully review each broker's experience, their proposed transaction timeline, how they would market the property, and the qualifications of the team you'd be working with.

Why go through all this trouble if you're planning to sell off-market? Because you can learn a lot—about market conditions, comparable sales, cap rates, how prospective buyers will look at your property, what you might be able to do to get a better price, and so on. In the end, you'll be better informed to make a final decision as to whether to use a broker.

Is making the brokers do all this work ethical if you don't plan to use them? Absolutely. Brokers invest a lot of time trying to find prospective sellers. They should appreciate the opportunity to win your business, even if you're initially disposed against using their services. There is nothing wrong with coming right out and letting them know up front. For example, you could say: "I'm interested in selling my property and thought I should reach out. To be completely honest, I'm inclined to sell it myself, but I'm open to meeting with you and reviewing any proposal or analysis you'd like to share." Most brokers will not be put off by a statement like this. On the contrary, they are more likely to be grateful for the opportunity to change your mind.

Ultimately, using a seasoned broker to bring your multifamily property to market will usually add more than enough value to offset any commission. A good broker will almost certainly put your property in front of far more qualified buyers than you could reach on your own. They have the connections, reach, and marketing resources to solicit the most offers—and the more offers you get, the higher your sales price is likely to be.

In addition to helping you reach more prospective buyers and get the best price, brokers can be invaluable in many other ways. They can provide advice, prepare an offering memorandum, serve as an intermediary with prospective buyers, vet buyers, negotiate, help coordinate due diligence, and manage the entire sales process from beginning to end.

Step 4: Define a Timeline and Process

After you've settled on how to bring your property to market, you should define exactly how the listing process will work and what the timeline will be. This is another area where a good broker can add value. (The process and general timeline considerations are outlined in Chapter Fifteen.) You'll want to establish up front whether you're going to publish an asking price or use market pricing. You'll also want to decide whether you'll evaluate offers and enter into negotiations on a rolling basis or follow a predefined schedule. Consider how tours will be scheduled and managed, whether there will be a call for offers, whether you're going to include a best-and-final round, and how offers will be evaluated.

When evaluating offers, remember to consider factors beyond price. In the end, a high offering price is meaningless unless the buyer follows through and closes. Otherwise, you risk having to go through the entire process all over again. If you're working with a broker, they can vet buyers on your behalf. As explained in Chapter Fifteen, some brokers will use a buyer's questionnaire to help get a full picture of the buyer, including how serious they are about the property, and how likely they are to follow through and close.

Step 5: Manage the Due Diligence and Closing Process

Once you have your property under contract, it's important to follow through and do what you can to expedite every step of the process. This means being responsive and working cooperatively with the broker and seller. It's in your best interest as a seller to move as quickly as possible through the process, and you certainly don't want to be responsible for any delays.

In addition to being responsive during due diligence and the closing process, you should make sure the property continues to be operated as it would if you were going to retain ownership. Too many sellers make the mistake of letting a property languish once it's under contract. There are three important reasons not to let this happen:

1. A significant change in the property's performance can undermine the buyer's ability to secure financing. A material change can also diminish the value of the property, which would entitle the buyer to retrade.

2. Deals fall through all the time, and you may end up retaining the property. Any harm resulting from a period of neglect will create problems that you'll then have to deal with.

3. It's the just the right thing to do (and your reputation depends on it). Taking every measure possible to ensure that the property is conveyed to the buyer in the condition in which it was represented is the honorable way to conduct business. Besides, the investment community is a small world, your reputation is important, and any less-than-ethical behavior will taint it.

KEY TAKEAWAYS

- Your default position should be *not* to sell because there are significant advantages to a buy-and-hold strategy, including the avoidance of transaction and onboarding expenses, tax advantages, principal paydown, appreciation, and portfolio diversification.
- Reasons to sell may include the requirements of your business plan, a change in circumstances, personal preference, or risk mitigation.
- Selling a property involves preparing the property, assembling the appropriate documentation, choosing your listing approach, preparing a process and timeline, and managing the due diligence and closing.
- When selling, make calculated decisions that are rooted in an objective assessment and not driven by fear. Panic selling almost never turns out well.

Madison Barracks: Part XIII

Despite the many setbacks we experienced with our loan servicer, we were still executing on our plans and filling up units. Less than six months in, occupancy was up to 75 percent and still rising. The transformation of the Apartments at Madison Barracks caught the attention of another investor, who made an unsolicited offer to acquire the property. His timing was better than he could have imagined, since in light of the challenges we were facing, an early exit seemed enticing. However, there was still too much meat on the bone, and I wanted to see things through. Despite the frustrations and setbacks, I decided not to succumb to the temptation of a quick sale—it just didn't feel like the right thing to do.

I thanked the prospective buyer and told him I'd reach out if I changed my mind. What I didn't tell him was that the idea of selling actually ended up hardening my resolve and making me revisit the big picture. I decided that we needed to make a change. The service we were getting from our lender was so bad that it was undermining our ability to execute. Therefore, I decided to refinance much earlier than planned and reached out to a local bank I had a good relationship with.

At this stage of the property turnaround, I was concerned that an appraisal might not come back high enough to replace the debt, let alone to allow us to pull out cash. But after everything that had happened, I felt I had no choice.

Fortunately, the appraisal came back at $5.7 million "as is" and $6 million "as completed" (after we completed work that was already underway). Given that we had owned the property for just six months, I was pretty happy with those numbers!

Based on the results of the appraisal, our new lender agreed to provide us with a mortgage of $4.8 million, which would allow us to pull out about $100,000, plus give us access to the money the lender had withdrawn from our account. Although this was much less than we had planned in our original underwriting, given the circumstances and the fact that we were refinancing so far ahead of schedule, I was super excited. The new lender also had less stringent insurance requirements, which would save us about another $20,000 per year—and most importantly, we wouldn't have to deal with that terrible loan servicer anymore. Hallelujah to that!

With the help of the cash infusion from the refinance, we began to map out the next phase of renovations. Meanwhile, we kept bringing units back online, and occupancy continued to rise. Less than one year after closing, we hit our target occupancy of 90 percent. Capital improvements progressed slowly but steadily and continue to this day. I still think it's going to take the better part of a decade to get things where I want them, but we're off to a great start.

The Apartments at Madison Barracks was a challenging project, but overcoming setbacks and finding ways to move forward are a big part of becoming a multifamily millionaire. Improving a community and providing a better place for the residents to call home are fulfilling achievements in and of themselves.

On top of everything else, I was able to acquire and improve the apartment complex where I had once been a renter—something I would never have imagined in my wildest dreams. How cool is that?

Chapter Twenty-Three
CONCLUSION

*If you're going to live, leave a legacy. Make a mark
on the world that can't be erased.*

—MAYA ANGELOU

Congratulations! You've reached the final chapter of *The Multifamily Millionaire, Volume II*. We've covered a lot of material in an effort to arm you with as much information as possible and maximize your chances of success. We wouldn't expect you to retain everything you've read, but hopefully Volumes I and II of *The Multifamily Millionaire* will serve as good references that you can return to again and again.

In closing, we'd like to share a few final thoughts before you head off into the multifamily world to take down some big properties. The first is that it's no accident that the subtitle of Volume I promotes financial independence while that of Volume II promotes the idea of creating generational wealth. The first great milestone in real estate investing is financial independence, which will allow you to become self-reliant and have the freedom to live the life you choose.

This is an admirable goal and a dream that many real estate entrepreneurs share—one that can be achieved only through hard work and sacrifice. If you have joined the ranks of the countless investors who have achieved financial freedom through multifamily real estate investing, that is a tremendous and life-changing accomplishment. Congratulations!

The next major milestone in multifamily investing is *generational* wealth, which can elevate you to an entirely different level. Generational wealth is no longer about your own financial independence: It's about lifting up those around you. It's about providing a better life for your loved ones and for future generations.

This is the stage we've reached in our own investing journeys. We have achieved financial freedom through real estate. We are no longer investing for ourselves; we are doing it for our children, for their children, and for the other special people in our lives. We are doing it to give back, make a difference, and leave a legacy. We also share a passion for education and want to help as many other people as possible achieve their own financial freedom and generational wealth, which is why we wrote *The Multifamily Millionaire.*

Most of the people who will read these books are blessed to live in a time and place where it is possible for anyone with enough grit and ingenuity to start with nothing and become a multifamily millionaire—to achieve financial independence and then create generational wealth through real estate. It is our sincerest hope that these books be a valuable resource if you elect to embark on this difficult but ultimately rewarding path, and we wish you nothing but the very best on your journey. As we said in the preface, we don't want you to do what we've done. We want you to do more.

Now get out there, roll up your sleeves, and crush it!

If you found value in this book, we would be so grateful for your positive review on Amazon.com. Thank you.

ACKNOWLEDGMENTS

The authors would like to acknowledge the following individuals for taking the time to do peer reviews of select chapters in Volume II of The Multifamily Millionaire. Their excellent feedback and insights helped make this book the best it could be. *THANK YOU.*

Adam Beckstedt, Welkin Equity

Keri Bednarz, Elevate Commercial Investment Group

Nathaniel J. Carroll, Bowers & Company CPAs, PLLC

JC Castillo, Velo Residential

Chad Cudworth, Blue Steel Capital

Brian Hamrick, Hamrick Investment Group

Joseph Gozlan, Eureka Business Group

James Kandasamy, Achieve Investment Group

Michael Le, Bayou City Group

Anton W. Mattli, Peak Financing

Walker Meadows, Open Door Capital

Ryan Murdock, Open Door Capital

Jordan E. Morgenstern, Morgenstern DeVoesick PLLC

Tricia Murray, Washington Street Properties

Mauricio J. Rauld, Esq., Premier Law Group

Ben Suttles, Disrupt Equity

Addison F. Vars, III, Barclay Damon LLP

Mike Williams, Open Door Capital

Scan to leave a review or access bonus content

Leave a review on Amazon

Access the free bonus content

More from
BiggerPockets Publishing

Recession-Proof Real Estate Investing

Take any recession in stride, and never be intimidated by a market shift again. In this book, accomplished investor J Scott dives into the theory of economic cycles and the real-world strategies for harnessing them to your advantage. With clear instructions for every type of investor, this easy-to-follow guide will show you how to make money during all of the market's twists and turns—whether during an economic recession or at any other point in the economic cycle. You'll never look at your real estate business the same way again!

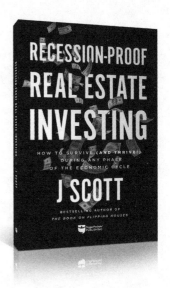

The Book on Advanced Tax Strategies

Saving on taxes means more money for you, your family, and your real estate investments. Learning tax strategies could be the easiest money you ever make! In this comprehensive follow-up to *The Book on Tax Strategies*, best-selling authors and CPAs Amanda Han and Matthew MacFarland bring you more strategies to slash your taxes and turn your real estate investments into a tax-saving machine.

If you enjoyed this book, we hope you'll take a moment to check out some of the other great material BiggerPockets offers. BiggerPockets is the real estate investing social network, marketplace, and information hub, designed to help make you a smarter real estate investor through podcasts, books, blog posts, videos, forums, and more. Sign up today—it's free! **Visit www.BiggerPockets.com.**

The Hands-Off Investor: An Insider's Guide to Investing in Passive Real Estate Syndications

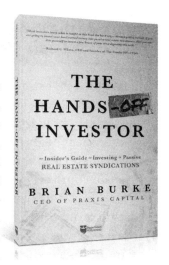

Want to invest in real estate but don't have the time? No matter your level of experience, real estate syndications provide an avenue to invest in real estate without tenants, toilets, or trash—and this comprehensive guide will teach you how to invest in these opportunities the right way. Author Brian Burke, a syndications insider with decades of experience in forming and managing syndication funds, will show you how to evaluate sponsors, opportunities, and offerings so you can pick the right ones and achieve the highest odds of a favorable outcome.

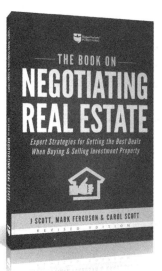

The Book on Negotiating Real Estate

When the real estate market gets hot, it's the investors who know the ins and outs of negotiating who will get the deal. J Scott, Mark Ferguson, and Carol Scott combine real-world experience and the science of negotiation in order to cover all aspects of the negotiation process and maximize your chances of reaching a profitable deal.

More from
BiggerPockets Publishing

Profit Like the Pros: The Best Real Estate Deals Made by Expert Investors

Remarkable real estate deals are happening all around us. Take a look behind the curtain to see exactly how investors have profited from their best deals ever! With twenty-five real-world stories from seasoned investors across the country, this book uncovers the secrets behind unbelievable real estate deals, from sourcing and funding to profiting. Author Ken Corsini—star of HGTV's *Flip or Flop Atlanta*—has distilled his best investor interviews to educate, entertain, and get your wheels spinning.

Long-Distance Real Estate Investing

Don't let your location dictate your financial freedom: Live where you want, and invest anywhere it makes sense! The rules, technology, and markets have changed: No longer are you forced to invest only in your backyard. In *Long-Distance Real Estate Investing*, learn an in-depth strategy to build profitable rental portfolios through buying, managing, and flipping out-of-state properties from real estate investor and agent David Greene.

The Book on Tax Strategies for the Savvy Real Estate Investor

Taxes! Boring and irritating, right? Perhaps. But if you want to succeed in real estate, your tax strategy will play a huge role in how fast you grow. A great tax strategy can save you thousands of dollars a year. A bad strategy could land you in legal trouble. With *The Book on Tax Strategies for the Savvy Real Estate Investor*, you'll find ways to deduct more, invest smarter, and pay far less to the IRS!

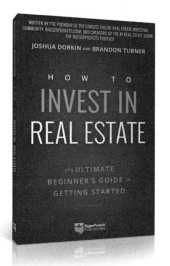

How to Invest in Real Estate

Two of the biggest names in the real estate world teamed up to write the most comprehensive manual ever written on getting started in the lucrative business of real estate investing. Joshua Dorkin and Brandon Turner give you an insider's look at the many different real estate niches and strategies so that you can find which one works best for you, your resources, and your goals.

CONNECT WITH BIGGERPOCKETS

and Become Successful in Your Real Estate Business Today!

Facebook
/BiggerPockets

Instagram
@BiggerPockets

Twitter
@BiggerPockets

LinkedIn
/company/Bigger
Pockets

Website
BiggerPockets.com